THE
GREAT UPSHIFT

HUMANITY'S COMING ADVANCE TOWARD PEACE AND HARMONY ON THE PLANET

Also by
ERVIN LASZLO

Science and the Akashic Field (2006)

The Intelligence of the Cosmos (2017)

Reconnecting to the Source (2020)

The Immutable Laws of the Akashic Field (2021)

The Wisdom Principles (2021)

Dawn of an Era of Well-Being with Frederick Tsao (2021)

The Survival Imperative: Upshifting to Conscious Evolution (2023)

Autobiography

My Journey (2001)

THE
GREAT UPSHIFT

HUMANITY'S COMING ADVANCE TOWARD
PEACE AND HARMONY ON THE PLANET

ERVIN LASZLO AND DAVID LORIMER
WITH CONTRIBUTIONS BY INTERNATIONAL THOUGHT LEADERS

The Great Upshift
Humanity's Coming Advance Toward Peace and Harmony on the Planet
Ervin Laszlo and David Lorimer

Print ISBN: 978-1-958921-52-4
EBook ISBN: 978-1-958921-53-1

Library of Congress Control Number: 2023943685

Published by Light on Light Press
An imprint of Sacred Stories Publishing, Fort Lauderdale, FL
Printed in the United States of America

TABLE OF CONTENTS

ROADMAP CLUSTER II. MAPPING OUR PATH FORWARD

ROADMAPS TO THE GREAT UPSHIFT — PART TWO:
UPSHIFTING OURSELVES

ROADMAP CLUSTER III. UPSHIFTING OUR HEALING

ROADMAP CLUSTER IV. UPSHIFTING OUR THINKING

INTRODUCTION BY THE AUTHORS

UPSHIFT OR DOWNSLIDE: WELCOME, CONSCIOUS ACTIVISTS!

Today's world is neither a happy nor a peaceful or even a sustainable place. We have entered a path of development replete with conflict and prone to multiple crises. Continuing on this path could lead to the sixth global extinction on the planet — one that is triggered by, and includes, the human species. If we are to remove the sword of Damocles from over our head, we urgently need to change paths. We must adopt better ways of conducting ourselves on the planet. We need to upshift our world, and for that, we need to upshift our consciousness.

The next phase of our adventure on this planet will be decisive. It could be an upshift to a better world, or a downslide to crisis and chaos. If it is to be an upshift, it must be carefully prepared and consciously guided. An effective and lasting transformation in the conduct of human life is not a simple matter. It is feasible, because in the final count it depends only on us, but it calls for conscious participation by a critical mass of dedicated people.

The great upshift could start small and then expand rapidly. It could begin with a handful of people reviewing the traveled path and looking for alternatives. On deeper reflection, they will find that there are feasible alternatives to the way we live and act on the planet — this compendium of insights by some of the most renowned thought-leaders of our time outlines the principal varieties. Opting for them grants us conscious evolution: the purposeful upshift that enables us to create a world in which all people can live in peace and harmony.

—Ervin Laszlo and David Lorimer

ROADMAPS TO THE GREAT UPSHIFT

PART ONE

UPSHIFTING OUR WORLD

ROADMAP CLUSTER I

THE BIG PICTURE

- *Keynote*: Myth-Perceptions, Mass Extinctions, and the Upshift to a New Civilization
- Our Conscious (R)evolution
- Upshifting Towards a Humanized Technology
- On the Cusp of a New Era
- Awakening the Power of the New Human Story
- The Spiritual Traditions and the Path Toward Peace and Harmony

CHAPTER 1

KEYNOTE

MYTH-PERCEPTIONS, MASS EXTINCTIONS, AND THE UPSHIFT TO A NEW CIVILIZATION

BRUCE H. LIPTON

Read the news or surf the Web, and you will observe that civilization is in a world of crises. Crisis ignites evolution! If today's headlines make you wonder about the fate of our planet, here is some news that may surprise you: from an evolutionary standpoint, we are exactly where we need to be. A scientific renaissance is taking us beyond economic collapse, climate change, religious and racial extremes, and the impending 6th Mass Extinction Event to reveal that such chaos is a natural step in an unfolding process, rather than the tragic end to a broken planet.

A new world is emerging right before our eyes. We are surrounded by evidence that civilization is poised on the threshold of a major evolutionary event ... Conscious Evolution.

Quantum Physics is precipitating a planetary wide evolutionary upheaval and ushering in a new version of reality. Quantum Physics is the most valid of all the sciences — virtually all the foundational hypotheses defining this science, introduced in 1927, have since been verified to be true. The primary difference between our earlier version of the Universe's mechanisms, defined in Classical (Newtonian) Physics, and the newer awareness offered by Quantum Physics, profoundly changes our understanding of the Universe.

Classical Physics is based upon a Newtonian version of the Universe as being subdivided into two separate realms: matter and energy. Historically, Science, built upon the foundation of separate material and energy realms, has become civilization's chosen "truth-provider," humanity's source of knowledge regarding the mysteries of the Universe. Of significance is the fact that this version of Science views Metaphysical abstract theories as having no basis in a material reality, dismissing Metaphysical philosophy as "religion."

The revision of modern Science is profoundly important at the current moment in time. The cultural consequences of a Classical Physics version of the Universe have precipitated the planet's 6th Mass Extinction Event. Five times in the history of the planet, life was thriving until some catastrophic event wiped out up to 90% of the web of life. The catastrophes were associated with natural events such as massive volcanic and earthquake activities, tectonic plate movements, and meteor impacts. The last Mass Extinction was 66 million years ago when a massive meteor hit the Yucatan peninsula. The collision upended the planet's web of life, eliminating 75% of all plant and animal species, including all the dinosaurs that roamed the land and seas.

For nearly 20 years, Science has been warning the public that human behavior is undermining the web of life and initiating a Mass Extinction.

A major factor contributing to this collapse is that the unbridled vora-
ciousness of modern civilization has trampled the Garden from which we
evolved. To sustain the demands of today's civilization, we need 1.6 Earths!
Obviously, this is an unsustainable reality contributing to today's global
chaos. Simply, civilization cannot survive if we do not change our behavior.
Fortunately, all we need to avert the impending 6th Mass Extinction Event
is ... Knowledge.

"Knowledge is Power" is a fundamental truth. Another way to express
the same idea: "A lack of knowledge is a lack of power." By definition, a
"misperception" contributes to a lack of knowledge and disempowerment.
I refer to societal misperceptions as "myth-perceptions," widely held false
beliefs/narratives shaping a traditional story that tends to explain natural
or social phenomena.

In 1967, my research on cloning stem cells contributed to pioneering
work in the field of Epigenetics, a new version of hereditary mechanisms.
Newly discovered epigenetic processes challenged the principles held
by conventional genetics and revealed that conventional genetic science
introduced fundamental scientific myth-perceptions that have distorted
our insights on the origin and nature of life. Today, those genetic misperceptions are provoking planetary upheaval.

The studies on cloned stem cells offered new insights on the molecular
pathways by which the mind controls genes (epigenetics) and behavior.
This research, fully described in *The Biology of Belief*,[1] introduces a "new"
biology in which beliefs (perceptions) control our lives. The new biology
fully complements the fundamental principle in quantum physics that
acknowledges "consciousness creates our life experiences."

While focusing on how consciousness shapes our individual lives, I
began to consider the consequences of a large population sharing the same
beliefs? They would physically manifest a culture shaped by their collective

perceptions. What if they created a version of life based on self-destructive misperceptions? As we are currently experiencing, they would manifest a Mass Extinction.

There are four fundamental scientific misperceptions, myths, listed below. Collectively, they are contributing to our own pending extinction.

- Myth Perception 1: Human Beings Are "Separate" from Nature
- Myth Perception 2: Life Is Controlled by Genes
- Myth Perception 3: Material and Energetic Realms Represent Separate Entities
- Myth Perception 4: Darwinian Theory's "Survival of the Fittest" Drives Evolution

The following is a summary describing the planet-altering influence arising from each of the above listed misperceptions.

▍MYTH PERCEPTION 1: HUMAN BEINGS ARE "SEPARATE" FROM NATURE

The misperception that human beings are separate entities from Nature was defined in the Biblical story of Genesis, which describes the 6-days of "creation." After five days of manifestations, the sixth day of creation brought forth the light, the sky, the Earth, the seas, and the forests, and then God created animals of the land … and man.

As described in the Bible, God said, "Let us make man in our image, after our likeness: and let them have dominion over the fish of the sea, and over the fowl of the air, and over the cattle, and over all the earth, and over every creeping thing that creepeth upon the earth."

After the creation of Adam and Eve, the Bible acknowledges that God blessed them and encouraged them to: "Have many children. Fill the earth and take control of it. Rule over the fish in the sea and the birds in the air. Rule over every living thing that moves on the earth."

Genesis emphasizes that humans were a separate creation, distinct from the origin of Nature. More significantly, the story granted humans dominion over Nature. How is that working out? Apparently, not well, for we are facing an impending man-made collapse of the planet's ecosystems, destroying the environment, and poisoning the air, land, and water. Clearly, the responsibility of "dominion" is not a well-developed character in human civilization.

Humanity didn't fare any better after Darwin's evolution theory successfully challenged the "truth" of the Church's Genesis origins. It was at this time that Science replaced the Church as civilization's "truth-provider." While Science offered an alternate origin story, its conclusion was the same as the Church's: there is no specific connection of humans with the rest of Nature. An evolution driven by random (purposeless) mutations means there is no reason, other than chance, to account for our existence. Both Science and the Church independently disconnected civilization from the environment in which we evolved.

The global chaos we are experiencing is a wake-up call from Mother Nature, alerting the world that dysfunctional human behavior is precipitating the impending 6th Mass Extinction. To survive on this planet, civilization must profoundly change its current course. The truths we now seek to survive the chaos will return us to a belief held by Indigenous people over 10,000 years ago: "Nature is a Garden, and humans are gardeners."

Gaia Theory, offered by James Lovelock, recognized that the Ear`' a living "system" that tends toward dynamic equilibrium `` harmony. For example, plants were the first life for`` Plants respire by breathing in carbon dioxide an` waste gas. As the planet's mass of plants increased, s content of oxygen. At high levels of oxygen, lightning ignited global fires. Nature's resolution for the oxygen imbalance was to introduce animals, organisms that respire by breathing in oxygen and releasing carbon dioxide. The respiratory interaction of plants and animals serves to balance atmospheric oxygen and carbon dioxide.

The origin of animals was not an accident. The new science of epigenetics reveals how environment engages genetic activity in manifesting organismal adaptations, a process that leads to the evolution of new species. When an environment is out of balance, Nature introduces a more powerful organism that will return environmental balance. However, the life of each newly introduced organism may also contribute to generating an environmental imbalance ... and the cycle goes on. The "new" biology emphasizes an alternative vision as to why we are here — environment managers.

Every organism plays an important role in maintaining ecological balance. As an example, when humans thought that wolves were a "menace" to their society, an aggressive campaign was launched to exterminate them. The result was a profound deterioration of the ecosystem with imbalances in the plant and animal populations, leading to an essential devolution of the local biosphere. When wolves were returned to the environment, their role in maintaining Nature's balance resulted in a complete restoration of the former natural environment.

Biologically, humans at the top of the Tree of Life are endowed to be the most powerful source of maintaining the Garden's harmony. Unfortunately, the culturally programmed belief that we are separate from Nature has removed responsibility for humans in tending the planet's environment. However, the inherent power humans wield over Nature is unarguably pressed in civilization's role in precipitating a global mass extinction.

In response to the planetary destruction caused by Myth Perception 1, civilization is being called upon to return to its evolutionary role as the Gardener, empowered to maintain ecological balance and rewarded with a bountiful harvest from Mother Earth. Civilization's urgent role is to reduce the destructive impact of our "footprint" in the Garden. In conjunction with technological innovation, humanity is offered an opportunity to more than survive. We can learn to *thrive* into the future.

▌MYTH PERCEPTION 2: LIFE IS CONTROLLED BY GENES

The belief that Genes control our lives was based on a famous 1944 experiment that transformed bacterial species with DNA extracts derived from other species.[2] Nine years later, Watson and Crick introduced the mechanism of how the DNA double helix encodes the synthesis of complex protein molecules, the building blocks of the body.[3]

Once Science established that genes programmed-controlled synthesis of the body's proteins, they were left with the question as to what "controls" the reproduction of the DNA. An answer was offered in an experiment where a DNA double helix was split into two single helices. When a single strand of the DNA was incubated in a solution of nucleic acid building blocks ("bases"), the single strand induced the creation of a complementary strand that recreated the original double helix. What controls DNA? DNA codes itself!

In 1958, Francis Crick published an article defining biology's Central Dogma, the belief that information in biology only flowed in one direction: From DNA to RNA to Protein. This model states that genes "control" our life characteristics, including our anatomy, physiology, emotions, and behaviors. This hypothesis became the foundation for the notion of Genetic Determinism. As the name implies, this belief acknowledges that genes "determine" the character of our lives. Humans, as the protein mechanisms at the end of the information flow, cannot go against the flow and influence the DNA.

The Central Dogma was an untested hypothesis when advanced by Crick. It has been repeated so frequently over the last 60 years that it has acquired that persona of being a fundamental "truth." However, epigenetic science invalidates the Dogma, which has now become a dysfunctional myth-perception. The world has come to misperceive the Dogma as a fundamental scientific fact, one that I taught to medical students years ago.

Consider the consequence of this theory: As far as we know, we didn't pick the genes we came with, and we can't change the genes if we don't like our characteristics. Add to that the belief that genes "turn on and off" by themselves. The public has become programmed with the belief that they are "victims" of their heredity, that traits carried in their family lineage will genetically determine their fates.

Epigenetics completely invalidates the disempowering myth of the Dogma and genetic determinism. Genes are simply molecular blueprints encoding the unique sequence of amino acids comprising the protein's peptide chain. The folding pattern of this linear peptide, which represents the protein's "backbone," shapes a protein's structure and function. The idea that genes turn on and off is false. As blueprints, genes are not "self-emergent;" they are incapable of controlling their own activity.

My research on cloned stem cells revealed that the chemistry of the culture medium, the environment in which cells are grown, controls their genetic fate. Culture medium is the laboratory version of blood. The fact that the environment controlled the cell's fate and genetics applies to all cells whether they are grown in plastic culture dishes or in human bodies (i.e., skin-covered "culture" dishes).

While the brain controls the chemical composition of blood, we are left with the fundamental question as to which chemicals should the blood contain. Epigenetic science emphasizes that the environment, and more importantly, our "perception" of the environment, controls the chemical composition of the blood, which in turn, controls gene activity. Since we are empowered to control our environment and perceptions, we are in control of our gene activity. The knowledge of epigenetic science transforms us from "victims" of our heredity to "masters" of our genetic expression.

It is important to note that less than 1% of disease is caused by genes and that 90% of doctor visitations are due to chronic stress. Stress-consciousness leads to high levels of stress hormones (e.g., cortisol) in the blood, a chemical environment that shuts down the growth and maintenance of the body, inhibits the immune system, and impairs conscious creativity. A world in stress is the driving force responsible for our current planetary health crisis.

When the public becomes fully aware of the implications of epigenetics, the fact that consciousness controls genes, they will be empowered to rewrite limiting and self-sabotaging behaviors that have taken control over their lives. The planet's health crisis would be resolved once the public applies the science of epigenetics to enhance the quality of their health, emotions, and creative abilities.

MYTH PERCEPTION 3: MATERIAL AND ENERGETIC REALMS REPRESENT SEPARATE ENTITIES

Newtonian (Classical) Physics subdivided the Universe into two separate and distinct realms: physical matter (atoms) and invisible energy (waves), with limited interactions between the realms. Essentially, matter can only be influenced by other forms of matter. The only acknowledged form of energy that impacts matter is referred to as "ionizing" energy, energy fields that alter matter such as electro-cauterization, UV radiation, and radioactivity.

Classical Physics does not recognize the influence of non-ionizing radiation such as consciousness and spirituality. However, this fact was profoundly challenged when it was recognized that positive or negative consciousness were respectively responsible for the health-impacting placebo and nocebo effects.

The newer science of Quantum Physics completely undermines the belief in a two-realm Universe defined in Classical Physics. In Quantum Physics, the Universe is a singularity, comprised of only one realm, energy, with matter representing a unique form of focused energy. Atoms are not made of physical particles (electrons, positrons, neutrons, and quarks); they are created from immaterial, nano-tornado-like, energy vortices.

Resolving the "secret of life," proteins, the anatomical building blocks of cells, are characterized by their unique 3-dimensional structure. The protein molecule's shape is derived from the folding pattern of its linear peptide "backbone." The folding pattern is generated by balancing the distribution of positive- and negative-charged amino acids along the linear peptide backbone.

The secret of life is movement. When a complementary environmental signal binds to a protein, the signal introduces a new electromagnetic charge that causes the protein backbone to reconfigure its folding pattern to accommodate a change in charge distribution. Movements generated by the protein's shape change drive the physiological behaviors that create life. The following equation summarizes the source of life:

$$Protein + Signal = Behavior$$

Conventional allopathic medicine, based on Classical Physics, focuses on material (chemical) signals, drugs, as the means of controlling biology. In contrast, energy medicine, based on Quantum Physics principles, emphasizes that invisible energy fields are the primary controlling signals shaping protein behaviors. Einstein emphasized the validity of this approach when he declared that "the field is the sole governing agency of the particle" (matter). The "mind" is the generator of energy "fields" that shape the character of our physical and behavioral realities.

An article entitled "The Mental Universe," published in the most prestigious scientific journal *Nature* by Physicist Richard Conn Henry of Johns Hopkins University, concludes with: "The Universe is immaterial — it's mental and spiritual. Live and enjoy."[4]

Quantum Physics acknowledges that consciousness is creating our life experiences. Then why is civilization precipitating its own extinction? The reason is that consciousness is derived from two functionally distinct and interdependent minds, the creative (self-) conscious mind and the programmable, habit-controlling subconscious mind.

The creative conscious mind that manifests wishes, desires, and aspirations only controls 5% of our life experiences, while 95% of our life is controlled by habits downloaded into the subconscious mind. Psychologists recognize that the majority of those programs that are downloaded into the child's subconscious mind before age 7, represent disempowering, self-sabotaging, and limiting beliefs.[1]

The reason why the conscious mind has limited control over our life experiences is that, in addition to being "creative," the conscious mind can "think." Thinking diverts the conscious mind's attention from controlling our behavior in the outer world, to focusing on thoughts within the mind. When the conscious mind is engaged in thought, it is disconnected from observing the current reality.

At such times, the subconscious serves as an "autopilot" that takes control over the operations of life, employing previously downloaded programs. While in thought, the conscious mind does not observe the behavioral programs being run by the subconscious mind. The relevance is that "invisible" subconscious habits control 95% of our lives, the majority of which sabotage our wishes and desires. Without the conscious awareness that we are running dysfunctional habit-programs, we perceive that we are "victims" in a world out of control.

The movie *The Matrix* is more of a documentary than a science fiction film. As emphasized in the movie, everyone's life is "programmed." This is a fact: 95% of life is controlled by subconscious mind programs (habits). Most of these life-shaping programs were downloaded into the subconscious before age 7, a time when the brain was predominantly functioning in the theta state (EEG). Theta is hypnosis. A child below 7 years of age acquires enculturation programs by simply observing and downloading behaviors of others, especially the behavior of parents, siblings, and local community.

It is significant to note that programs downloaded into a child's subconscious mind represent both the positive and negative behaviors of others. Acquired behavioral programs derived from observing others do not necessarily support our own wishes and desires, and yet, they do control the character of our lives.

In *The Matrix* movie, people are offered a blue pill, which when taken, maintains the character of their programmed lives. In contrast, a red pill allows people to escape their limiting programs. Science recognizes that falling in love with another person or a pet, or engaging in a labor of love, such as being a chef, a gardener, or an artist, keeps the conscious mind's attention focused on the present moment. Staying present, or being mindful, keeps the conscious mind engaged in controlling life, which cancels the need for the subconscious mind to serve as the "autopilot." When falling in love, the conscious creative mind stops "thinking" and is free to manifest the wishes and desires that create the honeymoon experience. This is how an "ordinary" life, in just 24 hours, can magically transform our experiences into Heaven-on-Earth.

Once the public becomes aware that their lives are primarily controlled by dysfunctional subconscious programs, they will be free to rewrite limiting subconscious beliefs and replace them with consciously creative programs supporting wishes and desires. If civilization was living a "honeymoon-driven" life, the whole planet would manifest the reality of Heaven-on-Earth.

MYTH PERCEPTION 4: DARWINIAN THEORY'S "SURVIVAL OF THE FITTEST" DRIVES EVOLUTION

Darwinian theory was poetically described by Alfred Tennyson as being "red in tooth and claw," a literary interpretation of the theory's emphasis that life is driven by "competition in the struggle for survival." Darwin based this aspect of his evolution theory on a philosophy defined by Thomas Malthus, an 18th-century British economist. The theory of Malthus concluded that food production would not be able to keep up with growth in the human population. This would result in a Malthusian Crisis that would eliminate excessive humans through disease, famine, and war.

Darwinian theory emphasizes that only the "fittest" will survive in this competition. His theory was predicated on a Victorian worldview that perceived the "fittest" to be those derived from upper class breeding. Citizens from the lower class, those that provided support for the upper class, were deemed expendable and would be eliminated through the competition to survive.

Unfortunately, Darwinian theory's focus on the "end" being survival does not define the "means" to get to that end. Social Darwinism legitimizes any pursuit necessary to survive, a scenario in which an Uzi in the hands of an extremist would triumph over the intelligence of an Einstein. This theory allows well fed people in Western nations to dismiss the starvation of millions of Africans as simply their failure to survive the struggle.

The problem is that the Malthusian competition hypothesis is a dysfunctional misperception. Science recognizes in animal populations that two parents provide for two parents, a reproductive strategy that stabilizes population growth.[5] More importantly, current science recognizes that evolution is driven by species cooperation, not by Darwinian competition.[6] When this new knowledge is understood by the population, it will stop the runaway dog-eat-dog rat race that is stressing civilization and the planet's ecosystems. Cooperation and the sharing of awareness in a community is the actual driving force that promotes the evolution of civilization.

Each of the here listed fundamental "myth-perceptions" is a primary contributor to humanity's dysfunction that is collectively precipitating Earth's 6th Mass Extinction. To survive the impending threat, the misperceptions currently held as societal "truths" must be replaced by an updated and more sustainable version of civilization. The turning point is the upshift that is emerging as people awaken to their inherent power, a new evolutionary force, for transforming the fear of an unwanted situation into the hope of new possibilities.

CHAPTER 2

OUR CONSCIOUS (R)EVOLUTION

JUDE CURRIVAN

I f past attempts to envisage the future are anything to go by, we likely have little or no idea of what will come.

Most forecasts of the future have been either iterations of the past, or a larger leap, often based on potential technological innovations, and now the consequences of the global environmental and existential threats we face. Yet, they still have been generally based on a currently prevailing worldview.

Few have been able to envisage what a future founded on a transformational understanding of nature or reality itself and our purpose and possible role within its evolutionary emergence might look like.

Nonetheless, we are on the threshold of such a radical and existential question, called to ask, 'What if?' such understanding might be imminent and its corollary, 'What then?'

It is, here and now, at a potential revelatory moment of collective choice and on the verge of a (r)evolutionary and transformational journey that we stand.

▌WHAT IF?

What if, instead of viewing consciousness as something we have and experiencing it at different levels of self-awareness, we come to understand as an empirical reality that mind and consciousness are what we and the whole world truly are?

What if we are about to discover, as wisdom teachings have maintained, that universal mind literally in-forms the appearance of our Universe, as merely its semblance and not its fundamental nature?

What if unity and its manifold expressions in complexity and diversity, rather than separation or uniformity, is indeed our existential reality?

What if we as a species no longer need to hope, trust, and have faith in such an aspirational possibility but come to understand, experience, and embody this essential realization?

What if science finally catches up and converges with wisdom teachings to provide scientifically-based evidence of the nonlocally unified nature of our entire Universe?

What if we're about to be presented with ever more compelling evidential confirmation that we're microcosmic co-creators of its unfolding and emergent coherent and unified intelligence, a finite thought form in the infinity and eternity of cosmic mind?

We are.

Such a 21st century scientific revolution is well underway, and its recent breakthroughs are rapidly expanding across all scales of existence. Increasingly, its discoveries across numerous fields of research from cosmology to biology, neuroscience, and the study of collective human behaviors and our innate nonlocal attributes will radically affect not only our view of the Universe at its smallest and largest scales but also at every level in between and vitally for our everyday lives.

Crucially, its findings are converging with spiritual experiences, indigenous and other perennial wisdom teachings, and numerous meta-analyses of supernormal and multi-dimensional phenomena into a cosmology of a conscious, emergent, and unitive Universe and a realization of our planetary home as also a sentient and evolving being — Gaia.

▌A UNITIVE NARRATIVE

This emergent understanding[7,8] is enabling an authentic and unitive narrative to underpin, frame, and empower our conscious (r)evolution, a collective we-volution.

Such a unitive narrative has been articulated, initially by members of the SDG thought leaders group of the Evolutionary Leaders circle,[9] and the tenets of its main and generic text, as follows, invite a collective choice to awaken from the illusion of separation to an experiential and conscious embodiment of its (r)evolutionary call and the potential for a future that works for all:

The unfolding evolutionary story describes how cosmic mind, articulated in a universal 'language' based on digitized and vitally, meaningful, in-formation and pixelated at the most minute scale of existence, literally and actively in-forms the entire appearance and manifest forms of our Universe. The holographic principle, so named by extending research from black holes to a universal scale, is also providing compelling cosmological evidence that the Universe's in-formed reality manifests holographically, with its innate wholeness expressed in nested and relational complexity of its differentiated and diverse parts.

The mathematical signatures and dynamic patterns and processes of wholeness are being found at all scales of existence and through numerous fields of study ranging from cosmology, physics, and chemistry to biology, complex systems, and collective human behaviors.

Beginning 13.8 billion years ago, not in the old paradigm story of the implied chaos of a big bang, but as a beautifully ordered and incredibly fine-tuned first moment of an ongoing 'big breath,' a sentient Universe emerged. As space expands from its miniscule birth and time flows from past to present to future, life embodies a profound evolutionary impulse driven not by random occurrences and mutations but through resonant and harmonic interplays of forces and influences that are meaningfully and coherently in-formed and guided.

Gaia's continuing emergence is embodied in collaborative and synergistic relationships and dynamic coevolutionary partnerships on a planetary scale where, now, the conscious evolution of humanity may be realized as an integral part of our planet's own evolutionary progress and purpose.

On planetary and human levels, the universal and archetypal relationships now being evidentially revealed are also reflected in spirituality-based and wisdom traditions and in psychologist C.G. Jung's concept of the collective unconscious and representative archetypes: containing the whole spiritual heritage of humanity's evolution born anew in the mind of every individual.

Instead of the apparent separation of our inner and outer awareness, and devaluation of our inner perception, a unitive narrative values our inner cognition and invites us to inwardly hear the wisdom of our hearts. In doing so, it also honors and respects the complementarity of feminine and masculine attributes, relatedness, and balanced perspectives and empowers the co-creativity of their synergies within and between us. Thus, its unity expressed in diversity guides us to a wholeness of both the inner being and outer doing in our lives and supports us in integrating our innate health and wholeness, both individually and communally.

▌A COMING UNITIVE AGE?

A period centered around two and a half thousand years ago and lasting over more than five centuries has been called the inception of the Axial Age, which has continued until now. Characterized by a series of nascent spiritual and philosophical teachings, institutionalization of religions, and shifts from communal to individual values, it also involved secular innovations including coinage, leading to wider and greater complexity of trading and societal structures.

Ushering in radical changes, nonetheless, the insights of the Axial Age all sought meaning and purpose for human existence. All recognized non-physical dimensions of reality and aspired to integrate inner and outer experience of life. Generally, while promoting the actualization of personal agency, they also emphasized the good of the whole, which included the sustenance of planetary well-being.

Yet, I would suggest that no philosopher or revelatory teacher of those times did nor could anticipate the nonlinear emergence of the sweeping technological and global changes that have continued to unfold.

The progressive secularization of our collective world-view and our sense of self through a prevailing scientific and technological perspective of materialist separation, while bringing physical benefits has, nonetheless, dis-membered our psyche from our earlier roots and communal sense of belonging and resulted from the consequential disconnection in chronic trauma.

Now, though, the evidence-based and emergent cosmology of a living Universe that meaningfully exists and purposefully evolves as a nonlocally unified entity is inviting us to awaken to realize that we are inseparable from each other, Gaia, and the whole world. It is calling us to re-member who we really are and heal the trauma of our perceived separation into the whole-being and belonging of our true nature and is empowering us to consciously evolve to the beings we can become.

Given, too, the immediacy of our global communications and the cultural potency of horizontal meme transfers, the possible dawning of a new and Unitive Age may emerge far more rapidly than did that of its Axial predecessor.

However, I would also suggest a likely similarity in the systemic nonlinearity and inherent unknowingness as to how such a unitive based future might unfold and embody its (r)evolutionary potential.

So, rather than attempt to forecast possible specificities, which I feel are enigmatic, I'll now go on to instead consider how we might best enjoin its potency, to consciously evolve and be guided by principles of personal and collective unitive awareness.

Such awareness embraces unitive values, the 'into-greation' of complementary feminine and masculine attributes, and naturalizes multidimensional perception and communications as integral aspects of our whole-being and belonging to the whole world. Its guidance also invites us to mature through our integral embodiment of mind, heart, and purpose, to become conscious co-evolutionary partners with the ongoing emergent impulse of Gaia and our entire Universe.

▌UNITIVE VALUES

The most foundational tenet of the emergent unitive narrative is that mind and consciousness are not something we have, but what we and the whole world fundamentally are. The realization of this universal unity and its expression in radical diversity vitally recognizes our interbeing and belonging with the whole community of Gaia and with the entire Universe and its imbued consciousness, meaning, purpose, and evolutionary flow.

It consequently also invites a range of unitive-based values and resultant ethical behaviors that are love-centered and inclusive.

These are the same values that the most profound of spiritually-based traditions teach and on which indigenous wisdom and healthy communal behaviors are based. They call for us to recognize that we are naturally part of a universal web of life, rather than separate from it.

These include reverence for all life. This embraces, honors, and respects not only people and other biological organisms but also those who Native American teachings refer to as 'all our relations,' including the body of Gaia, our Sun and Moon, our ancestral lineages, and spiritual and unseen realms.

Another is a deep and felt sense of what is fair and just, that which sociologists appreciate is embodied in us and expressed from early childhood. While young, we deeply care about such authenticity and truth. Yet, our societies, when based on a worldview and mind set of separation, teach and show us otherwise.

Reciprocity is another value which the Q'ero people of Peru call *ayni*, ensuring the mutuality and balance of give and take, in taking no more than what fulfils a need and, especially when that is provided by Gaia, to reciprocate with gratitude.

All of these values are based on an experienced kinship and participation in a world where there is differentiation, complexity, and diversity but which is essentially whole and its constituent parts inseparable and as embodied in the principle of *ubuntu*, a Nguni Bantu term that can be translated as 'I am because you are.'

Perhaps the most fundamental unitive value is founded on this recognition. The so-named 'golden rule,' to treat others — and our planetary home Gaia — as we would wish to be treated ourselves, is a value that lies at the heart of the core teachings of all major religions and spiritual traditions.

Unitive awareness also inherently honors and respects the complementarity of feminine and masculine attributes, their innate and powerful relatedness, and the benefits of including and balancing their perspectives and contributions. As such, the emergence of a new Unitive Age empowers the co-creativity of their synergies within and between us and enables us to achieve outcomes that are 'greater than the sum of their parts.'

Each of us naturally embodies both, in left-brain analytical and right brain intuitive ways of knowing and in the complementarity of mind-based and heart-based perception — with our hearts having as large a neural network of in-formational connectivity as our brains.

Our current socio-economic structures and organizations have, though, generally based themselves on mechanistic perspectives of separation and competition and hierarchical and dominating characteristics generally viewed as 'masculine,' with these having been predominant approaches and aiming to maximize quantitative performance.

Often continuing to use mechanistic terms to measure effectiveness, human beings are resources, cogs in the 'machine.' Business plans are blueprints for action, with key performance indicators focused on aligning all parts of the machine to its aims for success, almost completely monetarily based. Unchecked, these perspectives competitively and greedily have driven over-consumption, environmental desecration, biodiversity depletion and pollution, inequalities, conflicts, and epidemic levels of stress and dysfunctional behaviors.

In recent years, though, a growing, and now urgent, recognition of their limitations and unsustainability is coming to the fore. Together with inner personal development in the service of self and co-creative leadership and organizational purpose, there is an increasing appreciation of an imperative to integrate behavioral traits generally viewed as feminine, such as inclusion and cooperation.

Such integration stimulates transformational change from the inside out, engendering distributed intelligence throughout organizations and expanding relationships from the individual Me, to encompass the organizational We and a planetary perspective and stewardship of All. In doing so, it also ushers in and co-creatively propagates a synergistic balance of the best and continuing benefits of the past, predominantly masculine, organizational behaviors with feminine attributes.

The following eight attributes which I consider to be natural to such unitive perception, and of course able to be embodied by both men and women, are still unusual in our collective practice. Yet, consciously encouraging and nurturing them is, I believe, vital for a potential future that works for the good of the whole:

- *Servant-leader* — expresses the 'servereignty' of serving the good of the whole rather than the sovereignty of controlling the whole
- *Soul-model* — authentically embodies the highest coherence of the whole rather than role-modelling from an ego-based sense of status
- *Seer* — perceptive co-creator of the highest purpose and meaning of the organization
- *Sensor* — intuitively sensing what is calling to come through and emerge, and then responding and expressing its purpose rather than imposing control
- *Shaper* — facilitating the emergent evolutionary 'shape' and embodiment of the organization
- *Space-holder* — enabling and empowering diverse inclusivity and belonging and individual / collective worth, value, and meaning throughout the organization and beyond

And where appropriate:

- *Stirrer* — intervening as, when, and how sensed to co-enable progressive and optimal positive change, increased capacity, resilience, and thrivability
- *Shaker* — intervening as, when, and how sensed to initiate (r)evolutionary transformation

▌EXPANDING AWARENESS TO OUR WHOLE-BEING AND BELONGING

The so-named nonlocally unified reality of our universe has been effectively recognized as settled science by the award of the 2022 Nobel Prize for Physics to three researchers whose experimental work over many decades has validated what was an early prediction of quantum mechanics and, indeed, a necessary prerequisite for quantum phenomena to universally manifest.

The nonlocal mindfulness of our Universe naturally encompasses multidimensional levels of sentience. As attested to by universal wisdom teachings and myriad direct experience over millennia, we have inborn abilities to engage and communicate with and, vitally, to learn from them. Our intuition can then also be recognized as an inborn 'superpower' to which all of us have access, and nonlocal supernormal phenomena, attributes, and perception such as telepathy and remote viewing can be considered to be attainable too in certain states of awareness. Further, those meaningful 'coincidences' that Carl Jung called synchronicities, when paid attention to, also denote nonlocal connectivity, nonetheless without violating the causality crucially embedded within space-time. Naturalizing this birthright offers a greater embodiment of our potential whole-being and a realization that we fundamentally belong as micro-cosmic co-creators of the unitive sentience of our entire Universe. It also beckons us to a future where we can evolve to consciously become co-evolutionary partners of its and Gaia's ongoing emergent impulse and potential.

WHAT THEN? SEEING THROUGH A UNITIVE LENS

To paraphrase novelist Marcel Proust: "The real voyage of discovery consists not in seeking new landscapes but in having new eyes."

Our world-views underpin and frame our behaviors, and our behaviors also influence our world-views. So, progressively changing our perception, to view and so experience the world through a unitive lens, has the potential to (r)evolutionize our consciousness while, alongside, unitive approaches can actively support processes of change.

When I co-founded WholeWorld-View[10] in 2017, aiming to serve the understanding, experience, and embodiment of unitive awareness to serve this evolutionary purpose, our embryonic community recognized that what was required could be expressed by a three-fold call to action: Act Local, Feel Global and Think Cosmic.

At each level of the dynamically interdependent, interpenetrating, and holarchic levels of acting, feeling, and thinking from a unitive perspective, we asked why it matters to do so.

In acting local, the tenets of relating, belonging, involving, and sustaining came to the fore, providing place-based fractals (both physical and also virtual) of caring and co-creative communities to synergistically link up and lift up together.

In asking the same question of feeling global, responses that appreciated that "we look after what we care about" and "we care for what we relate to" emerged. Realizing that we and our planetary home Gaia are inseparable invoked, thanks to visionary Michael Lindfield, the embrace of the concept of being Gaian, a profoundly sensed invitation to experientially belong as microcosms of Gaia's sentience and evolutionary purpose.

In doing so, we can learn from the profound wisdom of our planetary parent, as we seek to consciously evolve our societies, organizations, and economics to undertake regenerative healing and being based on life and unitive eco-nomics. As I describe in *The Story of Gaia*:

> Our planetary home only uses the energy needed for all she achieves. She fits form to function with underlying simplicity, exquisite beauty, and intricate precision. She recycles everything with no waste. She shares and in-forms her skills locally and globally. She embodies collaboration throughout her biosphere, appreciating healthy competition and encouraging holarchic cooperation and evolutionary purpose. She exults in diversity and knows it to imbue resilience and collective genius. And she exists, evolves, and thrives within the wholistic limits and emergent opportunities of her planetary gaiasphere. And she's been doing so for over four billion years.

The evocation to think cosmic elicited that, as our entire universe exists and evolves as a nonlocally unified entity, we literally are its micro-cosmic co-creators and ourselves fundamentally embody its existential meaning and evolutionary purpose. Further, our conscious (r)evolution to embody unitive awareness invites us to become co-evolutionary partners in an ongoing, universal, and planetary journey of discovery, transformation, and emergent possibility.

CHAPTER 3

UPSHIFTING TOWARDS A HUMANIZED TECHNOLOGY

KINGSLEY L. DENNIS

But for those of us who have thrown off the myth of the machine, the next move is ours: for the gates of the technocratic prison will open automatically, despite their rusty ancient hinges, as soon as we choose to walk out. — Lewis Mumford

The arrival of a mechanized society has long been a feared specter. From philosophers (Jacques Ellul) to historians (Lewis Mumford) to humanist psychologists (Erich Fromm), the specter and spectacle of the megamachine was ominously on the horizon. It was feared that individual liberty within mass society would slip away from the control of the individual, the fear of losing individualism and privacy against a faceless machinic environment. The first wave of so-called progressive technology that arrived was an abundance of technique, management, and consumption. Society itself was in danger — still is in danger — of becoming the Machine, a grand overarching architecture based upon advancing technologies and governed by an elite technocracy.

These fears and anxieties still remain thanks largely to such pronouncements as have been made by Israeli historian Yuval Noah Harari. The fear of an automated future brings redundancy to human life and meaning. Recently, Harari announced that the immediate future holds little hope for a new underclass of 'irrelevant' and 'useless' people. In previous centuries, says Harari, people revolted against exploitation, oppression, tyranny, etc.; now, they fear becoming irrelevant. He has stated that: 'If we are not careful, we will end up with downgraded humans misusing upgraded computers to wreak havoc on themselves and on the world.'[11] Huge numbers of individuals will find themselves living in a society that doesn't need them anymore — or so the prognosis goes.

Yet, this narrative is not set in stone. It is a prediction based upon present trends according to a world of increasing materialism, consumption, and capitalistic drives. It is a world based upon the past and the present, but not the future. In the opinion of this author, it is a redundant projected timeline, for it is not based upon the hope of the many but the greed of the few. With our present and emerging technologies, a revitalized hope can be brought to bear upon the citizens of this planet.

Hope is a vital aspect of any social change. It has been said that the worship of progress based upon present trends is an alienation of hope. Real hope for change is a state of being, an inner readiness. It is the *humanization of hope* that I speak of here. It is a rallying cry against the encroaching forces of dehumanization that speak loudly of transhumanism and synthetic, silicon futures. Certain groups and agencies are speaking about a Fourth Industrial Revolution, and yet, their visions are based upon machines, mergers, economics, and efficiency. They do not present a human-centric future but one where a new industrial, automated future makes an allowance for the human being but only as periphery to the primary race of great technological change. This de-centering of the human being from the core of life is a grand mistake and misplacement. The future shall be human, or it shall not be. A humanized technology is what is required for taking humanity further into the 21st century. Otherwise, a great misbalance may occur between human relations and the world we find ourselves within.

Contrary to a humanized technology is a dehumanizing one, that is, a tech-architecture and ecosystem of non-visible codes, algorithms, and machinic intellect that makes decisions upon which depends the freedom and quality of life of the individual. This unseen and almost ungovernable dependency is alienating, disquieting, and apathetic to the human condition. Any future technologized human civilization needs to redefine the ordering and organizing potentials of technology into facilitators, assistors, and a secondary management architecture (rather than as the primary management system). In other words, the technological architecture is to be fully decentralized and assisting humans from the background, upon request, and within industry to facilitate human working conditions. Technology should never be a substitution to a human life, but an enabler of human needs and potentials.

Furthermore, a humanized technology is one that supports and assists the egalitarian nature of human society as opposed to instigating and sustaining hierarchical, elite societal stratifications. A humanized technology can only be a unifier and never a divider or segregator. Efficiency within humanized technology is never at the expense of the individual or the quality of their life but is an amplifier of these in support of human well-being.

Efficiency and economy have become dirty words within the present-day technological society. When we think of such concepts we are reminded of cold, dry mechanization and scientific management principles. Until now, technology has not been sufficiently aligned to the needs of the changing human condition upon this planet. We need a new relationship to our devices, our digital networks, and digital assistants before we end up being compelled to adapt to this machinic environment rather than it adapting to a human one.

Any sufficiently advanced species visiting this planet could be forgiven for thinking that a terraforming project is underway for adapting the planet Earth for a machinic intelligence or AI (Artificial Intellect) form of species — the highly dense electromagnetic environment, the masts and antennas, the cameras and surveillance systems, the monitoring satellites, etc., etc. In 1987, the English poet Heathcote Williams published his epic poem 'Autogeddon' about the impact of the automobile. In it he wrote:

> If an alien was to hover a few hundred yards above the planet
> It could be forgiven for thinking
> That cars were the dominant life-form,
> And that human beings were a kind of ambulatory fuel cell:
> Injected when the car wished to move off,
> And ejected when they were spent.[12]

The same can be said for the world of today if we replace 'car' with 'technological infrastructure.' Only the object of containment has changed; yet the subject of the containment has remained the same. If humanity is to transform itself from being 'a kind of ambulatory fuel cell' within the megamachine, then we need a recalibration of what technology means for human life.

The organization of human life is about quality rather than quantity. This needs to be programmed into the 'intellect' of our technologies. The attraction of automated convenience does not necessarily speak to our quality of life. Furthermore, convenience does not speak of contact and communion. In these years ahead, we shall be redefining what it means to be a human being. We shall also be asking ourselves what the social contract is — and we will need to deal with the new digital elephant in the room. Our social contract will have to become expanded to include our technological assistants and even perhaps the new denizens of AI. What it means to be human, and the human social contract, will most likely need to be redefined within the coming years of civilizational readaptation.

▌UPSHIFTED RELATIONSHIPS WITH TECHNOLOGY

A new orientation is in the making as humankind steps across the third decade threshold of the third millennium. The infantile obsession with our new toys and gadgets will need to be put aside, or put down, as we step into an adolescent phase. A renegotiation will be required so that the promises that technology holds for the human race can be brought to fruition rather than lingering within the infantile stage of centralization, control, censorship, conquest, and craving compulsions. A humanized technology plays a supporting role rather than a dominating one and does not seek to place human civilization within a cage of instrumental power. A humanized technology acts as a custodian to the adaptive needs of the human being. It does not devise means of subtly and slyly nudging and steering the individual into expected outcomes through a biased digital architecture, nor does it seek to make gains from the individual's privacy, data, or any other personal information, as has been well documented within the world of surveillance capitalism.[13]

In the coming years, humanity will no doubt seek a form of transcendence to go beyond certain social rituals and practices that are becoming redundant due to the welcomed arrival of specific forms of automation. The relief from particular forms of manual labor, as well as other types of monotonous work, can bring the average person out of a vicious cycle of dependency and allow new freedoms and creative explorations. New avenues of economic management can establish different roles for workers and release them from past drudgery. Young children can learn programming and coding skills so that they become their own architects of the future, a new generation of programmers that have ethics as a principal moral code that then becomes coded into the intellect of the machines. Yet, this all assumes a move away from top-down corporatization and governmental censorship over technology, its patents, exploration, and utilization, and this presupposes a shift in human consciousness itself.

Technology is a mirror to the human condition. It reflects us back to ourselves: our preoccupations, dreams, desires, and visions. If certain incumbent belief systems and ways of thinking are not transcended, then there is the danger that technologies will come to reflect the infancy of human thinking. We shall need to elevate our capacity for envisioning and truly wanting the values of compassion, collaboration, connection, and conscious awareness if we wish our technologies to assist us in transitioning to an *upshifted* future. If humanity becomes more aligned with a human-centric, value-driven future, then our technologies will reflect this. There is not one without the other. Humankind is in symbiosis with its creations and must be the ones to first set the moral, ethical, and conscious example. The rest will follow.

We can have a world of information, diagnoses, analyses, contact, and much more, at our fingertips. We can become more *Homo sapiens* (wise) as well as *Homo "ludens"* (playful). Wisdom and joy can become an integral part of our technological engagement *if* we can get the balance right. Our digitally assisted explorations into the farthest depths of space and sea; investigations of climate and environment; and engineering marvels and architectural splendors can steer us forward into new insights. The human being alongside technological assistance can envision and construct a world currently beyond our imaginations. It can be done, but only if the right path is taken at this juncture in our human story. We are at a most critical and important time for the future of the human species — we are entering into a merger with another form of intellect, and in this, we need to ensure that the form, manner, and style of intelligence across the planet remains primarily organic based.

Planet Earth is in coherence with organic life, and it would be unnatural to demote organic intelligence in favor of an artificial form of intellect. That is why this essay speaks of the hope of a humanized technological future. The primary concern has to be for the well-being of organic life on the planet, as well as for the planet itself. Present and future economic investments, alongside human efforts, time, and focus should be aimed at developing and establishing a technological environment that assists in liberating humanity from the chores and tasks of previous dependencies. This liberation can then trigger a new explosion in creative industries, imaginative explorations, and innovative pursuits hitherto not made possible for economically indentured societies. This could lead to a cultural renewal appropriate for laying the groundwork for a 21st century planetwide yet decentralized human civilization, a human civilization that is free from the shackles of outdated belief systems, power/control structures, and hierarchical greed.

Yet, this liberation also requires a liberty of mind, body, and consciousness. We do not need to become cyborged or transhumanly tweaked. Neither do we necessarily need to implant devices inside our bodies. These are fashions and consumer conveniences that we have been led into believing will better our days. Yet, we can move beyond this ritualistic and immature thinking into a new era of technological comprehension, collaboration, and closeness. We can transcend ourselves through the inner world of the human being whilst orientating our outer world through a technological partnering, a partnership that is balanced, in harmony and equilibrium, and not overseen by a small, elite, technocratic group.

A humanized technological future must be egalitarian and offer broad-ranging opportunities for all, regardless of class or social identities. In short, the only certifiable technological future is one that unifies rather than divides; promotes development and not alienation; and compels individuals to greatness rather than apathy. There is hope for a future of humanized technology, yet the consciousness shifts need to be occurring now so that the groundwork can be laid with appropriate values, ethics, and equitable vision. These are amongst the *upshifts* that can be promoted and shared for the world of today so that they may illuminate the world of tomorrow.

CHAPTER 4

ON THE CUSP OF A NEW ERA

MICHAEL ELLIS

A s we stand now on the cusp of a new era, we should take stock of the world we inhabit. Twenty years ago, life on our planet was entirely different. The phenomenal rise of corporate science and digitalization and the unprecedented boom in technology have completely transformed our society. The world we live in now is data-driven, where every piece of information is collected, collated, and monetized. This has led to a fragmented world. We are exposed to billions or trillions more electromagnetic frequencies than we were exposed to two decades ago. The harmful effects of radio-frequency radiation on living beings and on the environment have been well documented, and the 5G Space Appeal calls for greater caution in the deployment of technology.[14]

Yet, despite these concerns, 5G is the technology that forms the communication basis of the Fourth Industrial Revolution. It is the backbone of a new age of innovation, where artificial intelligence, big data, and the Internet of Things converge to create a hyperconnected society.

The implications of these developments are vast and far-reaching. We must take stock of the world we are building. As we move forward, we must be mindful of the potential dangers of this new era. We must strive for a world that is both innovative and safe, a world where technology serves the needs of humanity and not the other way around. It is only through a concerted effort that we can achieve this collective responsibility to safeguard our future. So let us stand together, as we face the challenges of the future head-on and build a world that is worthy of our hopes and dreams.

▮THE GREAT RESET

The concept of the Great Reset, introduced by the World Economic Forum (WEF) in May of 2020, proposes a fundamental restructuring of our economy and geopolitical relations, based on the belief that every element of nature and every life form is part of a global inventory, managed by a benevolent state, owned by wealthy elites, via technology. As Klaus Schwab of the Great Reset has said, "You will be free and be happy." Is this truly the path to a better future? The integration of technology into our daily lives presents a host of challenges. One of the most pressing challenges is the displacement of human labor, as machines and algorithms replace workers across the board. This will potentially lead to mass underemployment and unemployment, leaving many struggling to make ends meet.

The issue of privacy and data protection is another area of concern, as our personal information is increasingly collected and analyzed. The rise of social media has only exacerbated this problem, with personal data often being harvested and used for targeted advertising or other purposes without our consent. However, perhaps the most worrying issue of all is the impact that technology is having on our physical and mental health. It is becoming increasingly clear that the sedentary lifestyle associated with our increasing "screen time" and the mental strain of being constantly connected to technology are taking an enormous toll on our well-being.

We must prioritize education for life, well-being and health, creativity, and human values to ensure that everyone can thrive. At the heart of this, there must be a recognition of the basic rights and needs of all people, regardless of their level of education or socioeconomic status.

As we have become ever more focused on the material world, the significance of the soul has receded into the background. But what is the soul, and why is it so important? At its core, the soul is the essence of who we are as human beings. It is the source of our deepest values and beliefs, and the wellspring of our creativity and inspiration. Without the soul, we are reduced to mere automatons, devoid of the depth and richness that make life worth living. So how do we reconnect with the soul in an era dominated by materialism and electromagnetic fields? The answer lies in a fundamental shift in our priorities and values. We must learn to prioritize our inner lives, cultivating practices and habits that foster connection, compassion, and meaning.

THE GLOBAL REVOLUTION IN THE SPHERE OF HUMAN CONSCIOUSNESS

Humanity is at a crisis point, and we are facing tremendous challenges, including singularities of enormous importance impacting the survival of humanity. Transhumanism aims to enable every human to be part human and part artificial intelligence.

The need for a "global revolution in the sphere of human consciousness" has been espoused by many thinkers throughout history. One prominent example is Vaclav Havel, who was a Czech writer, philosopher, and politician. In a 1990 address to the U.S. Congress, Havel said, "Without a global revolution in the sphere of human consciousness, nothing will change for the better in the sphere of our being as humans, and the catastrophe toward which this world is headed, be it ecological, social, and demographic or a general breakdown of civilization, will be unavoidable."

The idea of a shift in human consciousness has also been discussed in the context of environmental issues. In 1992, a group of 1,575 scientists, including 99 Nobel Prize winners, signed a document titled "World Scientists' Warning to Humanity." More recently, in November of 2017, a new warning was issued by 15,364 scientists from 184 countries who agreed to offer their names as signatories. The warning states that "humanity is now being given a second notice...time is running out" and calls for "changes in our stewardship of the Earth and the life on it."[15]

The concept of the interconnectedness of all life on Earth has been discussed by many spiritual and philosophical traditions, including Buddhism and Indigenous cultures. The idea that humans must live with, rather than upon, nature has been articulated by many thinkers, including Sir Mark Oliphant, an Australian physicist who was instrumental in the development of nuclear technology. He believed that the use of nuclear weapons in war would have catastrophic consequences, potentially leading to the destruction of humanity. In August of 1945, the U.S. dropped atomic bombs on the Japanese cities of Hiroshima and Nagasaki, which resulted in the deaths of over 200,000 people. Sir Mark Oliphant was shocked and deeply troubled by the use of the atomic bomb and, consequently, removed himself from the Manhattan Project. Sir Mark also wrote about the need for a "messianic revolution" to create awareness of the "one-ness of life on Earth" and the "need for change." The need for a global revolution in human consciousness is crucial in addressing the challenges that we face as a species. We must re-evaluate ourselves as the prime cause of the problems we are facing and rediscover the profound value inherent in every single human being.

Ultimately, what is required is a complete shift in the paradigm, involving science, education, and health, to a complete understanding of humanity and our relationship with the cosmos. Ecological sustainability, peace, and health must become our basic requirement, and we must ensure that every member of the global population has access to advanced education including education for life and education on health, values, and creativity enabling them to participate in building a sustainable future for all.

▌CONSCIOUSNESS

> *I regard consciousness as fundamental. I regard matter as a derivative of consciousness.* — Max Planck

We live in a self-referential, organizing, informational, biological universe where physics is no longer a materialistic science.

Dr. William Braud, a major contributor to parapsychology and transpersonal psychology, states that a new epistemology would implicitly question the assumption that a science characterized by inviolable "scientific laws" can, in the end, adequately deal with causality. Is consciousness real in some nontrivial sense? Can it be "causal"? His experiments and studies suggest that consciousness may be causal.[16]

▌THE QUANTUM FIELD

Now is the time to explore the mind of the universe and cross the final frontier into the mind of GOD. The need for a global revolution in human consciousness is crucial in addressing the challenges that we face as a species.

We are currently at a bifurcation point. Ervin Laszlo says, "There are tremendous Holotropic attractors within the Universe, which by their very nature, enhance emergence and integration." He also says that the holotropic attractor accounts for nature's tendency to create wholes that are more than the simple sum of their parts. Considering the emerging vision, matter, life, and mind are consistent elements within an overall system of great complexity but coherent and harmonious design.

According to Laszlo, "The biosphere is born within the womb of the universe, and mind and consciousness are born in the womb of the biosphere. Nothing is independent of anything else."

Our very nature should be in harmony with the rhythms of the planet. We dwell on a living planet that has its own ways of inspiration, expiration, breathing, and circulation. We are interlinked through our extensive interpretation of how we experience our lives. This experiential model of perception is reinforced by our neuronal connections and ways of thinking.

▌THIS IS THE CHALLENGE

How do we get out of the conditioning of the morass of entangled minds and linked fields of consciousness to our heritage of true reality?

Firstly, we are not alone. We are energy beings connected with energy systems reaching the furthest corners of the universe. Our chronobiology and our rhythms beat with the pulsating rhythms of our heart, our brain, the phases of the moon, the sunset and sunrise, the vibrational pulse of planet earth, sunspot activity, the waxing and waning of the tides, the slow rotation of the earth through the zodiac, and the precession of our planet around the galactic center of the Milky Way. The energy meridians of our bodies and the light emitted by our bodies synchronize with star systems in our Galaxy.

The consciousness which we observe in ourselves and the natural environment and the supportive infrastructures we create around us are all connected. A change in one person can affect the whole Biosphere and the whole cosmos. As Margaret Mead said, "Never doubt that a small group of thoughtful committed citizens can change the world; indeed, it is the only thing that ever has."

However, the change we talk of is radical and of a different proportion and synthesis.

It partakes NOT of philosophy or technology created from a perceived inanimate universe. We have forgotten that deep connection with nature, and we live in a state of separation. Virtual reality cannot in any way accommodate a reality in any sense. Indeed, we need those "aha!" moments and that sense of oneness with the totality of all things to be alive and enlightened.

The next great leap for humanity will be when we seek to actualize the noetic possibilities within each human frame of reference. There is much more in us than we possibly can imagine. We are creatures of a living universe. The challenge is to give people information and to wake them up to the truth of their well-being, their spirituality, and their souls and to the realization that we have infinite capacities to heal ourselves. We must realize that we have an infinite capacity to change the realities that we experience. We must realize that the power of a coherent mass of people far exceeds the power of a small cabal who wishes to materialize our planet and change the total DNA of it. This realization should be accompanied by forms of new ways of understanding the depths and significance of the human psyche.

In *The Undiscovered Self*, Jung wrote, "The structure and physiology of this brain pose no explanation of the psyche." Jung emphasized the sacredness and significance of the human psyche as being more important than anything else. He saw the psyche and soul as being worn away by materialism and the onslaught of technology. We must give, as Jung said, "deference and significance to the paramount importance of the human psyche."

AND THIS IS WHERE WE START

We should start with the recognition of the significance and importance of individual and collective action in the political sphere. The opportunity is now. Now is the time for people to wake up and speak out.

Our lack of active participation in politics does not exempt us from the responsibility for the results. Individuals need to recognize that political decisions and actions affect everyone, regardless of whether they participate in the political process. By failing to participate in politics, individuals not only limit their ability to influence political outcomes, but they also miss the opportunities to hold elected officials accountable and to shape public affairs.

PARADIGM SHIFT

The measures aimed at preventing ecological catastrophe and transition to sustainable development, whether it be technological, economic, or ecological, will be doomed to failure unless we free ourselves from the old scientific, intellectual paradigm.

Max Planck said that "science progresses funeral by funeral." This means that the way society looks at life and creates and maintains itself is at the expense of everything else and the way that reality is perceived. This is also related to the way science is created.

The paradigm changes when a new reality is created by new ways of thinking. This is called a paradigm shift. This is very much tied up with institutionalized bias. Institutional bias is the way that systematic biases exist within organizations where there is inequality of treatment and outcomes for different kinds of people. Norms and values are taken for granted and shape the behavior of individuals who conform to institutionalized scripts. This is very much reflected in mass transformation and mass hypnosis when the public mind unconditionally accepts news items and the imposition of regulations by authority figures including professors and scientists.

▎THE LOTUS SUTRA AND THE MYSTIC TRUTH

Consciousness, as expressed in the great spiritual traditions, is a process by which awakening occurs. Spirituality, which has existed for thousands of years, must now be extended to an infinite progression.

The Lotus Sutra is regarded as the greatest teaching of the Buddha. It is also a massive cosmic treatise on the nature of the universe. It expresses, in terms of the lifespan of the Buddha, the infinite progression and existence of all sentience in the Multiverse. This Universe is the quantum Buddha field of perfection and compassion where the Thus Come Ones, Tathagatas, or Buddhas in the Lotus Sutra are omnipresent.

There are myriads of these Buddhas in the universe. They represent the Holotropic forces and attractors that maintain the Universe in its purpose and its balance. The essence of creativity is expressed through these Buddhas in terms of infinite light. When we look through the James Webb telescope, we see before us billions of galaxies even within a small amount of space. Indeed, what we are looking at is the mind and the mystic principle of the great law itself. This is expressed in the Lotus Sutra as "the Mystic Law."

Nichiren Daishonin, the Buddha of 13th century Japan, says this mystic law is completion, beauty, perfection, truth, and light. It is the law which expresses the manifestation of totality. It is the one within all and all within one. Nichiren makes it quite clear that this is a cosmological principle which integrates the totality and enables each person who chants "Nam-Myoho-Renge-Kyo" to come into direct connection with the ultimate truth or law by which all can attain enlightenment. The Lotus Sutra sees the totality of existence as being alive. The Lotus Sutra also sees the creation of everything occurring in an infinitesimal moment in time.

Nichiren also expresses the powerful concept of Ichinen Sanzen, which describes the principle of each infinitesimally small moment of human life containing within it the totality of all existence and the infinite potential for all future creation. Indeed, the universe is recreating itself at every infinitesimal moment, and we are simultaneously a part of this process.

The perfection in Buddhism is very much tied up with concepts of value and ethics, which are expressed in ancient Greek philosophy as goodness, beauty, and truth.

▌THE NEED FOR RE-EVALUATION

We need to re-evaluate ourselves in terms of the nature of consciousness and use these proclivities that have been expressed through Buddhism and other spiritual teachings to understand who we are and how we can go forwards. I believe the most important thing we can do now is to inspire people with our message of liberation and renaissance of the spirit.

We require a new spirituality encompassing a consciousness of oneness in which all life maintains itself at the expense of everything else. In other words, we are all connected. The enormous turning will be an integration of spirituality with ecology and technology. We need to see ourselves as holistically, inextricably connected in mind, body, spirit, society, and environment.

A planetary culture implies that science, technology, healing relationships, economics, government, and education are seen from the broadest perspective. They should not be nation-based, but globally based, inspiring new holistic ways of thinking to enhance our connectedness, going beyond "isms" and ideologies, and recognizing the sacredness of all life. This new planetary based culture includes the creation of new art, literature, and music and the development of a life philosophy that is based on the universal principles inherent in human activity.

CROSSING THE FINAL FRONTIER

Following the end of WWII, Einstein said that, if humanity is to survive, there must be a substantially new manner of thinking.

As humanity continues to evolve, we are faced with a new paradigm that encompasses a consciousness of "oneness" where all life on Earth is connected and not separate. This new frontier represents the next Copernican revolution, as we initiate Planet Earth into the field of the living universe. This also requires the interface with extra-terrestrial civilizations, especially the galactic forms of life, in order to foster communication and peaceful relations.

We possess the key to understanding and are now able to cross this final frontier by realizing that the universe is a self-referential quantum Akashic field of information. This information is holographic and implicate, meaning that space and time are no longer the dominant factors determining existence.[17]

Hidden within the context of the field is the source of all, including love, beingness, purity, creativity, and essence. It is the source of good, truth, and beauty, expressed in Platonic ideals. It is the essence from which all things manifest.

The universe is subtly enhanced and organized through attractors, a concept introduced by Ervin Laszlo. The universe has a subtle purpose of creativity, formation, and emergence where the totality becomes more diverse and creative and is enhanced through teleology. This entails the production of a myriad of different sentient and insentient forms.

The enlightened Tathagatas of the Universe, as expressed in the Lotus Sutra, are all-knowing in the sense that the Universe itself is self-referential and all-knowing, and these beings partake of the fundamental functioning and well-being of the Universe. Their function is to create a basic harmony and core of beauty, love, and truth in the totality of the Universe. This concept has been described in the Indian Vedas and Buddhist teachings as the spiritual core of enlightenment inherent in the Universe. The spiritual core of enlightenment is the basic law or process on which the Universe is based. It is a creative process, and this ultimate law is the mystic truth that coordinates and engenders truth through sentience, which becomes more sentient when expressed through celestial or ultra-Buddha beings who embrace the Universe in totality.

The Lotus Sutra, one of the greatest teachings of Buddhism, describes in detail the structure of the living universe, the ultra-humans and extra-terrestrials, and Buddhas that are part of the universe. The Tathagata, literally the Thus Come One, or Buddha, is the expression of the basic Buddha nature of the Buddha-field of the Universe, which is the totality of the universe expressed in Buddhist terms. This understanding of the Universe is supported by an understanding of the quantum field. Now is the time for us to break through the eggshell of organized religion into the spiritual truth of the living universe.

This is our planetary and human initiation. We are at the point of galactic initiation of Planet Earth into the living universe. We have the potential to understand and communicate with other intelligent life forms, and to work together to create a harmonious and peaceful existence for all beings in the Universe. It is time for us to cross the final frontier and enter the mind of God.

CHAPTER 5

AWAKENING THE POWER OF THE NEW HUMAN STORY

GREGG BRADEN

For the first time in recorded history, we stand on the threshold of losing the cherished qualities that make us human. Technologies are being adopted and policies are being written with the power to erase our cherished memories, to eliminate the uncertainty of our emotions, to override our skills of critical thinking, our unique ability to self-regulate the systems of our body, and to replace our natural bodies altogether with synthetic biology.

Advances ranging from artificial intelligence and virtual reality to tiny robots the size of a single bacteria, combined with a belief that machines are superior to the human body, have placed us on a course for the inevitable — a collision between technology and natural biology and the role they play in our lives. The showdown is happening now. The outcome will change us forever. The laws are being drafted, and the social conditioning is being implemented, which will forever lock us into one of two possible futures: 1) a dystopian world of hybrid human-machines where we've traded our emotions and fallibility for speed and efficiency, or 2) our awakening to the highest expression of our natural abilities and what it means to be fully human.

USE IT OR LOSE IT

The technology poses a threat that may best be described through a brief idiom in the biological sciences. It simply states, *"Use it or lose it."* This idiom reminds us that we lose our natural abilities when we don't use them. The neurons in our brain, the cells of our body, our ability to think, remember, and solve problems, as well natural systems, such as our immune response, all begin to atrophy and become useless when we replace them with synthetic chemistry and computer chips. With this fact in mind, we're faced with the question that philosophers and science fiction writers warned we would encounter as the consequence of our technological evolution: How far do we allow the human-machine merger to go? *How much of ourselves do we give away to technology?*

Are we willing to sacrifice the cherished human qualities that set us apart from all known forms of life in exchange for the speed, durability, and efficiency of computer chips in our brain and performance enhancing sensors in our natural blood? Are we happier when we do so? Are we healthier? Do we lead more fulfilled lives? Perhaps most importantly, if we replace our natural biology with machines today, what unknown capabilities and untapped potentials do we lose forever?

We can't begin to answer these species-altering questions until we first answer something even more basic: What is it that are we giving away? What capacities have we yet to discover that we will lose by merging ourselves with machines and AI? The danger in replacing our biology with machines is that we cannot say with certainty what we lose when we do so. We cannot say because we simply don't know. Experiments with cloning technology may help to illustrate what I mean here.

THE UNSOLVED MYSTERY

In 1996, the scientific community made an announcement that sounded like the plot of a futuristic sci-fi thriller. On July 5th of that year, the *Roslin Institute* in Scotland, a renowned animal research facility, announced the birth of a domestic sheep named Dolly. While she was not the first animal in history to be cloned, Dolly was the first animal to be cloned from an adult cell taken from a specific body part (a somatic cell), rather than the much-publicized type of cell known as an embryonic stem cell.

At the time of her birth, Dolly appeared as any other sheep of her kind. She looked like a sheep. She lived like a sheep, and she was healthy enough to mate and produce six lambs during her brief life. At the age of four, however, something strange and unexpected began to happen to Dolly. Her body began to break down and deteriorate. First, she developed a form of arthritis that was managed through the use of drugs that reduced the painful inflammation in her joints. Within three years, however, her arthritis progressed and was further compounded by a progressive respiratory disease that made it difficult for her to breathe. On February 14th, Dolly's life ended as she was euthanized.

At the time of her death, she was 6 and a half years of age — only half of the 11 to 12-year lifespan that is typical for her species. The obvious question in the scientific community was why? What happened to Dolly that brought a premature end to her successful cloning? The honest answer is that no one knows for sure. While there are theories regarding the length of her telomeres and how her age compared to the age of the sheep that she was originally cloned from, at the time of this writing, scientists still cannot say with absolute certainty why Dolly's body began to break down at half of her species' lifespan. It's this uncertainty that is one example of a warning flag that should caution us when it comes to engineering natural processes.

While we're obviously not sheep, and replacing elements of the human body with machines is not cloning, there is a principle here that applies in both of these instances. In both cloning and the replacing of living systems with artificial technology, the common denominator is that natural processes are being overridden and bypassed. In both instances, Nature is artificially interrupted and overridden, and something yet to be identified is lost in the process. What element of natural life is not understood and was lost in Dolly's cloning? Are we missing a similar element in our movement toward replacing the natural blood, neurons, and tissues of the human body with chemicals and machines?

The technology that has brought us to this crossroads is no secret. On the contrary, it's being ushered in openly and proudly. Mainstream media, slick marketing campaigns, and some of the largest technology companies in the world are touting the adoption of human-replacement technology as "inevitable progress." Some scientists, politicians, and philosophers have even gone so far as to say that the merging of artificial technology with natural biology is the next step in human evolution. American inventor and author Ray Kurzweil, for example, tells us, "When you talk to a human in 2035 you'll be talking to someone that's a combination of biological and non-biological intelligence." If Kurzweil is right, we have only a few short years to determine our future relationship to technology.

▌WE ARE THE TECHNOLOGY WE'VE BEEN WAITING FOR

There is an elephant in the room that many in the scientific community are reluctant to embrace or even to acknowledge: Within each of us lie dormant abilities and extraordinary potentials far beyond what was believed to be possible in the past. The technologies that are designed to replace our biology actually mimic the existing functions that our cells and natural systems already perform, except we do it better. Diverse fields of study ranging from human evolution and genetics to the emerging science of neuro-cardiology and heart intelligence reveal that we are a highly advanced, highly sophisticated, "soft" bio-technology with the ability to self-heal, self-regulate, self-generate, and rejuvenate every organ, each gland, and all tissue in our bodies. While the artificial computer chips and nano-sensors are fast and efficient, their capacities are limited by the physics of the material of which they're made, and they cannot be scaled beyond the limits of their atomic structure. The plasticity of human cells, neurons, and tissue, on the other hand, have demonstrated their capacities and have yet to reveal the upward limits of their scalability.

Once we know the power and truth of our superhuman potentials, the trans-human technology that steals our humanness begins to look much less appealing, and much less urgent. The reason: *We are the technology we've been waiting for!* Through these discoveries, for the first time in our existence, we have the opportunity to know what it means to be pure human, and with that knowledge, we are reminded of the qualities and values of our humanness that are rare, cherished, and worth preserving.

CHAPTER 6

THE SPIRITUAL TRADITIONS AND THE PATH TOWARD PEACE AND HARMONY

KARAN SINGH

Peace and harmony have been sought by humanity ever since the dawn of civilization. Yet, the whole of human history, from the very earliest times, is replete with wars and violent conflicts from the tribal right up to the international level. All religions preach peace, but, in fact, religion has been one of the major sources of violent conflict through the centuries and remains so even today, despite the worldwide growing Interfaith movement in which I am actively involved. Science was supposed to help establish peace, but it has created increasingly deadly weapons of mass destruction. Communism, socialism, capitalism, democracy — all claimed the desire to establish peace, but all invariably waged war. Even as I speak, dozens of local and regional conflicts are raging around the world, and thousands perish every month as a result, not to speak of the seemingly unending fractured and devastating war between Russia and Ukraine.

As against these negative situations, however, all the great spiritual traditions of the world tell us that there is, deep within our consciousness, a creative power that, if invoked and nurtured, can bring about a benign transformation in our thoughts and behavior. The lives and teachings of saints and seers from all the great religions of the world bear this out, and though it may be unrealistic to expect such capacities in ordinary people, it does impel us to look deeper into this holistic philosophy of peace in its varied dimensions. I have identified five dimensions of peace which need our consideration, looked upon not as parallel lines but as concentric circles, beginning and ending with the only two irreducible and indivisible units — the individual at the one end and Planet Earth that we inhabit at the other.

Let me start with the entity with which we are expected to be most familiar, ourselves. It is a common misconception that just because we are aware of our outer existence, we really know the depths of our own psyche. In the East, it has been accepted for thousands of years that the outer personality is simply an ever-changing and temporary habitation for an inner, immortal spark — call it the soul, the Atman, or whatever. In India, there has developed over the last thirty centuries an entire science of introspection and inner development known by the generic term Yoga, a psycho-spiritual discipline designed to unite the divinity immanent and the divinity transcendent, of which the outer physical exercises known by that name in the West are simply a small part. With the development of depth psychology in the West, particularly with C.G. Jung who must be ranked as one of the most creative thinkers of the 20th century, and with the unique heritage of Zen masters in Japan, modern psychology has at last realized that our conscious minds are simply like the surface of an ocean, constantly buffeted by waves and typhoons, harboring in its depths numerous creatures, friendly as well as hostile.

The spiritual and mystic traditions of humanity are informed by the belief that there resides deep within us a divine spark which is capable of being fanned into the blazing fire of spiritual realization. As the seer of the Upanishad proclaims: "I have seen that great Being shining like a sun beyond the darkness. It is only by knowing this that we can cross the ocean of darkness and death." This quest constitutes our spiritual challenge as human beings endowed with an unquenchable thirst for the greater reality pervading our everyday consciousness.

This inner spiritual link is the true foundation of the Interfaith movement. It binds the entire human race into a single family, cutting across all barriers of nationality and religion, caste and creed, sexual preferences, and social and economic status. What the Hindus call *antarik shanti*, Buddhists the *Bodhi Chitta*, Chinese the *Tao*, and Christians the 'Peace that Passeth Understanding' is, therefore, the first pre-requisite in our quest for peace. How we achieve this, whether through *Jnana* Yoga, the way of study and contemplation; *Bhakti* Yoga, the way of emotional outpouring towards a personalized manifestation of the Divine; *Karma* Yoga, the way of dedicated works and good deeds; *Raja* Yoga, the way of internal spiritual practices, meditation, and ecstatic gnosis; or a combination of these various paths, will depend on the inner and outer configuration of each individual's life situation. But the point is that the effort consciously has to be made; spiritual progress does not occur automatically without strenuous inner effort, any more than training for the Olympics can be achieved without prolonged and vigorous physical disciplines.

The second circle in which all of us move is the family, which is still the most fundamental social grouping and, despite its widespread erosion in the West, remains the bedrock of society. If our family relationships are full of conflict and struggle, we are unlikely to be able to find inner peace or make any meaningful contribution towards establishing it in society. Family relationships have two basic dimensions, the spouse-spouse relationship and the parent-children relationship, in both of which tension and strife are becoming increasingly widespread. An important point here revolves around the status of women. In many contemporary societies, their status is still far from satisfactory, and women tend to be relegated to an inferior position. In the West, one sometimes gets the impression that the pendulum has swung in the opposite direction, perhaps to compensate for past injustices. What is needed is a harmonious balance between the two. In the Hindu tradition, we have the remarkable concept of *Ardhanarishwara,* Lord Shiva as half male and half female. This creative fusion is ideally reflected on the social plane in the concept of the wife as *ardhangini,* equal sharer and partner in the adventure of life.

With regard to the tension between generations, one reason it is getting more pronounced is that the pace of change has accelerated. As a result, there is an increasing psychological gulf between children and their parents. Here again, the interests of harmony are best served by steering a middle course between the parental domination of traditional societies and the virtual alienation of children in the West. Young people today are imbued with great talent, and there needs to be a continuous inter-generational dialogue so that the creative energies of youth can be harnessed to the quest for a sane and harmonious global society. In this context, Peace Education must find a place in the curricula of schools and colleges around the world. In our quest for peace, we have to begin with our immediate family, as that is the experimental workshop in which we can learn the virtues of understanding and love, compassion, and co-ordination. It is a microcosm of the larger global society defined in Hindu scriptures as *Vasudhaiva Kutumbakam,* the World as a Family.

As we move beyond the family circle, we come to the third dimension in our quest for peace, which involves the wider society in which we live. There are many areas here including religious communities, caste affiliations, linguistic groupings, professional associations, political bodies, and so on. In the present age, we necessarily interact with a wide spectrum of such social groupings, and in our interface with each one of them, we have to work towards a peaceful settlement of disputes and a creative interaction of different visions and opposing viewpoints to prevent conflicts from erupting. Each of these areas can contribute to the growth of social cohesion but is also potentially a source of acute conflict as we see from our own experience in India and other countries. A purposeful movement towards a more equitable economic order is also essential if the social tensions are not to overwhelm large portions of the planet. Ultimately, a world in which the top 5% appropriate 95% of the world's wealth is not a sustainable paradigm.

The rapid changes in technology have brought about a major change in the texture of social intercourse. Gone are the virtually self-sufficient villages or the professional guilds of artisans and craftsmen bound together by their commitment to a common undertaking. Much of modem production tends to be impersonal, and the growth of industrial slums in many parts of the world represents a potent source of social tension and conflict. The growing specter of the malign underworld of drugs and drug-related violence, and the shameful trafficking in human beings, represent a grave hurdle in our quest for social peace and harmony. Unless there is a concerted drive to eradicate poverty around the world, these tensions will surely erupt into deadly conflicts that will engulf even the affluent nations.

We come fourthly to the political structure that has played such a predominant role in human history over the last few centuries — the Nation State. Although its claim to total sovereignty has become increasingly untenable, the nation state is still the most powerful form of social organization in our present civilization. Here again, its record has been mixed. While it has certainly led to great progress and cohesion, it has also resulted in endless conflicts between nations and between various ethnic, linguistic, and political groups within nations. Today, on the one hand, we have the extraordinary spectacle of nationalism being transcended in the development of the European community, a truly historic event in human history where nations which were at war with each other for centuries (and through their colonial rivalries kept the whole world in turmoil) have at last overcome their animosities and have moved rapidly towards a common market, free travel, a common currency, and a common parliament. On the other hand, we have witnessed the disintegration first of the Soviet Empire, and then of Yugoslavia, both of which broke up into their often mutually antagonistic constituent ethnic units, while secessionist movements are creating zones of tension and strife around the world.

This dual process of the reassertion of sub-nationalism and the transcending of nationalism is one that is likely to continue through the 21st century. The larger threat of the Cold War erupting into a nuclear holocaust has once again emerged with the Russia-Ukraine conflict and disturbing developments in North Korea. There is enough inflammable material and modern weaponry in Europe and Asia to keep the fires of conflict burning for several decades. Somehow, the whole process has to be contained within a larger framework, whether of regional groupings like the European Community, ASEAN, SAARC, or the ossified United Nations itself, which is in urgent need of updating and democratization, though its specialized agencies are doing excellent work.

This brings me to the fifth dimension, the quest for world peace. This is now no longer merely a mystical vision or an idealist Utopia, it has become an imperative for the very survival of the human race. The growth of weapons technology has been so awesome that, with nuclear weapons, we can destroy not only the human race but also all life forms on this planet. Even non-nuclear conflicts like the Gulf Wars have caused massive causalities and appalling damage to the biosphere and the environment of our planet. It is, therefore, essential for us to find mechanisms for a peaceful resolution of disputes between nation states.

This links directly with the Interfaith movement, which in modern times may be said to have begun in 1893 when the first Parliament of the World's Religions convened in Chicago, and Swami Vivekananda made such an abiding impact. During the 20th century, several Interfaith organizations developed including the International Association for Religious Freedom (IARF), the World Council of Religions for Peace (WCRP), the Temple of Understanding (ToU) — of which I am Chairman worldwide, the United Religions Initiative (URI), and the Chicago Group. There were a whole series of Interfaith meetings around the world in the last century. In 1993, the Second Parliament of the World's Religions met again in Chicago, exactly a hundred years after the first one. In 1999, the Third Parliament was held in Cape Town, South Africa, and thereafter moved around the world (after over two decades, it arrives back in Chicago in August of 2023 for the 130th Anniversary). A remarkable event took place in 2000; the United Nations held the Millennium World Peace Summit for Spiritual and Religious Leaders in New York in the main hall of the United Nations building where I had the privilege of presiding over its First Plenary Session.

The Interfaith dialogue involves Interfaith prayers, roundtables, seminars, symposia, and interaction at many levels. It is particularly important that Interfaith values are reflected in educational curricula around the world. Exclusionist and monopolistic claims to religious truths must give place to a more balanced and inclusivist approach. A great deal of work is being done in the various faiths. Beautiful temples, mosques, gurudwaras, churches, and other places of worship are being built, but the Interfaith movement, as such, is yet nobody's baby. Unless the Interfaith movement comes center stage, things are not going to fall into place in the global society emerging before our very eyes.

The question is not *whether* we are going to have a global society, but *what* sort of global society it will be. Will it be based upon exploitation, negativities, crime, hatred, and fanaticism, or are we going to have a sane and harmonious global society based on Interfaith understanding and peaceful conflict resolution? Like the roads in Robert Frost's poem, or indeed in the Katha Upanishad thousands of years earlier, two paths now lie before us. One could lead through a concerted and multi-dimensional quest for peace and continuing Interfaith dialogue towards a sane and equitable world civilization in which the scarce resources of Planet Earth are used to provide the necessary material, intellectual, and spiritual inputs for a decent civilized life to all human beings. The other is the path of conflict and disharmony, fundamentalism, and fanaticism, which will inevitably result in the destruction of human civilization as we now know it.

As the great seer and evolutionary thinker Sri Aurobindo stressed so eloquently in his monumental works, what is needed at this stage of human destiny is neither a philosophy of total transcendence, which would leave human beings essentially powerless, nor a philosophy of immanence alone, which leaves the world at the mercy of the hostile powers. Rather, the contemporary discussion has to revolve around an integrated, holistic philosophy in which human existence is looked upon as a rare gift to be utilized both for inner development and for the welfare of society and the world, as well as for nurturing mother Earth. This, in turn, postulates the urgent need for a worldwide, multidimensional Interfaith dialogue.

Religion has been one of the major civilizational forces in human history. Much that is great and noble — art and architecture, dance and music, literature and moral codes, law and legal structures — can be traced back to one or other of the great religions of the world. At the same time, it is a tragic fact that more people have been killed, tortured, burned, and persecuted in the name of religion than on any other account, and the supreme irony is that each religion looks upon its version of the Divine as being compassionate and merciful. This essentially contradictory situation must not be allowed to continue into the nuclear age. It is now to be recognized that all the great religions of the world represent so many different strivings towards the Divine and that, in the final analysis, they all represent what the Veda postulates as *Ekam sad viprah bahudha vadanti*, the Truth is One, the Wise call it by many Names.

We may certainly believe and claim that our own path is the most appropriate, but that does not justify our condemning, persecuting, or murdering those who follow other paths. Let us accept with grace that for every religious belief there is a majority of humankind which does not accept it. Therefore, discarding fanaticism and fundamentalism that represent obnoxious aberrations of the noble paths of religion, let us adopt a philosophy that accepts multiple paths to the Divine, that not only tolerates other religions but also welcomes the plurality of human striving for the Divine. Unless we move conceptually onto a new dimension of Interfaith dialogue and harmony, any hope of an integrated human being living in a sane and peaceful global society will remain an evanescent dream.

This is an important precondition for the shift to the new consciousness that Ervin Laszlo, James Lovelock, Sri Aurobindo, and other thought-leaders have been elaborating in depth.

NOTES & REFERENCES

▌CHAPTER 1

1. Lipton, B. H. (2016). The Biology of Belief 10th Anniversary Edition: Unleashing the Power of Consciousness, Matter & Miracles. Carlsbad CA: Hay House.
2. Avery, O. T., Macleod, C. M., & McCarty, M. (1944). Studies on the Chemical Nature of the Substance Inducing Transformation of Pneumococcal Types: Induction of Transformation by a Desoxyribonucleic Acid Fraction Isolated from Pneumococcus Type III. *The Journal of Experimental Medicine*, 79(2):137–158. https://doi.org/10.1084/jem.79.2.137
3. Watson, J. D., & Crick, F. H. C. (1953). Molecular Structure of Nucleic Acids: A Structure for Deoxyribose Nucleic Acid. *Nature*, 171:737–738. https://doi.org/10.1038/171737a0
4. Henry, R. C. (2005). The mental Universe. *Nature*, 436:29. https://doi.org/10.1038/436029a
5. Cohen, J. (2001). Knife-edge of design. *Nature*, 411:529. https://doi.org/10.1038/35079203
6. Nowak, M. A., (2012). Why We Help: The Evolution of Cooperation. *Scientific American*, 307(1):34–39. https://ped.fas.harvard.edu/files/ped/files/sciam12_0.pdf

▌CHAPTER 2

7. Currivan, J. (2017; 2022). *The Cosmic Hologram: In-formation at the Center of Creation*. Rochester, VT; Toronto, Canada: Inner Traditions.

8. Currivan, J. (2022; 2023) *The Story of Gaia: The Big Breath and the Evolutionary Journey of Our Conscious Planet.* Rochester, VT; Toronto, Canada: Inner Traditions.

9. www.evolutionaryleaders.net/unitivenarrative

10. www.wholeworld-view.org

CHAPTER 3

11. Harari, Y. N. (2018). *21 Lessons for the 21st Century.* London: Jonathan Cape.

12. "AUTOGEDDON," the epic poem by Heathcote Williams, was originally published in *Whole Earth Review*, Fall 1987: 26–29. http://cfu.freehostia.com/Members/colin/autogeddon/

13. Zuboff, S. (2019). *The Age of Surveillance Capitalism: The Fight for a Human Future at the New Frontier of Power.* New York: PublicAffairs.

CHAPTER 4

14. INTERNATIONAL APPEAL – Stop 5G on Earth and in Space. https://www.5gspaceappeal.org/

15. Ripple, W.J., et al. (2017). World Scientists' Warning to Humanity: A Second Notice. *Bioscience*, 67(12):1026–1028. https://doi.org/10.1093/biosci/bix125

16. Braud, W., Dossey, L. (2003). *Distant Mental Influence: Its Contributions to Science, Healing, and Human Interactions (Studies in Consciousness).* Charlottesville: Hampton Roads Publishing; and Braud, W. (2000). Wellness implications of retroactive intentional influence: exploring an outrageous hypothesis. *Alternative Therapies in Health and Medicine*, 6(1):37–48.

17. Storoy, D. David Bohm, Implicate Order and Holomovement. Sebastopol, CA: Science and Nonduality (SAND). www.scienceandnonduality.com/article/david-bohm-implicate-order-and-holomovement

ROADMAP CLUSTER II

MAPPING OUR PATH FORWARD

- *Keynote*: The Upshifted Principles of Global Order
- Revolution from the Ground Up
- Ascending to the Age of Planetary Consciousness
- Upshifting the Future
- The Upshift Path to a New Paradigm World
- The Emerging Unitive Age
- The Key Principles of Mutual Aid
- An Upshifted Development Path: The Politics of Being
- Transforming a Death Economy into a Life Economy
- From 6th Mass Extinction to 6th Mass Evolution

CHAPTER 7

KEYNOTE

THE UPSHIFTED PRINCIPLES OF GLOBAL ORDER

ALFRED DE ZAYAS

L ike throughout the domain of human affairs, peace and progress depend on identifying the right priorities and pursuing coherent policies to achieve them. Principles of Global Order alone will not succeed in saving the world from Apocalypse. We must win the dis-information war, formulate a plan of action with concrete, pragmatic measures, and reclaim our democracy, day by day, step by step.

Multiple global problems threaten the survival of humankind, including the danger of nuclear war, the proliferation of weapons of mass destruction including bio- and chemical weapons, artificial intelligence, global warming, ecocide, pandemics, and natural disasters. On a different plane, we recognize root causes of many man-made problems, notably the dis-information campaigns driven by governments and the private sector, the Western focus on short-term profits at the expense of future generations, the impunity of transnational corporations and monopolies, deliberate deforestation, and pollution of oceans and rivers. There is a pattern of anti-ecological exploitation of natural resources that prevents the economic development of many nations in Asia, Africa, and Latin America, many under the yoke of monstrous foreign debt, which is facilitated by official corruption, tax havens, privilege, and structural violence and often is characterized by the narcissism of power, cynicism, greed, and plain human stupidity.

What should our priorities be? *Pax optima rerum* — peace is the highest good — was the motto of the Peace of Westphalia of 1648, which ended the murderous Thirty Years' War, an insane catastrophe that killed an estimated eight million Europeans. The First and Second World Wars together killed more than 60 million human beings. Where are the lessons learned? Did we learn any? A nuclear war would most likely destroy the planet, and there would be no victors. I am not sure that even Albert Einstein perceived the existential danger to all of humanity, even though in 1947 at a dinner party he is reported to have acknowledged his respect for the might of the atom — "I know not with what weapons World War III will be fought, but World War IV will be fought with sticks and stones." This quotation may be apocryphal, but *se non è vero, è molto ben trovato*. Back in 1933, Einstein and Sigmund Freud had exchanged letters on the thorny issue of why intelligent men start wars instead of sitting down and discussing possible options of peaceful coexistence. The League of Nations published the exchange in a famous book entitled *Why War?*[1]

Peace must be our priority, a global compact on education for peace and empathy, a paradigm-shift away from military-first economies to human security economies and away from the military-industrial-digital-financial complex, and a conversion into constructive social policies, job creation, and healthcare.

There are plenty of diagnoses of the many ills that plague humanity. We draw hope — from hope. We have faith in ourselves and in the capacity of humans to solve man-made problems. We are still surrounded by Nature in its glory — the mountains and lakes, rivers and oceans, forests and orchards, birds and butterflies, endless wheatfields, the ineffable beauty of sunrise and sunset. If we would only open our eyes, we could discover the logic of Creation. This mindset can be ours, if we want it. It is up to us to see the positive in things and to remain positive and optimistic, notwithstanding the incompetence and corruption of the politicians who govern over us.

We draw hope from the concept of law, a product of organized civilization. We do have a coherent rules-based international order in the UN Charter, which is akin to a world constitution. We have international treaties, monitoring mechanisms, fact-finding commissions, and local, regional, and international courts. This is more than just window-dressing, and yet, we know that justice is not mathematics, not self-executing. Alas, law is subject to subjectivity; it is NOT coterminous with justice. What we must do is to ensure that the rule of law evolves into the rule of justice, that the principle "might makes right" is replaced by "right is might."

There are many obstacles to the establishment of a just world order. In my book, *Building a Just World Order*,[2] I formulate 25 Principles of International Order, which build upon the UN Charter, international treaties, the Vienna Convention on the Law of Treaties, the Vienna Convention on Diplomatic Relations, the nine core human rights conventions, and Security Council and General Assembly Resolutions including 2131, 2625, 3314, 39/11, 60/1. The book draws from my 14 reports to the UN Human Rights Council and General Assembly, issued in my capacity as UN Independent Expert on International Order.[3] These 25 Principles provide a roadmap to peace and development and were described by the President of the General Assembly 2018–19 as a "magna carta for the 21st Century."

Building a Just World Order is the first book in a trilogy of human rights analyses. The second, *Countering Mainstream Narratives*,[4] documents the good and the bad in world governance. Indeed, we have institutions that have been created by the powerful to serve the powerful. We have courts that should be impartial but are in the service of the status quo. We have human rights treaties that have been hijacked by what I would term the "human rights industry." We have an Office of the High Commissioner for Human Rights that essentially propagates a Western hyper restricted view of "individual rights," otherwise known as "business friendly" rights, while neglecting the promotion and protection of collective rights. We observe non-governmental organizations that weaponize human rights for a variety of political purposes. We see courts that do not speak justice but are tools of "lawfare," of the destruction of human rights defenders and whistle-blowers like Julian Assange, human rights courts that use some human rights to destroy other human rights in the name of geo-political imperatives. We see an International Criminal Court that only indicts Africans and fails to investigate the war crimes and crimes against humanity committed by NATO forces in Yugoslavia, Afghanistan, Iraq, Libya, and Syria. The ICC will only have authority and credibility when it indicts George W. Bush, Tony Blair, Benjamin Netanyahu, and Mohammed bin Salman.

Whether we like it or not, we must acknowledge that many institutions entrusted with the promotion and protection of our rights have failed us and betrayed the planet. We are reminded of Juvenal's constitutional question — *"Quis custodiet ipsos custodes?"* — Who will guard over the guardians? Well, we must reluctantly recognize that when institutions are penetrated by intelligence services and corrupted by power and money, *only we can be the guardians.* We must take the responsibility on our own shoulders.

Meanwhile, the very language of human rights has been corrupted. We witness a continuing epistemological revolution as predicted by George Orwell in his dystopian novel *1984*: "War is Peace, Freedom is Slavery, Ignorance is Strength."[5] This is the paradox. Although many of us recognize double-think, listen to newspeak, and reject cognitive dissonance, many have accommodated themselves to the "new normal."

Yet, in this hardly uplifting scenario, there is always a silver lining. There are voices of reason, voices of ethical values, voices for peace, cooperation, solidarity, forgiveness, and reconciliation: Pope Francis, Eduardo Galeano, Illan Pappe, Joseph Stiglitz, Noam Chomsky, Naomi Klein, Arundhati Roy, Jeffrey Sachs, Richard Falk, Nils Melzer, Stephen Kinzer, Ron Paul, Howard Zinn, Vijay Prashad, Chris Hedges, William Blum, Glenn Greenwald, Michael Chossudovsky, Patrick Cockburn, Daniel Ellsberg, Dennis Kucinich, Diana Johnstone, Michael Hudson, Patrick Buchanan, Paul Craig Roberts, and so many others. Indeed, we are not alone in rejecting the "mainstream narrative" and the concerted effort by governments to rule by lies and censorship.

▍RECOVERING WORLD SANITY

My 25 Principles of International Order begin with the truism that peace is a fundamental human right, an enabling right that allows us to exercise all other civil, cultural, economic, political, and social rights. The principles demand concrete action to build the defenses of peace in the very minds that engender war. But in order to establish durable peace, we must first win the information war. We must fight censorship by government and by the private sector. Indeed, the U.S. Department of Homeland Security works hand in hand with Silicon Valley and social media in suppressing information and imposing "cancel culture" on dissidents. No need to burn books when a whistle-blower can be declared a heretic and persecuted, when a freedom-fighter can be called a terrorist, when a free-thinker can be defamed as unpatriotic, even as a traitor.

In the United States, freedom of speech activists must invoke the Freedom of Information Act to force government to disclose information that has been wrongly withheld from the public. We cannot exercise democratic choices when we only have half of the truth, when the government, under the pretext of "national security," engages in criminal secrecy and cover-ups. Indeed, secrecy facilitates aggression, war crimes, and crimes against humanity. Secrecy even facilitates genocide through a complex of fake news, fake history, false flags, and negationism — this was the case with the Armenian genocide, the Holocaust, Halabja, Srebrenica, and so many other crimes.[6]

If we are to succeed in winning the information war, we must have access to all relevant information, as stipulated in article 19 ICCPR. Principle 23 of my 25 Principles of International Order reads:

> The right to know and the right to access reliable information is an essential component of the national and international democratic order, and finds its legal basis inter alia in article 19 ICCPR. Government and private sector secrecy rules and cover-ups are enemies of the democratic order. Hence, whistle-blowers are necessary human rights defenders, because they disclose information about crimes and omissions of governments, transnational corporations and other non-State actors. Transparency and accountability are crucial to every democratic society and the rule of law.

A Charter of Rights of Whistle-blowers is urgently needed, as proposed in my reports to the Human Rights Council and General Assembly. The right of freedom of opinion and expression necessarily encompasses the right to publish research contrary to mainstream conceptions, and entails the right to be wrong. Penal laws that are enacted to suppress dissent and so-called "memory laws,"[7] which pretend to crystalize history into a politically correct narrative are totalitarian, offend academic freedom and endanger not only domestic but also international democracy (see my 2013 report to the Human Rights Council[8]).

The right to truth was recognized by the UN Commission for Human Rights Resolution 2005/66, which determined that there was an "inalienable and autonomous right" to truth,[9] in the United Nations Principles to Combat Impunity (2005), and in General Assembly Resolution 60/147. In 2011, the Human Rights Council created the function of a UN Special Rapporteur on the Promotion of Truth, Justice and Reparation.[10] While modern technology can advance the right to truth, it can also frustrate it. Access to information is already being manipulated in the digital world. Indeed, algorithms and artificial intelligence[11] applications have become a critical part of the information environment. We encounter them throughout the internet, on digital devices, and in technical systems, search engines, social media platforms, messaging applications, and public information mechanisms. While algorithms are potentially useful to facilitate access to information, they are already being misused, particularly by search engines that give visibility primarily to mainstream narratives and frequently suppress "non-conforming views."

If we are going to win the information war, we need to democratize the media and ensure that all views have a chance to be debated in the "marketplace of ideas." We need more independent journalists, investigative journalists, watchdogs, alternative media such as Grayzone,[12] Pushback, Intercept, the Real News Network, Counterpunch, Consortium News, Democracy Now, Truthout, Le Monde Diplomatique, etc. We need more independent journalists like the Australian Caitlin Johnstone in Melbourne, the Canadian Aaron Maté, the Scotsman Alan Macleod, the American filmmaker Oliver Stone, and the Australian filmmaker John Pilger.

In order to build sustainable peace, we as Americans must reject the dangerous propaganda against "enemies" that our government has itself conjured, we must reject unilateralism and face the reality of a multipolar world and the necessity of multilateral diplomacy. U.S. exceptionalism is obsolete and incompatible with the UN Charter.

Our "rules based international order"/UN Charter lays down the purposes and principles of the Organization in articles 1 and 2 of the Charter, which reaffirm the sovereign equality of states and the self-determination of peoples. As it says in the Preamble, "We the peoples of the United Nations, determined to save succeeding generations from the scourge of war ..." In order to do so, there is a treaty-based obligation to settle disputes by peaceful means (Art. 2(3)). There is also the prohibition not only of the use of force, but also of the "threat" of the use of force. Thus, every provocation, saber-rattling, menacing another State or people entails a violation of the Charter. Article 39 of the Charter also gives the Security Council the power to take action when there is a threat or breach of the peace. Propaganda for war and deliberate demonization of a perceived geopolitical rival constitute such a threat of the peace and furthermore contravene Article 20 of the International Covenant on Civil and Political Rights.

Regional arrangements similarly reaffirm the sovereign equality of states and its corollary, the prohibition of military intervention and any kind of interference in the Internal Affairs of States. Articles 3, 19, and 20 of the Charter of the Organization of American States reaffirm this principle of customary international law. Unquestionably, unilateral coercive measures such as economic sanctions and financial blockades amount to the use of force and are incompatible both with the UN and OAS Charters. The General Assembly and the UN Human Rights Council[13] have repeatedly condemned unilateral coercive measures as contrary to international law and as obstacles for States to implement their obligations under the ICCPR and ICESCR. This corresponds to Principles 16-19 of my 25 Principles.

Prevention is better than cure, and indeed, it is the function of the United Nations to prevent grievances from developing into threats of international peace and security. Hence, the UN should deploy preventive diplomacy and facilitate the peaceful settlement of disputes. One of the pillars of the UN Charter is the right of self-determination of peoples. Indeed, the realization of the right of self-determination has a crucial conflict-prevention function. Article 10 of my 25 Principles reads: "The right of self-determination of peoples as stipulated in the Charter and in common article 1 of the ICCPR and ICESCR is a fundamental principle of international law (*jus cogens*) and international public policy (*ordre public*)." All peoples without exception are rights-holders of self-determination. The duty bearers are all States members of the UN.

The exercise of self-determination is an expression of democracy, as democracy is an expression of self-determination. It attains enhanced legitimacy when a referendum is organized and monitored under the auspices of the United Nations. Although the enjoyment of self-determination in the form of autonomy, federalism, secession, or union with another State entity is a human right, it is not self-executing. Timely dialogue for the realization of self-determination is an effective conflict-prevention strategy.[14] The United Nations has an essential mediating role between States and peoples and should conduct self-determination referenda as a conflict-prevention measure because self-determination grievances often develop into a threat to the peace or a breach of the peace for purposes of article 39 of the UN Charter. The right of self-determination has not only a collective but also an individual dimension. Moreover, the right to call for and conduct a referendum is protected by article 19 ICCPR.

One right that the "human rights industry"[15] always forgets is the right to solidarity. As I elucidate in Principle 22 of my 25 Principles, everyone has the right to international solidarity as a human right.[16] Pursuant thereto, States have the duty to cooperate with one another, irrespective of the differences in their political, economic, and social systems, in order to maintain international peace and security and to promote international economic stability and progress. To this end, States are obliged to conduct their international relations in the economic, political, social, cultural, technical, and trade fields in accordance with the principles of sovereign equality and non-intervention. States should promote a culture of dialogue and mediation.

▌PLAN OF ACTION

Briefly:

- We must return to the spirituality of the Universal Declaration of Human Rights, which celebrates its 75th anniversary on December 10, 2023. The San Francisco NGO "Eleanor Lives" is devoted to revitalizing the legacy of Eleanor Roosevelt.[17]
- We must win the information war, denounce the mainstream media for its dis-information campaigns and for the unprofessional censorship that many newspapers and television networks systematically practice.

- We must devote time and energy to educating future generations. Indeed, a Global Compact on Education, including education for peace and empathy, is necessary.
- We must ensure that a Charter of Rights of Whistle-blowers is drafted and adopted by the General Assembly, because whistle-blowers are eminent human rights defenders.
- We must reclaim our democracy and demand transparency and accountability from our governments.

CHAPTER 8

REVOLUTION FROM THE GROUND UP

KEES VAN DER PIJL

When we think of revolution, the image rising before our eyes will tend to include large masses of people pouring into the streets, flags and banners, the roar of popular fury. Public buildings are taken over, the police retreats, and the army refuses to fire on the people. Such scenes have still been visible, most recently on the eve of the promulgation of the Covid pandemic. For French president Macron, to name but one embattled leader, the health emergency did not come a day too soon, as the Yellow Vest movement was merging with nationwide protest rallies against a proposed pension reform. In France, as in many other countries, a restive, indeed rebellious population was tamed by the restrictions announced to deal with what was claimed to be a deadly virus outbreak.

As I write, the 'pandemic' has subsided (it was officially declared over by the World Health Organisation), but not its consequences. An ill-conceived, possibly maliciously intended vaccination campaign using insufficiently tested gene therapies has begun to ruin the health of the several billion people who were effectively compelled to take it. This is the greatest medical scandal in history, as Christine Andersen, member of the European Parliament, has stated, a crime against humanity without precedent.

▌A REVOLUTION DEFINED BY COUNTERREVOLUTION

The question that arises is how the world population will respond to the evidence that is bound to come out sooner or later. The origins of the virus in biological warfare research, its release, the suppression of simple, readily available medication (hydroxychloroquine, ivermectin), unprecedented restrictions including curfews and school closures — it will all come out into the open one day alongside the pinnacle of it all, the criminal dissemination of crippling, in many cases deadly, inoculations marketed by pharmaceutical giants Pfizer, Astra-Zeneca, Moderna and Johnson & Johnson — the 'big four' of what may turn out to be the greatest mass murder in human history.

Again, this will inevitably come out. And then what?

To begin to understand, we should recognize that the imposition of the lockdowns was a counterrevolutionary step, intended to stem the tide of popular revolt that was rising across the globe. The ruling classes of the world, for all their differences, were confronted with what appeared to be a potentially uncontrollable revolutionary movement, disparate for sure, but unmistakeably no longer controllable by the routine techniques of economic concessions, distraction, and the like. Even the politics of fear that had been thought out in the 1990s had to switch gear. Given that the fear caused by terror incidents in the wake of '9/11' was eroding, the 'virus route,' explored since the late 1980s, offered itself as a replacement. Unlike other possible states of emergency, in the name of war or climate change, epidemics can be dealt with by repressive packages that have been in place for often more than a century. In addition, the health angle was above suspicion, initially at least.

Yet choosing this approach, as we can see today, carries its own risks. Once a growing number of people begin to see that the invocation of public health is a false one, hiding a political programme aimed at repressing popular aspirations, there will be a precipitate loss of confidence in the medical authorities down to the local doctor. This is not to suggest that either the disciplinary project as such, or the recognition of it in the people's mind, were ever a single undertaking, coherent, and free from internal contradictions and retarding influences.

What counts is the overall thrust of the process set in motion by the choice to aim for a health panic, justifying any measures in the name of combating it. This specific counterrevolutionary thrust has also fundamentally affected the nature and forms of the ongoing revolt, which was bound to resurface. The revolution this time will no doubt include 'large masses of people pouring into the streets, flags, and banners,' but at the core, as a process of fundamental social change, it will be something else if it is to succeed and usher in as new era of human development.

FROM THE SINGLE BODY TO THE LARGER STRUCTURES

This will be the first revolution in history which has at its root people's concern, indeed an existential concern, about bodily health, one body after another. As we can see today, there is a definite rise in concern over basic health. This takes the form of an intensified attention to what we eat and its nutritional content. In addition to the search for uncontaminated food, vitamin and mineral supplements are in high demand. Not coincidentally, the authorities and the large businesses they are in hock with are responding to this with the propagation of new techniques of growing food without land use, and at even faster rates, as well as eating insects, and steps to try and shift the food supplement and vitamin market to large companies or suppress it altogether. Such steps, however, only highlight government untrustworthiness when it comes to taking care of people's physical well-being. The new ecology movement has already moved too far into the sphere where people themselves have taken responsibility for their bodily and mental well-being for government repression to be effective. Let me note in passing that this has little to do with CO_2 and/or global warming, fossil fuel use, and other issues that seem to have more connections to geopolitics or, again, are motivated by the need to discipline the population.

The quest for biologically clean and nutritious food, the attention paid to vitamin and mineral intake, and focus on regular physical activity will not remain confined to a lifestyle issue. It is increasingly obvious to more and more people that the food industry is using human bodies as dumping grounds for substandard nourishment. Just as importantly, the large medical infrastructure, hospitals, and doctors, as well as the pharmaceutical industry, are recognised today as purveyors of medicine dependency rather than health care. Having lost the trust of more and more people in the Covid scam, the medical profession will increasingly face neglect as a reorientation to autonomy regarding one's health and well-being spreads.

For this to spill over from a middle-class concern to a larger popular cause, the economic consequences of such a shift must be taken into account. The cost of medical care and insurance has in many countries spiralled out of control, accompanied paradoxically by steps to limit the choice of treatment or even the doctor administering it. However, if the willingness to rely on health authorities diminishes, this becomes an illogical expenditure. Why pay huge insurance premiums if one mistrusts the practitioners? So, the next step would have to be extending community control of doctors' surgeries, in combination with the propagation of healthy lifestyles. Ultimately, a (re-) nationalisation of hospitals, medical insurance, and the pharmaceutical industry would have to follow. This is just one route that leads straight from the starting point of a self-conscious concern over bodily and mental well-being.

Of course, we would not be looking at institutions and companies of roughly the original size now under a nominal state-owned management. The fact that people themselves are becoming the self-conscious guardians of their health, sharing knowledge and experiences with each other, greatly reduces the need for extensive and often prohibitively expensive industrial medical treatments. Whilst the allopathic treatment infrastructure is reduced in size (most drastically, the pharmaceutical industry, which is mostly busy with advertising and PR anyway), small-scale establishments relying on traditional medicine in combination with the most successful advances in modern medicine would take their place. Of the innovations that should be included in an up-to-date medical regime, ivermectin would be a case in point, as well as of course probiotics and (tightly regulated) antibiotics.

▍HABEAS CORPUS

There is no need to negotiate abstract principles of democracy even in this first stage of a revolutionary change of society. The one (wo-) man, one vote principle is already contained in the very starting point of the transformation; it is inherent in its corporeal launching ground. This refers to a classic democratic principle (*habeas corpus*, "let your body be yours") and is only given a broader content with each step that leads from the individual health/food/lifestyle concerns to its broader ramifications.

A second branch of extending bodily responsibility into the economy would be food supply. Here, too, a 'microphysics' of revolution (to use

Michel Foucault's phrase) that begins at the level of the individual(s), from the ground up, is in order to reward that responsibility by a steady supply of nutritious quality foodstuffs. The farming community in each country has a large role to play here. Currently, farmers are squeezed by banks and fodder companies who push them towards a capitalist way of producing: as fast and cheap as possible. Wide use of growth hormones and antibiotics (even as preventative food supplement) reduce the quality of livestock and make them susceptible to disease. On the other hand, farmers face large supermarket chains that have pushed the price of a liter of milk below that of the equivalent of water. Farmers' markets instead of supermarket chains, which sell mostly fattening, over-sweet, over-refined snacks, should be encouraged as part of catering to a growing demand for health food. The supermarkets and the factories supplying them with mostly over-processed foods are also links in a chain that includes large-scale trade ventures as well as banks imposing profit requirements on whoever relies on inputs or credit from them.

DUAL POWER

In the past, the socialist experience was one-sidedly state-oriented. For every activity, there was a bureaucratic shadow institution setting targets and measuring performance. There is no need to review the entire Soviet-style economy and its society here, except that it stands in stark contrast, in every respect, to what I call a revolution from the ground up. Still, some classical themes of the revolutionary suggest themselves. I just mention the notion of dual power. This was the stage in which people no longer obeyed the established authorities but began to lend their ears to the emerging authorities of the revolution. Once dual power extended to the apparatuses

of state violence, the old order was doomed, and the new one took over —
however, with the consequence of reproducing the old apparatuses, sometimes, and even enlarging them.

In a microphysical revolution, this duplication and reproduction will
not take place. For what arises in opposition to the existing state apparatus and the large-scale economic structures it obeys is not an alternative,
equally large state in combination with vast economic entities (as in the
command economy of Soviet state socialism). On the contrary, the revolution is a one (wo-) man affair. This also removes the need to seize power
in the existing state before any improvement can be decreed from above.
Against this notion of one-off revolution, which in the past distinguished
a revolutionary from a reformist wing in any insurrection, the revolution
from the ground up overcomes this dichotomy. It does not have to reach
for the control panel immediately, and potentially prematurely, to be successful. Every step on the way of restoring a natural way of life is meaningful in itself and leads to immediate improvements proportional to the
structural change achieved.

Once the larger structural consequences of a shift in lifestyle come into
view (taking possession of medical institutions and food distribution), we
enter more dangerous waters. For with them, arise more serious challenges
that may provoke counterrevolutionary violence. Yet, unlike a top-down
one, where it is all or nothing, this revolution can also retreat and wait for
better times.

▌COMMUNICATING THE REVOLUTION: THE IT BREAKTHROUGH

The Information Technology (IT) revolution meanwhile leads to steady
spread of insights concerning the issues raised here. The availability

on a world scale of Internet data provision without the gatekeeper role of media editorial boards is a revolution that can only be compared to the invention of book printing that laid the foundation for the Church reformation by allowing people for the first time to study the Bible themselves. Digitization and the Internet make it possible to take every vote and make every decision in full transparency. It should be obvious that the reason why Julian Assange, the publisher of the Wikileaks materials, is slowly being murdered by the Anglo-American state is not the 'free press' — which is practically monopolized by the billionaire class. It is the principle of transparency that he has put into practice and that heralds a new age beyond that of diplomatic and commercial secrecy. The obvious implications for permanent surveillance of those in positions of responsibility as delegates of the people need not be spelled out here.

Of course, today, the trend is still in the opposite direction, the surveillance of populations by states. Hence, this is not a matter of abstract contemplation. Either humanity will regain its freedom, or it will be led into digital slavery. Since the latter is inconceivable for a growing number of people, an alternative social order will have to be introduced to take the place of a bankrupt capitalism. The preparations and experiments with which this will be realized, and the constant feedback, will eventually result in a radical democracy with digital planning.

One structural obstacle to the revolution from the ground up I have described was that the billionaire classis was shielded from the population by an intermediate class cadre performing tasks for the oligarchy. In the 1970s, the cadre was pushed to the left under the impact of a militant working class which, in the balance with their immigrant colleagues, still by far had the upper hand. This gave a forward-looking technocracy a progressive push. The neoliberal counteroffensive then rescinded the class compromise with organized labor and gave the urban cadre, or rather, one fraction of it, the privileged position it enjoys today.

Nevertheless, much will depend on how this relatively privileged urban cadre will respond to the lockdowns by which governments the world over have countered the unrest among the lower classes and the marginalized populations. However, the IT revolution has given cadres, as well as the rest of the population, the means for active engagement in politics based on information. In this regard, the May 68 movement itself has laid the theoretical foundation for a revolution of a new type.

In his manifesto, *The Society of the Spectacle,* French philosopher Guy Debord wrote that a seizure of power ending the capitalist regime will not be analogous to the way the capitalist bourgeoisie itself came to power. The bourgeoisie emerged as a 'class of the economy,' of economic development; it was a dynamic force, concentrated in the cities and linked to (interloper) trade and early manufacture outside the purview of the guilds. The stagnant agricultural economy of late feudalism with its low productivity was no match for this ascendant class. The 'proletariat' in capitalism, on the other hand, in the sense of the class that seeks to abolish class society as such, will not come to power likewise as a 'class of the economy,' surpassing the predatory dynamics of capital by increased productivity. Worker socialism and state socialism as its ultimate historical embodiment have demonstrated that this is impossible. Even the Soviet Union and its bloc, commanding unprecedented natural resources, with a highly developed technical and scientific elite and a superior education system raising the rest of the population to literacy and cultural development, eventually proved unable to overtake the capitalism of the West.

According to Debord, therefore, the progressive forces can only become superior to the bourgeoisie on the basis of their ability to see beyond the capitalist horizon, as a *class of consciousness.* The very fact that life more and more revolves around information is a unifying force. Since the concern with clean living, proper nutrition, and active life is spreading across all groups and classes of society, this is the most powerful unifying movement the world has seen. The whole of society is increasingly organized around the digital infrastructure; everything revolves around the one universal currency, information. There will be an exponential spread of information concerning health in every respect, and ramifications into the health industry as we know it and the food production and distribution along monopoly-capitalist lines. This will generate a political culture that moves away from the bourgeois culture of possessive individualism, a myopic individualism that takes no responsibility for the broader questions of human survival.

What commends the idea of a microphysical, from the ground up revolution most is that it is in full swing.

CHAPTER 9

ASCENDING TO THE AGE OF PLANETARY CONSCIOUSNESS

PAVEL LUKSHA

▎TRANSITING THE EVOLUTIONARY CRISIS

About seventy years ago, humanity entered the period of Great Acceleration[18] — though factors leading to it had been in play for centuries if not millennia. The growth of population size, collective human wealth, and technological complexity including computational capacity has been enormous. But so has been the environmental footprint on all planetary systems, as humanity has transcended the majority of "planetary boundaries,"[19] with one of the worst impacted systems being the biosphere.[20]

What could be the future dynamics of this process? We are in the phase of evolutionary instability, on the cusp of multiple future trajectories that could occur in the next 100 years. Techno-optimists suggest that the ongoing exponential growth of technological capacity will lead to the technological singularity resulting in the rise of the god-like superintelligence.[21]

Other theories indicate two possible future dynamics of the human civilization:

- "The decline curve" — upon reaching the peak level of development and complexity, the human system enters into an irreversible decline caused by the damage to the environment and depleted natural resources;[22]
- "The S-curve" — upon reaching the inflection point, the human system will stabilize on the new level of development & complexity, where a more balanced and harmonious existence is possible.[23]

The notion of the "decline curve" is rather pessimistic and is more of a gloomy threat to be avoided. The concept behind the "S-curve" offers a more positive outlook and enables us to examine the factors that will facilitate a smooth transition into the desired future. This second perspective is likely non-negotiable: the very discourse on "paths to a better world" presupposes that humanity is capable of completing such a journey.

The possibility of an evolutionary transition of humanity was perceived and anticipated since at least the beginning of the 20th century by thinkers such as Vladimir Vernadsky,[24] Teilhard de Chardin,[25] Sri Aurobindo,[26] and Barbara Marx Hubbard.[27] As we search pathways into better futures, it is crucial to confront the limitations of humanity's mode of existence on the planet. We are evolving into a planetary species, and to ensure our survival and well-being, we need to take responsibility for the planetary processes.

Konstantin Tsiolkovsky[28] and a group of Russian cosmists observed that human evolution is an ongoing process — the possible next stage for future humans is to abandon "the cradle of planet Earth" and become a multi-planetary "cosmic species." Our future descendants would adapt to life on other planets, in other solar systems, and in interstellar space, and their technologies, societies, and even physical bodies will undergo dramatic changes that are yet unimaginable. Will our descendants continue to increase their technological power and project their control over matter and energy onto solar systems and whole galaxies, as per the Kardashev[29] scale? Or will they prefer to adapt their bodies to new habitats, potentially creating immortal "angel-like" energy bodies, as Tsiolkovsky envisioned?

However, this future stage of human evolution remains purely theoretical, despite current plans to settle on the Moon and Mars. The environment of both celestial bodies is far more hostile to human bodies than the most unwelcoming habitats on Earth, and our civilization does not yet possess technologies to ensure the long-term survival and thriving of human habitats there — in particular, we are not capable of creating artificial ecosystems that can indefinitely maintain themselves. To reach the stage when humanity is able to live on other planets and become interplanetary, we must first truly become a planetary species that is able to establish circular economies, manage natural ecosystems sustainably, and form thriving love- and peace-based communities across our planet. Harmonious coexistence between humans and nature with the support of technologies is crucial for the sustainable future within and beyond the boundaries of Earth. Among other things, recognition of the complexity of the biosphere, adoption of the post-anthropocentric worldview, and learning to coexist peacefully with millions of other species is key to our evolution towards becoming a cosmic species.

So, we need to overcome our collective limits to planetization,[30] including anthropocentrism that disregards the interconnectedness of all life on Earth, our linear and fragmented thinking that fails to account for the complex and interconnected nature of planetary systems and processes, and our preference of competitive relationships and violence to solve problems. We must develop the planetary consciousness that enables us to live and act as a planetary species, in alignment with Earth and its systems.

PLANETIZATION AND PLANETARY CONSCIOUSNESS

Three major stages of planetization in human history can be described that have defined our role as a planetary species:

- The Archaic stage was associated with the migration of *Homo sapiens* across the planet. Around 15–20 thousand years ago, our ancestors spread all over the land and came into contact with almost all types of living ecosystems (most of these migrations were driven by fluctuations of climate, forcing humans to move closer to the equator or to return to polar regions at different stages). Only a handful of remote territories (such as Hawaii, New Zealand, or Antarctica) remained untouched, but in the end, even they were reached and inhabited. From the biological perspective, *Homo sapiens* is a super-invasive species, unparalleled among the large multicellular organisms. Our invasiveness was shaped by the unique evolutionary ability of our species: we evolve not by genes and bodies alone (as all other species during evolution) but primarily by our material and spiritual cultures.

- The Modernity stage is associated with the development of large human communities that grew as people transitioned to a settled way of life. It was no longer primarily people themselves who moved around the world, but material flows — goods, artifacts, or seeds — as well as knowledge. The network of trade, military, and political communications of the great empires linked the planet together. The first wave of global connectivity was largely completed by the mid-19th century and has only been qualitatively reinforced since then.

- The third stage, which could be called Noospheric (also "regenerative"[31] or "biosphere-centric"[32]), involves the emergence of institutions that coordinate the lives of people and technological systems across the planet. So far, these institutions have largely regulated the lives of humans themselves, from political freedoms and patent laws to the cost of fuel and access to new entertainment. However, it is increasingly clear that, without creating conditions that ensure the viability and flourishing of non-human planetary systems, our species will unlikely survive on Earth. Humanity must take responsibility for its environment and help the planet find a new balance — that is, not only manage the processes of human civilization itself, but also do so in coordination with the natural processes of the biosphere, atmosphere, hydrosphere, and lithosphere.

According to Vernadsky,[33] the transition to a Noospheric stage requires certain conditions. In addition to the obvious factors such as the dispersal of humanity across the landmass, and increased connectivity and exchanges between territories, Vernadsky believed that equality, justice, and democratization should be promoted, scientific knowledge should be freely developed, and education should be accessible to all. According to Vernadsky, abandoning wars on Earth was also a critical factor.

Teilhard de Chardin saw the Noospheric stage and the transformation of humanity into a geological force as the part of a larger evolutionary process that encompasses all life on Earth. For him, the Noospheric transition or planetization was manifested as "the formation of an organico-social super-complex" in which all life will be united in a single consciousness,[34] the culmination of human evolution. In Teilhard de Chardin's view, the emergence of a planetary consciousness and the realization of our interconnectedness with all life on Earth is the key to a sustainable and harmonious future.

While these and many authors have emphasized the importance of the transition to planetary consciousness for the future of humanity, the essence of this concept and how it can be achieved remain enigmatic. It is crucial to deepen our understanding of what planetary consciousness entails and how it can be fostered.

One possible typology of planetary consciousness in human civilization suggests that it is manifested on three levels:

- Level 1: *Planetary consciousness as conceptual mindset* involves the cognitive ability to comprehend our interconnectedness with the planet and its systems. It includes the capacity to understand global human and non-human systems, recognize the connection between the local and the global, and think in a systemic, long-term, and evolutionary manner. This level can be observed in various knowledge fields, including cosmology, geology, biology, and "big history."
- Level 2: *Planetary consciousness as a set of practices* involves acting in the best interests of planetary systems, both locally and globally. Examples include taking ecological and climatic responsibility, implementing circular and regenerative economics, supporting planetary movements and global institutions, and adopting new models of governance that recognize non-human systems as legal entities.
- Level 3: *Planetary consciousness as a way of being* is characterized by the ability to empathize with planetary processes, sense belonging to a larger planetary organism of life and love, and integrate the "mind of Gaia" in daily actions and communications. This level of consciousness is manifested within various practices of compassion of Buddhist and Abrahamic traditions, Taoist practices of non-doing, and more.

However, we should refrain from associating planetary consciousness solely with individual efforts to comprehend planetary processes. Planetary consciousness is formed not only (and maybe less so) at the individual level, but also at the level of the whole species. Many scholars, including

Aurobindo, Teilhard de Chardin, and Turchin and Joslyn,[35] argued that the development of collective intelligence is the next systemic transition in the evolution of complex systems on our planet and that it is inevitable in the process of planetization of our species (Teilhard de Chardin emphasized that the rise of collective intelligence will not result in the suppression of individuality, but in the enhanced personal spiritual evolution).

To what extent is planetary consciousness cultivated by us, whether individually or collectively, and to what extent is it manifested within us? A recent perspective by Adam Frank and colleagues[36] suggests that planets themselves are extremely complex, sentient, and even "super-intelligent" beings. Considering these ideas, it is highly likely that planetary consciousness may already exist within the planet itself. This consciousness is manifested through the coordinated operations of all planetary systems and the intensive exchange of information across all levels of organization of matter (similarly to "embodied consciousness" in individual organisms). Then, we do not need to invent planetary consciousness — our task is to connect with the consciousness of the planet itself and align with it in our individual and collective existence.

The traditional scientific narrative of human evolution portrays humans as "spontaneously" emerging from their primate ancestors through a combination of random genetic mutations, then working their way "up" towards dominating all other species and becoming a superior species of the biosphere. However, if we accept Frank's hypothesis of the "super-intelligent" planet, we can speculate that the evolution of life on Earth is not random, and the development of the biosphere and the planet has some direction. It is then plausible that humans are "created" (or teleologically evolved) by the biosphere and the planet to serve their specific role as "organs" of planetary evolution. Our science and technology, our efforts to coordinate biospheric and other planetary processes, then can be envisaged as our early attempt to fulfill our evolutionary goal. As a part of this perspective, humans are also "organs of awareness" of the planet and the universe.

▌AWAKENING PLANETARY CONSCIOUSNESS IN HUMANKIND

Planetary consciousness is manifested and held in humanity through the various systems of collective coordination, from legislation and cultural norms to the architecture of cities and technological infrastructure. Social institutions themselves, in particular, the ones that govern human practices of everyday life (e.g., eating habits, hygiene, or even religious rituals), are the very forms of the embodiment and preservation of collective consciousness. What if these systems and institutions were reorganized from the perspective of planetary consciousness? What major changes would allow planetary consciousness to take root at the scale of humanity?

There are several major directions where such transformation should unfold, and all of them adhere to the same principle: following "the sense of evolution" or the forces of Life and Love themselves (that embody the sense of evolution). In practice, it means cultivating the ability to be more alive and loving on a personal and community level and creating social structures that are life- and love-affirming.

Different aspects of this principle can manifest themselves in transitions such as:

- *Deep Democracy*: decision-making (politics) and resource allocation (economy) that is fair and inclusive towards diverse human individuals and collectives (including the diversity of genders, ages, ethnicities, belief systems, etc.).
- *Open Knowledge*: knowledge creation and distribution (through media, science, technology, etc.) that allows important knowledge to be

distributed as freely as possible, used and verified as openly as possible, and protected from manipulation and distortion.

- *Regenerative Economy*: production and distribution on principles of circularity and regeneration that create conditions conducive to life (including rewilded ecosystems as well as intentionally designed eco-systems that support human presence).

- *Post-Anthropocentric Governance*: decision-making representing inter-ests (and "voices") of key species and ecosystems and, later, elements of abiotic planetary systems (rivers, mountains, etc.).

- *Non-Violent Existence*: governance that minimizes systemic violence on all levels of society (from domestic violence to inter-faith and ethnic conflicts) and reduces chances of new military conflicts to zero.

All these changes require a plethora of systemic innovations in areas of production, administration, and jurisprudence. The most crucial element, however, is the massive transformation in the cognition and capacities of people involved. Therefore, educational systems play a vital role in foster-ing planetary consciousness.

As a Global Education Futures report indicated, "education is the most sophisticated social practice of intentional evolution ... still widely underutilized," and therefore, we need to evolve "our capacities to learn and lead in such a way as to co-create our healthy and desirable future together here on Earth and beyond."[37] Several educational practices can be cultivated to establish planetary consciousness:

- *Collaboration and Co-Creation-Based Learning*: learning to work together towards shared goals and to solve problems in collaboration.

- *Empathy-Based Learning*: learning to understand and share the feelings of others, to foster a sense of connection and compassion for all beings, including the planet itself.

- *Intercultural and Interfaith Learning*: learning to recognize various cultures and belief systems, appreciate the diversity of human experience, and cultivate a global perspective, building a sense of global community.
- *Nature-Based Learning*: learning to connect with the natural world, understand our interdependence with all living things, and cultivate a sense of respect and stewardship for the natural world.

It is important to acknowledge that education is also a tool for holding onto the past paradigm. Therefore, it is necessary to create not only new content but also new organizational forms for learning. Learning must take place in communities that see an evolutionary transition as their own task. The transformation of these isolated groups into a global learning ecosystem will allow us to build up the critical mass for the rise of planetary consciousness in humanity.

I believe that a crucial step in facilitating a transition to planetary consciousness is the establishment of an entity that I refer to as the "University for the Planet." Drawing on the original meaning of "university" as an institution capable of engaging with the world at large ("universum"), this networked educational and developmental institution would serve as a catalytic agent for the transition to planetary consciousness. It could coordinate global efforts while simultaneously working with small local groups to spread planet-centered methods of thinking and practice through teaching and project-based initiatives. The University for the Planet would not only be a place of learning for humans but also for the technological environment (including AI and robotics) and living non-human systems such as ecosystems and bioregions. The University can become an "operator of transition," an essential tool for advancing beyond the current barriers of human evolution and spreading planetary consciousness across the planet.

CHAPTER 10

UPSHIFTING THE FUTURE

CHARLES EISENSTEIN

Let us capitalize *the Future* to indicate its status as an archetype, for in the modern era, it has taken on a significance beyond mere "times to come." In contrast to non-modern cultures' conception of time as cyclical, spiral, or fractal, modern time-binding weds the future to a notion of progress. The Future is a glorious estate in which humanity has become the Cartesian "lords and possessors" not only of the material world, but of the social world as well. The Future was to be a perfect society of material abundance, endless leisure, engineered happiness, perfect health, and perhaps even physical immortality. This, the conquest of death itself, would be the ultimate triumph over nature, and so figures prominently in current iterations of transcendentalist thought (such as transhumanism and the singularity).

This Babelian project of taking Heaven by storm lies in ruins around us. But as we stumble through its wreckage — political decay, economic inequality, depression, addiction, domestic violence, militarism, poverty, chronic illness, and ecological degradation — we find everywhere the green shoots of an unreasonable hope poking through the rubble. The hope is not that some miracle technology will fulfil the Cartesian promise after all and deliver us unto the paradise of total control. The green shoots draw directly from the humus of a larger intelligence in which the human being may participate.

Progress in the modern era has been a function of *know-how*, thus the close link between science and technology. If you know how it works, you can take command of it. What you can predict, you can, potentially, control. The technologies of the future do not depend on knowing how, because they do not depend solely on human intelligence. Someone else, something else, knows how. They partake in organic intelligence.

Recent advances in biology offer examples of organization without control. I mean organization in the literal sense of the formation of organs. Contrary to expectations, there is no material repository in the genes or elsewhere that instructs cells how to build a body. Nothing directs them to build an eye here and a limb there. They just know what to do. They do not work off a blueprint.

The dreams of progress-qua-control are not entirely in vain; each has a correlate in a new era of organic intelligence. The main difference is that in the new story, human progress is indivisible from planetary metamorphosis: progress of all life on earth. You see, there is a germ of truth in the linearity of the modernist idea. Life enacts an arrow of time. It runs the opposite direction of 20th-century physics' devolution toward ever-greater entropy: it moves toward ever-greater order, ever-greater complexity. Life moves toward life. Life creates the conditions for more life. Earth becomes more and more alive. Biodiversity intensifies through the epochs. Of four billion years of life on earth, three billion were exclusive to unicellular life forms. Trilobites appeared only half a billion years ago, which is also when plant life began to colonize the continents. Terrestrial megafauna like dinosaurs appeared several hundred million years later, followed later still by the first flowering plants. Mammals are even more recent, perhaps 100 million years old, So, animals and plants, ecosystems as we know them today, have only been around for less than 5% of earth's history. Life has indeed, in this sense, progressed. Life has a timeline. Humanity's future is to rejoin that timeline, and to participate in the further efflorescence of life.

To many people, it has seemed that the human species, or at least human civilization, has been a curse on the planet. They say, "Earth would be better off without us." Or in the face of ecological crisis, they say, "Earth will be fine; it is humanity that might go extinct." These sentiments are unavoidable when humanity is wedded to a vision of its destiny that requires dominating and subduing life. When we understand our destiny to be participation in the further unfolding of life, beauty, and complexity in the cosmos, no longer are we a burden to earth, but a gift. In that story, we bring our gifts to bear toward making that destiny a reality.

In the old story of progress, the role of the human being was to tame the wild, simplify complexity, and dominate the earth, which was an environment, a source of resources, a domain over which we were to ascend to unchallenged sovereignty. In the future, we would engineer the weather, specify what would grow where, and bring the whole earth under an orderly plan.

In the new-and-ancient story, the human being works to heal the lands and waters that have been harmed. We use material and ritual technologies to maintain a dynamic and fruitful balance in the community of life. We watch and listen for what wants to be born on earth. How can we further enrich life? In coming centuries, deserts bloom anew, marine dead zones come back to life, forests reclaim their ancient domains, and species thought to be extinct reappear. We bring the full power of our ingenuity to cleanse the world of plastic, toxic chemicals, and radioactive waste.

The new story of progress — human participation in the efflorescence of beauty, complexity, and life in the cosmos — is not only a redirection of ends, but it is also a revolution in means. Understanding our companionship with intelligences outside and beyond the human, creative possibilities, that is to say, technologies, arise beyond our *know-how*. We gain allies to help us accomplish the "impossible." For a long time, an ideology of force-based causality has narrated to us what is possible, leaving many powers and potencies in the margins of civilization's reality. I speak here of psi phenomena, over-unity energy technologies, various forms of energy healing, and "technologies" involving dream states, psychedelic substances, focused attention, ritual, water, sound, and light, and so forth. Science-as-we-have-known-it casts them all into disrepute, because they resist its legitimizing framework of explanation: reduction to the operation of forces.

I call the above-mentioned technologies, *technologies of reunion*. They allow us to stand no longer apart from a dead material world, pushing it around by force. Paradoxically, they also fulfil the authentic aspirations that underlie the vain strivings of the program of control. We might heal our bodies without forceful chemical and surgical interventions. We might communicate over great distances through direct connections between minds. We might travel between the stars with methods more akin to trance than to rocket propulsion. We might access enormous energy without burning fuel. We might even, in a sense, conquer death: not through preserving the body but by connecting with parts of ourselves beyond the body as we know it. In the future, we will not be so afraid to die, and we won't run a whole civilization based on the manic phobia of death. That, indeed, is the most harmful consequence of the story of the separate self that underpins our civilization.

A new story of the human being is no mere intellectual construct. It co-resonates with a state of consciousness. The story cannot change unless the extended being of mind and body changes with it. The new ends and means that are available to us express more fundamental changes. Therefore, I will add one more element to upshifting the future: peace. None of the technologies of reunion will be anything but marginal when war mentality still pervades the field of human consciousness. Even with existing, conventional technologies, none of our problems are difficult to solve. But because we spend most of our energy opposing one another, all of our problems are impossible to solve. War mentality bears deep links with force-based causality and force-based technology. War is their inevitable expression. A fit habitation for technologies of reunion is a culture that has moved past us-versus-them thinking, violence-based solutions, good-versus-evil narratives, and the habits of judgement. To ignore these and focus only on the wonders of free energy devices or psi technologies or even regenerative agriculture is to perform, to adopt a phrase, technological bypassing.

Peace, as an active principle and not a mere absence of conflict, is another word for reunion: Peace with the rest of nature. Peace with each other. Peace with exiled parts of ourselves. Peace within society and without it. It is not the absence of conflict; it is that conflict is no longer the default response to a problem. Similarly, force-based technology will not disappear; no longer, though, is it the dominant mode of relations with the world. Upshifting the future, simply put, is to rejoin the world, to come home, to participate in its intelligence, and to know ourselves as life's gift to life.

CHAPTER 11

THE UPSHIFT PATH TO A NEW PARADIGM WORLD

ANNELOES SMITSMAN

▮ THE META-CRISIS

We are entering times of catalytic tipping points. Life on planet Earth is radically shifting in ways we are not prepared for. We are reaching critical limits of adaptation. Add to this increasing wealth inequalities, worsening geo-political tensions over scarce resources, increasing risks for nuclear escalations, the renewed arms race, and rising populist and separatist movements — it is evident that major actions are urgently required.

The planetary crisis is the meta-crisis of our time — that is, multiple tipping points now start to converge. Tipping points create nonlinear change dynamics that can radically shift the structures of reality as we know it. When the caterpillar reaches its limits to growth, its metamorphic transformation becomes a tipping point for the emerging butterfly. In similar ways, humanity has reached its limits to exponential growth.

Although we cannot compare the planetary crisis to the metamorphosis of a caterpillar, there are sense-making perspectives that can help us approach the meta-crisis transformationally. The call for systemic transformation is loud and clear.

- What can we learn from the caterpillar about metamorphic transformation for becoming a species with a lighter footprint?
- How can we embrace our own metamorphosis to mature as a planetary conscious species?

Like the caterpillar, we have no idea what it means to experience life from a butterfly perspective. During systemic transitions — when the old structures of the caterpillar world are dissolving, and the new structures and sensory organs of the butterfly have not yet fully formed — life may seem unclear and uncertain. During this mushy phase, it is important that we allow ourselves to cocoon, to grow the new connective structures and sensory organs of our future potential. Only then do we become our evolutionary next step.

The meta-crisis is the onset of our metamorphic transformation, which is precisely why I believe there is reason for *active hope*. For the first time in human history, people from all over the world can directly get involved in the making of an entirely new civilization. Furthermore, our technologies and science have advanced to the point that we can bio-mimic and Cosmo-mimic Nature's genius and apply this to our societal development. By applying the wisdom of living systems we can create:

- Economies that operate as thriving learning ecosystems;
- Political systems that operate as planetary neural networks;
- Cultures that operate as planetary sensory organs; and
- Educational systems that operate as nurseries for actualizing our collective intelligence potential.

The meta-crisis is the quest of our time to become the 'solutionaries' for a thriving world and future. We are also sense-making organs of Gaia, our planet. Our life-given human capacities are precisely tuned for us to create meaning from information, and wisdom from knowledge. Our bodies are part of Gaia's vast intelligence and her evolutionary process. For the myriad bacteria and viruses inside us, our bodies are like a planet. Within us live entire galaxies teaming with life.

When you allow yourself to relax into unitive consciousness, your experience of the world and reality can profoundly shift. You may then experience how the universe from its smallest elements to its vast galaxies is a living network of relationships with infinite creative potential. We are *that* universe; life is fractal. We are part of a universe of consciousness that is alive with meaning and has an innate directionality towards wholeness.

Do not try to solve the meta-crisis, instead *enter* into it. Embrace it. Let yourself become part of it. Go deeper into the heartbeat of life. Experience yourself *as* life. Become receptive to the wisdom of our universe, and allow this wisdom to upshift your perspective, understanding, and response. Now solutions can emerge that are integral and transformative, and not based on trying to fix a problem.

Relate with yourself and others as future humans of the emerging new era. Contribute to the maturation of human consciousness by embracing your metamorphic transformation. Allow the sensory organs of butterfly consciousness to form within your consciousness — so you may start to experience life from the next step of our evolutionary development as a species.

BECOMING CONSCIOUS OF OUR SYSTEM ARCHETYPES

To mature as a species, it is imperative that we learn from earlier civilizations — so we may become wiser together. The Industrial Age was built from mechanistic archetypes and extractive economic models that operate at the cost of vital planetary boundaries and social thresholds.

A system archetype is the underlying structure of the interconnections and interdependencies of a system, which influences the degrees of freedom in a system and how the elements of a system interact. For example, the archetype of a hierarchic system manifests as imposed goals and top-down control with restrictions for how people can interact, share information, and enact change. Hierarchic archetypes generate rigid, dualistic, and divisive patterns of behavior.[38] A system archetype that is decentralized and participatory will respect people's autonomy within the system, and support interdependencies through open information sharing, and inclusive decision making.

Each system archetype creates its own growth dynamics. A system archetype designed for exponential growth risks exponential collapse when the resource nexus of the growth curve becomes undermined, and carrying capacities are exceeded. Extractive growth models remove and extract more value from their systems than what is returned or can be regenerated.

A system archetype for regenerative growth follows a cyclical path that allows ecosystems and their resources to renew and regenerate. Regenerative growth models add back more value than what has been removed, used, or extracted. To build post-carbon societies that are regenerative by design, we need to know what system archetypes we operationalize for growth and development.

The informational architecture of complex living systems provides essential lessons for how to operationalize system archetypes that are regenerative and thrivable by design. Living systems operationalize an architecture of wholeness, which is cosmologically given and remains sourced from nonlocal implicate orders of consciousness that are informationally unified.[39] In other words, the archetypes of living systems are regenerative and thrivable by design.

Living systems access and utilize the quantum potentials of the universe for renewal, transformation, and evolutionary development. Quantum potentials can also be considered as the imaginal potentials of living systems that enable the emergence of new diversity and new choices from Cosmic coherence.[40] As such, living systems can evolve to higher orders of complexity in ways that contribute to the generativity of life.

Mechanistic systems, by contrast, are designed from linear goals and objectives that are informationally divisive and disconnected from the nonlocal implicate orders of consciousness.[41] As such, mechanistic systems become more rigid and destructive over time — that is, unable to renew or evolve from within, and unable to diversify from Cosmic coherence (i.e., informational wholeness).

Mechanistic systems also impact the people who are working in and for such systems, by creating systemic thrivability barriers[38]. In other words, mechanistic systems behave contrary to the evolutionary capacities of living systems.

Mechanistic growth models became standardized during the Industrial Age — and still are today — driving rapid technological development and industrialization. Path making for a better world requires awareness of the system archetypes we operationalize.

The archetypes of living systems are dynamic, responsive, holonic, non-linear, and cosmologically sourced from the implicate orders of consciousness. In other words, the archetypes of living systems are evolutionary by design and fundamental for our thrivability.

▌FACING OUR SYSTEMIC BLIND SPOTS

To better understand the origin of the mechanistic archetypes, we need to consider the implications that the Newtonian scientific worldviews had on the industrialization of our world. Newtonian sciences upheld the view that the universe is like a gigantic machine — operated by rigid and deterministic laws. The Newtonian scientific worldview was also adopted by social scientists, economists, politicians, judiciary, and policy makers who sought ways to better govern and control a world of seemingly separate entities that compete for survival.

The technological advancements of the Industrial Age were made possible (in part) because of this mechanistic approach. Although modernization has brought many benefits and opportunities, it also caused enormous ecological and social debts. Economists tend to refer to such costs as 'externalities,' which are not accounted for in mainstream economic models. Hardly any of the products and services we purchase today are based on a true price that accounts for the true costs and impacts.

The meta-crisis is a direct result of the mechanistic growth archetypes that became the dominant operating systems for our societal development. To resolve the root causes of the sustainability crisis, the transformation of the underlying mechanistic growth archetypes is imperative. Realistically, this will only happen if the underlying political and economic paradigm shifts to one that is focused on planetary security and collective well-being. Future generations depend on us to face our systemic blind spots.

▌THE UPSHIFT PATH

The human species is a fascinating experiment of nature. As a species we are one, and yet, in our oneness we are also incredibly diverse — just like the universe. The evolutionary path of life is coded for creative diversity. Our societies are becoming increasingly complex, and not just because of technology or population growth. Increasing complexity over time is the evolutionary pattern of the universe. Trying to regress to earlier states of less complexity is simply not an option.

Nature has a brilliant pattern for ensuring that increasing complexity does not implode from within, and thus becomes self-destructive. It is called 'evolutionary coherence', which is also the secret key to communicating from the underlying wholeness of emerging diversity. I like to describe evolutionary coherence as follows:

> Evolutionary coherence is a dynamic state of harmonic resonance and spontaneous collaboration between the diverse elements and relationships of complex living systems. A natural state of attunement to the innate wholeness and unity of life.[42]

We can also think of evolutionary coherence as an invisible conductor. When we are in the pattern of evolutionary coherence our experience of complexity becomes enjoyable, rich, harmonic, and multi-dimensional. Our body knows when we are in coherence with life — our breath becomes deeper, our nervous system relaxes, our heart rhythm coheres, our vision naturally expands, and we can access our innate resources for thriving.

The path towards deepening evolutionary coherence is already given. It is the wave that brought our universe into being and continues to in-form the evolutionary direction of life. As soon as we shift out of the old dualistic separatist mindsets and stop competing for domination, we can rejoin the Cosmic wave of evolutionary coherence once more.

WE ARE FRACTALS OF A QUANTUM UNIVERSE

Cosmologist Jude Currivan offers a reinterpretation of the laws of thermodynamics as laws of informational dynamics.[43] Doing so reveals how the evolutionary patterns of our universe emerge from nonlocal Cosmic orders that are informationally unified and fractally in-form the evolutionary process of life.[39]

To live wiser on the planet, we need to realize what universe we are living in. The Cosmic architecture of the universe is finely tuned, not through immutable laws, but through interwoven networks of relationships that make life possible. We literally bring each other forth, and we are the living systems through which the universe actualizes its cosmological potentials.

The meta-crisis is the outer manifestation of the mechanistic system archetypes of our societal development, which reflects our earlier reductionistic understanding of the universe. We can design better systems that support, and even enhance, the carrying capacities of our planet and the maturation of human consciousness.

▌REALITY IS NONLOCAL

Physicists John Clauser, Alain Aspect and Anton Zeilinger were awarded their 2022 Nobel Prize in Physics for their experiments with entangled photons, establishing the violation of Bell inequalities and pioneering quantum information science. Their research confirms that the universe is fundamentally nonlocal, which also implies that it is locally not real.[44] In other words, we live in a quantum universe whereby nonlocality is the underlying principle of reality, and not locality as was long presumed by mainstream science.

Nonlocality is a principle of quantum physics, yet not easy to comprehend. Classical physics suggests that physical reality is local, which means that a measurement at one point in space cannot influence what occurs at another point in space, if the distance between the points is large enough.

However, as the scientific research of John Clauser, Alain Aspect, Anton Zeilinger (and other physicists) confirms, physical reality is fundamentally nonlocal. What this means is that under certain conditions the measurement of one particle will correlate instantaneously with the state of another particle, even if the physical distance between the particles is many light-years away. Nonlocality also implies that particles at more fundamental levels of reality are informationally correlated and entangled.[43]

Although we live in a quantum universe, mainstream society still operates by and large as if we live in a classical and mechanistic universe. Quantum principles can be mind boggling to comprehend. However, living systems operate by these principles all the time, as does our body. Physicist Arkani-Hamed went even further by stating that "space-time is doomed," to express how space-time itself appears to emerge from more fundamental layers of reality for which new principles in physics are required to better understand this.[45]

By accepting how nonlocality — instead of locality — is the underlying principle of reality, we may finally upshift out of dualistic and mechanistic worldviews. Only then can we truly start to co-create our world with the wisdom of living systems, systems that developed by utilizing the quantum capacities of the universe.

Nature is a collective intelligence that has grown from billions of years of networking and embodying the quantum potentials of the universe through complex living systems. This collaborative intelligence has made life on Earth — including human life — possible.

As one of the youngest species of our planet, it is time for us to step up, grow up, and become Earth wise. We have it within us to contribute to the evolution of life on Earth, rather than harm it. We are nature, too.

▍THE EARTHWISE CONSTITUTION FOR A PLANETARY CIVILIZATION

The upshift to a planetary civilization requires actionable solutions, based on the wisdom of living systems. We can become the people who shift the needle from collapse to thriving. We can become the people whom our Earth needs and on whom future generations can depend. We are the future ancestors of the next civilizations. What can you do today to accelerate the upshift to a new paradigm world?

To address the root causes of the sustainability crisis, we created the EARTHwise Constitution for a Planetary Civilization.[46] It opens with:

We, as future ancestors of a planetary civilization, commit to co-creating thrivable worlds and futures with the wisdom of living systems, in partnership with life and our Earth.

The Constitution is open source and freely available and serves as a:

- Cosmic Compass and social contract for co-creating our worlds and futures with the wisdom of living systems.
- Meta-attractor and evolutionary blueprint for cohering and aligning myriad of movements, projects, and initiatives through a common vision and focus.

Constitutions are not just for countries made by people. Living systems have an innate constitution for their evolutionary development, which is their informational architecture that fractals the wholeness of life. To affirm this, Article 3 of the EARTHwise Constitution states:

We acknowledge how our universe exists and evolves as a single unified entity, an undividable wholeness. This evolutionary principle helps us understand life as a unified reality, whereby energy-matter and space-time are complementary informational expressions of consciousness.

▌THE UPSHIFT TO A PLANETARY CIVILIZATION

Maturation is a complex and nonlinear learning process. Systems often appear to regress to earlier stages just before jumping to new stages of development — especially when new developmental structures and capacities have not yet formed sufficiently for embodying the emerging new potentials and degrees of freedom.

From a developmental perspective, temporary regressions are not a set-back but an integration of earlier structures and capacities into newly developing ones. The rise of former archaic systems and authoritarian archetypes could indicate that our species is at the forefront of a new developmental stage. We are each developing future humans of an emerging new era.

To complete this essay, the following guidelines may be offered to support our upshift capacities:

- *Inspire Transformation*: Facilitate experiences that unite and help people connect with their future human potential of the emerging new era for the upshift to a new paradigm world.
- *Act as a Solutionary*: Respond to challenges creatively and empower transformative solutions through wisdom-based actions that connect us to the larger possibilities of life.
- *Empower the Shift to Planetary Consciousness*: Act from planetary consciousness by offering an integral perspective of the challenges and opportunities of the meta-crisis.

- *Engage Nature's Genius*: Partner with nature's collective intelligence and the pattern of evolutionary coherence for developing our capacities for thrivable worlds and futures.
- *Become the World You Wish to Live in*: Opt out of that which causes harm and division and opt into that which helps heal and regenerate our world and planet.

CHAPTER 12

THE EMERGING UNITIVE AGE

ROBERT ATKINSON

The superficial boundaries between us are breaking down. Long-standing silos of separate knowledge systems are crumbling. Multiple interconnected global crises are forcing us to acknowledge the reality of the whole and the power of its evolutionary impulse. There is much to give us assurance that this dark night shall pass.

This is a time of bridge-building and partnering, a time to expand existing circles of unity into larger and more inclusive circles of unity that fully embrace and reflect the entirety of the whole. The reconstruction of human society and all its relationships, including with all other life forms on the planet, is the uppermost challenge of our time.

▌A UNITIVE WORLDVIEW

We are experiencing the birth pangs of the culminating stage of a long evolutionary process that has forever been in motion. The perennial wisdom in the Hermetic principle of "As above, so below" is derived from a holistic, unitive worldview which has been prominent in some circles throughout time and sees all Creation as one whole.

Everything on the micro level reflects everything on the macro level. As Plato also noted, "Perhaps there is a pattern set up in the heavens for one who desires to see it, and having seen it, to find one in himself." This unitive principle has always supported the purpose and direction of an evolutionary impulse yet is only now coming into public awareness.

Science and spirituality, formerly competing knowledge systems, are now being understood as complementary ways of knowing the mysteries of the universe. Both recognize a common force guiding evolutionary progress toward a consciousness of wholeness. Both emphasize the interconnected nature of all things as part of the same reality. And more and more people today are discovering this pattern in and around themselves through their own experience of wholeness.

This principle addresses the divide between duality and nonduality, confirms that the individual and the collective mirror one another in their essential nature and processes, and explains how all things are interconnected.

▌A 19TH CENTURY TIPPING POINT

As part of an evolutionary flow that brings about periodic leaps of consciousness, in the middle of the 19th century, during a time of discord, disunity, and inequality in Persia, Baha'u'llah, founder of the worldwide Baha'i community, renewed the spiritual teachings that have guided the peoples of the world throughout the ages with a comprehensive revelation that focused on unity as the way of healing the ills of an ailing humanity.

He proclaimed, "Regard the world as the human body which, though at its creation whole and perfect, hath been afflicted, through various causes, with grave disorders and maladies... The mightiest instrument for the healing of all the world is the union of all its peoples."

Unity is the all-encompassing, over-arching principle that all progress in the world depends upon. It is the natural outcome of an organic process of restoring seemingly opposing forces to their inherent wholeness. He further said, "The well-being of mankind, its peace and security, are unattainable unless and until its unity is firmly established."

At the same time, Baha'u'llah acknowledged a pattern in the unfolding of evolution that makes progress a nonlinear spiral-like process consisting of phases of ups and downs. He said, "The oneness of humanity will be achieved in evolutionary stages replete with strife, chaos, and confusion." This holistic - and realistic – view accounts for and explains why a recurring process of personal and collective transformation is necessary throughout the cycles of evolution.

Although evolution is by no means a straight line, the wholeness of Creation is undeniable. Abdu'l-Baha, son, successor, and interpreter of Baha'u'llah's teachings, provided a succinct clarification of this unitive worldview: "The evolution of existence is one. The divine system is one. Whether they be small or great beings, all are subject to one law and system." All things in the entirety of existence make up an interdependent whole, a oneness in which everything in the whole is an inseparable part.

In this unitive consciousness, reality is one, and all seeming differences and distinctions are imaginary. What brings *us* to this unitive consciousness is directly experiencing a universal pattern that all versions of the transformation process follow.

▌A UNITIVE PATTERN WITHIN US AND AROUND US

There is a pattern found in mythology, mysticism, ritual, and psychology that centrally locates transformation within its core, connects us to the cycles of nature, and heightens our awareness of the responsibility that comes with having the direct experience of this pattern in our lives. This results in a desire to "give back" and "lift up" others in whatever ways we can.

This pattern defines a life lived deeply, by confirming that all are governed by the same natural law, what Pierre Teilhard de Chardin called "a single energy at play in the world." It shows how evolution in all realms is tied together, and all of Creation is an indivisible wholeness.

In mythology, Joseph Campbell made popular the *monomyth*, or journey of the hero, drawing from the archetypes of the world's myths to form the pattern of *departure – initiation – return*.

In ritual, Arnold van Gennep identified the pattern that all rites of passage follow in guiding the young person from dependence to interdependence through *separation – transition – incorporation*.

In mysticism, Evelyn Underhill described *the mystic way* as a universal, androgynous journey of spiritual transformation following a pattern that leads from *awakening* to *purification* to *union*, resulting in living in harmony with the whole.

This is not just a pattern haphazardly chosen in a variety of settings, but a pattern that is part of our internal make up. Psychologist Carl Jung found that as the archetypes embedded in our unconscious are released by life experiences and we become conscious of them, through great struggle, we eventually are able to merge opposites into a new whole. This forms a pattern that he called the "individuation process" and takes in the stages of *birth of the ego – death of the ego – birth of the whole self.*

In mapping the contents of the collective unconscious, Jung helped clarify that the whole spiritual heritage of humanity is contained within us and is born anew in the mind of every individual. This inner blueprint for transformation is designed to guide us along our way through the difficulties of life and back to a consciousness of our innate wholeness.

This universal pattern is also found within the basic structure of story itself. Beyond beginning – middle – end, on a deeper and more meaningful level, this pattern consists of *beginning – muddle – resolution*. It is the muddles, or challenges, we face that represent the core of the transformation process, enabling its completion, or resolution.

In *A New Story of Wholeness*, this is described as a blueprint for living into wholeness, with three parts, *call to wholeness*, *path of purification*, and *return to wholeness*. Personal transformation is intricately connected to collective transformation. Both lead to the other, and both naturally result in a desire to contribute to the betterment of the world, what Kabbalists call Tikkun Olam, the work of repairing the world, or restoring the world to *wholeness*.

We are all capable of living into this wholeness; it is an innate capacity, as Evelyn Underhill said: "The germ of the transcendent life, the spring of the amazing energy which enables the great mystic to arise to freedom, is latent in all of us, an integral part of our humanity."

But achieving this potential requires a conscious effort to lift ourselves out of complacency and beyond the illusions that deceive us. This inner pattern also helps move us across a continuum of states of consciousness as we experience a broader and deeper reality through our challenges and struggles. From this perspective, all states of consciousness are interdependent links of a chain within the same whole.

Our journey to wholeness takes us across the side of the continuum built upon a *consciousness of duality* from separation, and all that leads to, to the other side of the continuum built upon a *consciousness of wholeness* leading us from connection and cooperation to gender equality and economic equity to unity in diversity – all interconnected stepping-stones to peace. This side of the continuum shows us the mysterious hidden wholeness that the Buddha referred to: "All things originate from one essence, develop according to one law, and are destined to one aim."

▌EXPRESSIONS OF A UNITIVE WORLD

As we enter further into humanity's unitive age, the natural culmination of our evolutionary trajectory that will unite humanity as one family, we will see more of the desire, the deep commitment, to carry out our lives in service to the whole.

Shifting our focus from the part to the whole, we become convinced that what is best for one is what is best for the whole. Most importantly, we will see a moving away from means that begin and end in disunity toward means that bring about unity in everything we do. Here are a few examples of how this will transform every aspect of our lives.

- Though justice typically separates victim from perpetrator, it is meant to maintain the inherent balance of life. *Unitive justice* is justice that brings about unity [see Chapter 32 in this book].
- Though healing typically focuses on ailing parts, it is meant to make whole again. *Unitive healing* is healing that brings about unity.
- Though economics typically creates a system of haves and have nots, it is meant to be a system for maintaining well-being. *Unitive economics* is economics that brings about unity – by eliminating the extremes of wealth and poverty.

- Though knowledge is typically separated into distinct ways of knowing, it is meant to help us understand the world we live in. *Unitive knowledge* seeks to bridge interdisciplinary boundaries to bring about unity, as with science and spirituality.

- Though language can be used to divide or unify, it is meant to communicate common understandings. *Unitive language* is language that brings about unity.

- Though patterns are typically seen separately, they are meant to highlight connections in apparent randomness that also have a common source. A *unitive pattern* is a pattern that brings about unity – by connecting with other apparent random patterns that have their common source in the unitive system of natural law.

- Though narratives can result in either disunity or unity, they are the neutral form, structure, or pattern a story is told in. *Unitive narratives* are narratives that bring about unity [see Chapter 2 in this book].

- Though governance can separate, it is meant to bring people, communities, and nations into closer cooperation. *Unitive governance* is governance that brings about unity.

This bullet list could go on and on, as our emerging unitive age depends upon achieving and maintaining harmony and unity in all endeavors. Unity is what most characterizes the spirit of our age, just as the Ten Commandments and the Beatitudes did for their time. Achieving this wider unity on a global scale in the social, cultural, and economic spheres means living by common values and principles that assist us in becoming one human family.

Unity cannot be achieved without wholeness; wholeness requires equality between women and men, balance between wealth and poverty, freedom from all forms of prejudice, harmony between science and spirituality, and protecting nature as a divine trust.

These unifying principles are so interdependently tied together that the realization of one depends upon the realization of all the others. Each one is also a prerequisite for fulfilling the age-old vision of peace on Earth.

▌UNITY IS THE OUTCOME OF THE EVOLUTIONARY IMPULSE

The good news, and what gives us hope for the future, is that consciousness evolves toward unity and wholeness. All things have unity as their natural purpose. Humanity's spiritual evolution is directed toward unity. Unity of purpose is central to the evolutionary impulse. Humanity will reach its apex of consciousness when we collectively reflect the perfect harmony, unity, and wholeness that already exists in all the diversity of creation. Unity is necessary for maintaining the wholeness-in-motion of all things that are. This knowledge of a hidden thread of wholeness connecting, supporting, and uniting all things in existence is at the mystic heart of all sacred traditions and is now the leading edge of scientific understanding.

Only the unitive action we all take now will allow a gentle path to peace on Earth. Love is the sacred activism of our time, binding all hearts together. We are on the verge of this unitive worldview becoming as commonly accepted in our time as nationalism was in the past.[47]

CHAPTER 13

THE KEY PRINCIPLES OF MUTUAL AID

GAUTHIER CHAPELLE

M utual aid has been everywhere, since the dawn of time, in a much clearer way than we imagined at the start of this investigation.

Mutual aid acquires its power in a hostile environment. This results in a competitive advantage: it allows living things to better survive threats.

Mutual aid cannot be grasped without taking into account the different levels of organization, which can be summed up by the words of D. S. Wilson and E. O. Wilson: 'Selfishness beats altruism within groups. Altruistic groups beat selfish groups. Everything else is commentary.'

Mutual aid reaches exceptional levels in humans: it is powerful, deeply rooted in us, can be deployed on a very large scale, but remains flexible (with a high sensitivity to external conditions thanks to epigenetics and culture).

Mutual aid is a powerful, but fragile and sometimes dangerous force which appears under very specific conditions, and which disappears or becomes toxic (pathologies, closures, etc.) when the conditions are no longer met.

Mutual aid is deployed in the living world in many shapes and sizes (symbiodiversity), both in the mechanisms and in the evolutionary paths that lead to its emergence.

The architecture of mutual aid (including among humans) therefore resembles Russian dolls where, as the dolls get bigger, they become more complex, and different sizes of dolls can cooperate with each other. All of these dolls form an ever-changing network of multicolored networks.

Mutual aid is the main source of innovation in life, at all scales, and has been since the emergence of life. It is the key to the diversification of living things, and one of the pillars of natural selection.

Finally, competition finds its place in this context. It remains the second major pillar of natural selection, helps strengthen mutual aid between organizations, and is used by organizations to delimit their territories or make their needs known. But it is energy costly and risky, which makes it unreliable when it comes to engaging in an effective and sustainable 'struggle for life.'

▌THE FUTURE OF MUTUAL AID?

The lessons we drew from exploring what we call mutual aid, and which includes all the ways in which living things associate with each other, can be summed up in a few key points.

First, there is the evidence that mutual aid and competition have been everywhere, between individuals and between species, since the dawn of time. Helping each other is deeply rooted in us as humans, both in our biological heritage and in the cultural practices which are interwoven with our biology, and it comes naturally to us. As recent studies have shown, cooperation has been a central theme in popular narratives around the whole world for tens of thousands of years. But the problem of our society is that it has fallen under the influence of a powerful culture that only allows for individuals and competition.

Next, although it may seem counterintuitive for competition-ridden society, it is shortages, crises, and hostile environments that make mutual aid emerge. We find this principle on two different time scales. First, it is found in our own lives when we encounter a very stressful situation or when we have to react to a disaster. In an emergency, people self-organize without panic and help each other in a remarkably effective way. All that is left in them is the acute awareness of being human, of needing security, of needing to help the other. Self-help and altruism emerge spontaneously, as was observed on September 11, 2001, in New York, or at Bataclan in Paris in 2015.

All this happens very quickly, in a few hours or a few days. Then, on the long time-scale of biological evolution, a hostile environment brings out mutual aid between organisms, simply because those which adopt solitary or selfish strategies are much less likely to survive.

Thus, a collapse perspective leads us to envisage not so much a rose-tinted future paradise of mutual aid and altruism but rather a situation where human groups who do not help each other will have less chance of survival. The standard of living of an average European is equivalent to 400 'energy slaves,' meaning that each European consumes on a daily basis an amount of energy equivalent to a work force of 400 healthy people. If these 'energy slaves' (fossil fuels) diminish or disappear, we will have to start working much harder, while also accepting that our standard of living will fall substantially. We will then rediscover the effectiveness of working in a group and realize that it was precisely wealth and abundance that allowed the emergence of selfish and individualistic behaviors. In other words, in our present environment, the help of the other is not necessary, and competitiveness does not involve real risks.

We also saw that mutual help in a group, however spontaneous and powerful at first, can quickly collapse if not reinforced by social norms such as rewarding altruistic people, punishing cheats, and good and bad reputation, as well as the basic need to feel security, fairness, and trust within the group. Consequently, we can suppose, and we observe in fact, that while occasional serious disasters lead to the emergence of prosocial acts (solidarity, altruism, mutual help), over time, if a basic institutional structure doesn't form between the reconstituted individuals, social chaos can easily come back and degenerate into deadly conflict.

The challenge for the next few years, then, is to demonstrate the toxicity of our competitive culture, to denounce it, and to transform it. We need to appreciate that a culture of mutual aid can be fragile and hard to sustain. It requires a lot of practice and willingness until effective 'invisible architectures' have been put in place to support it. But the result is worth the effort: mutual help is powerful and can move mountains. 'We are not saints, but we are sometimes good team players,' says the psychologist Jonathan Haidt.

▌WHICH GROUPS?

Every group of individuals (family, nation, company, association, religion, or whatever) has a kind of skin or membrane — a self — that defines it, that protects it from the world outside and filters what it agrees to let in or out. Sometimes, the membrane becomes watertight, and the group 'closes in on itself,' considering what is external to it as foreign, even hostile, or simply non-existent. Individuals within the group then lose their reciprocal relationships with individuals outside, whose subject status becomes transformed into that of an object, in relation to which anything is permitted. This is what happens between supporters of football teams, between religions, between countries at war, or between humans and animals.

How can we rebuild the connections with those and with what is around us, so that they are mutual, trustworthy, secure, and equitable? That is the big undertaking of our time. It's in our interest to do whatever is needed to strengthen our relationships with others, both humans and non-humans. To do this, we need to examine the various membranes that constitute us, learn how to make them porous (stop them from becoming exclusive), and discover more extensive ones, so transforming beings who seem distant into subjects within our enlarged community.

The challenge will be to juggle with this interweaving of identities so that we can get through the storms ahead without allowing our feelings of sadness, fear, or anger to transform into forms of aggression. During a major upheaval of the social order, and consequently of the norms that structure that order, we can always count on the very solid 'membranes' of small groups, which we can form relatively easily (family, neighborhood, village, even associations, and so on). However, we should also be aware that even if a reference group such as the nation contracts or disappears, it doesn't stop us from feeling, and bringing to life, much more extensive 'membranes' that include all of humanity and everything that lives. We can feel compassion and empathy freely for whomever it may be.

This question of the membrane and its radical enlargement occurs in a very practical way in relation to refugees and migrations. The spontaneous rejection of some outside the 'nation' membrane, as long as this membrane is still meaningful, can be understood (among other reasons) by fear of scarcity ('There won't be enough for everybody; we'll end up fighting each other.') or the anxiety of losing one's identity ('Do they share my values? I'm not willing to compromise them.').

It is normal that accepting a stranger causes fear at times. Opening one of our protective membranes (family, city, nation, etc.) to strangers is always a risk. But openness and welcome can be cultivated, and it is possible to become 'competent' through learning how to manage these membranes. Also, you only need to spend an evening with some Sudanese refugees to discover people 'like us,' with the same concerns, emotions, and needs.

Governments call this great phenomenon of migration a 'crisis,' but what has happened since 2015 is only the small beginning of a great movement that will become much larger in the course of the century. Projections for 2050 suggest a figure of 200 million displaced persons because of climatic factors (floods, droughts, etc.), and many more if one considers all the other reasons (wars, epidemics, etc.) The political apparatus seems to have no way of preparing for the long term, showing how far it was not designed for such purposes. Still worse, by 2050, we French, Belgians, or Swiss may find ourselves forced to migrate or to seek asylum in Norway, Finland, or Russia because of global warming or the explosion of one or more nuclear reactors. If we look at today's African refugees, we see the human condition as it may be for most people in the twenty-first century.

Migrations have been characteristic of humanity for hundreds of thousands of years. If we were not so powerfully wired for empathy and mutual assistance, we, beardless, immature little monkeys, totally vulnerable at birth, would have been dead long ago. Our ability to cooperate, to make groups and societies, has made us one of the most widespread species on Earth.

However, there is a serious obstacle to the implementation of mutual aid in a group. This is hierarchy. Many animals are able to coordinate and divide tasks, but only humans (or, more accurately, some human cultures) have developed social structures in the form of vast hierarchical pyramids. While this recent mode of organization has proved effective in stable and predictable situations – such of the military, or building cathedrals or rail-ways – it is both inadequate and ineffective when the situation becomes complex and the environment changes.

As Marc Halévy, a physicist, philosopher, and business consultant, points out: 'By definition, a hierarchical pyramid structure is the easiest way to connect x points to each other. The simplest, so the stupidest. How do you expect information originating from thousands of actors to be han-dled, at the required level of complexity, by the ten people on the board of directors?' With the bewildering level of complexity of our huge societies, we seriously need to question the appropriateness of such architectures of power. They not only make us far more vulnerable and less resilient in the event of major disruptions, such as those in the electricity grid, or pro-longed strikes affecting supply chains, but their rigidity makes they them-selves become factors in aggravating disasters.

The occasional attempts to build 'team spirit' in companies has no real effect; the hierarchical pyramid structure encourages 'everyone for them-selves.' Our obligation is always to become more successful and find ways to climb up the ladder. Sébastien Faure, an early 20th century anarchist teacher, already noted more than a hundred years ago: 'So, what one sets in motion, with a system of ranking, is: among the people at the top, vanity, presumption, contempt of the inferior, and in any case careerism; among the people at the bottom, envy, discouragement, unwillingness to make an effort, resignation.'

In addition, 'top-down' decisions regularly generate a feeling of unfair-ness — for example, on the issue of differences in how people are treated in relation to salaries. A feeling of fairness, however, is one of the three ingredients (along with security and trust) necessary for the emergence and maintenance of mutual aid. Consequently, even if mutual aid manages to keep going in such pyramidal structures, it is systematically inhibited by the decision-making and power mechanisms inherent to this type of structure.

In recent years, as noted by management specialist Frédéric Laloux, new organic and decentralized organizational methods have been developed. In a striking convergence with colony-based living organisms (such as ants or mushrooms), these organizations rely on both local and interconnected intelligence, making for resilience and cooperation. Our society is progressively moving (and it is high time that it did so) from 'power over' to 'power with.'

Empathy, compassion, reciprocity, trust, and the subtleties of group dynamics cannot be felt through a book — they have to be experienced. We have all felt significant moments of mutual help at a difficult time, received a helping hand, felt a hand on our shoulder, perceived a look of gratitude or the thrill of being part of a group. For Carolyn Baker, 'It is important to know our neighbors, not only for security purposes, but to know what they might need from us that they may be too proud to reveal. Are you sure that your neighbors have enough to eat?'

We need each other, and appreciating this leads us to admit and express our vulnerability, both as individuals and as social groups. The capacity for resilience comes from the bonds that people have woven with those around them. This is 'social capital.' When bad news comes, it is important not to feel alone, and not to feel that the people around you don't know how to react as a group. We need to learn, experience, and teach the art of being together from now on, and as quickly as possible.

CHAPTER 14

AN UPSHIFTED DEVELOPMENT PATH: THE POLITICS OF BEING

THOMAS LEGRAND

A NEW DEVELOPMENT PARADIGM

As an environmentalist working on tropical forest conservation and climate change, I have realized there is so little we can achieve within our general development paradigm that emphasizes economic growth. To live in harmony on this planet, we need a profound reorientation of our priorities, not only as individuals, but also as societies.

The systemic crisis we are facing points to an overall obsolescence of this development path. It is also a civilizational crisis as this model itself is embedded in a specific cultural program: the modern paradigm and its set of values — materialism, reductionism, individualism, humanism, anthropocentrism, scientism, etc. — that set us apart from one another and nature. We have all the technical solutions we need, but we are lacking the right mindsets and values, as well as a new vision of the good life.

Humanity is now called to undergo a profound and long-awaited cultural evolution, which is in essence spiritual, "*a change of mind and heart,*" as the Earth Charter said at the beginning of the new millennium. In fact, the evolutionary crisis we are facing results from an imbalance between humankind's material and technological power and the relative underdevelopment of the consciousness, wisdom, and ethics we need to manage this power and the increasing complexity it has brought to our world. Humanity has seen its power multiply, to the point that many scientists consider human beings to have become the dominant influence on climate and the environment, characterizing a new geological epoch called "anthropocene." But our development path has not allowed the kind of human growth necessary to build a wiser society that makes good use of this power.

The Earth Charter proposes a new vision of progress, which can support this human evolution. It affirms that "when basic needs have been met, human development is primarily about being more, not having more." While recognizing that material prosperity and securing basic needs can enable the transition from "having" to "being," particularly in western societies, I would argue that human development is always about "being more." In fact, "having" is a means, not an end itself, and "being more" may be the key to ensure everyone can meet their basic needs for two reasons. First, investing in personal development at scale, especially for poor people, can have an important positive impact on the development of poor countries, as shown by the example of Nordic European countries and their "popular enlightenment" ("folk-bildung") education policies in the nineteenth century. Second, "being more" may also be the key to build more solidary and equitable societies as pointed out by Indian spiritual and humanitarian leader Amma: "In today's world, people experience two types of poverty: the poverty caused by lack of food, clothing and shelter, and the poverty caused by lack of love and compassion. Of these two, the second type needs to be considered first — because, if we have love and compassion in our hearts, then we will wholeheartedly serve those who suffer from lack of food, clothing, and shelter." Moreover, the paradigm of economic growth is rooted in western modernity and its strong materialistic values. Many low-income countries and communities — such as Bhutan's Gross National Happiness, or Bolivia's and Ecuador's living-well/ good living political philosophies — may be more naturally inclined than western countries toward development paradigms that reflect a "being" focus, that are closer to their own cultural values. Failing to recognize these "being" aspirations before basic needs have been met (assuming they probably never were from modern standards) seems like a highly condescending, dehumanizing, and erroneous vision.

I call this new development paradigm that emphasizes "being more" as our main collective goal the Politics of Being. It recognizes that life is a spiritual journey and aims at aligning our institutions with our true reason for being here on Earth: becoming who we are, the best and most complete version of ourselves. It also acknowledges the rights of nature: all living beings have the right to be.

The primary objective of governments should be to provide the means for each being to express its full potential, achieving its deepest healthy aspirations, while cultivating human qualities and values. The latter echoes the conclusion of American political economist Elinor Ostrom, who is arguably the most influential scholar in institutional analysis at the moment. In her lecture for the reception of her Nobel prize in economics in 2009, she summarized the most important lesson she drew from fifty years of research:

Designing institutions to force (or nudge) entirely self-interested individuals to achieve better outcomes has been the major goal posited by policy analysts for governments to accomplish for much of the past half century. Extensive empirical research leads me to argue that instead, a core goal of public policy should be to facilitate the development of institutions that bring out the best in humans.

Rather than enacting our assumed selfish, greedy, and competitive nature, our social institutions should be designed in a way that supports the cultivation of virtues as sages from Aristotle to Confucius have traditionally emphasized.

▌REDESIGNING OUR INSTITUTIONS FOR "BEING"

Think about how our retributive justice systems — founded on the logic of "punishment" — bring out our instinct for retaliation, while restorative justice invites everyone who is part of it — the victim, the offender, and community members — to practice human qualities such as understanding, listening, awareness, courage, and responsibility. Such restorative systems are not only more effective and cheaper, but they also nourish our humanity with systemic implications for all other dimensions of our lives. Can you imagine democratic governance systems freed from party politics, corporate interest, and polarizing social media algorithms? What if the latter supported citizen participation, effective deliberation, and decision-making, as well as the practice of civic virtues such as a sense of service, respect, non-violent communication, openness, and the search for truth and the public good instead of pitting one half of the population against the other? What if instead of filling brains with knowledge, our education systems supported the awakening and actualization of children's true being and helped them to grow as authentic human beings in all their dimensions, supporting cooperative learning rather than competition and the understanding of the world as an interconnected whole through topic-based learning rather than cutting it into separate disciplines?

This is not only feasible, as many examples attest, but it also is increasingly recognized as the most promising way forward in all these sectors. I can go on. The rising healthcare costs of an aging population affected by chronic diseases invites us to move away from a health paradigm focused on sickness to one centered on prevention and well-being, in which individuals are empowered to adopt healthier lifestyles, thanks to greater mental health. In complex and fast-changing environments, there is growing evidence that values-driven organizations, as well as more decentralized and adaptable organizations based on trust, empowerment, and the development of human socio-emotional capacities are particularly suited to thrive.

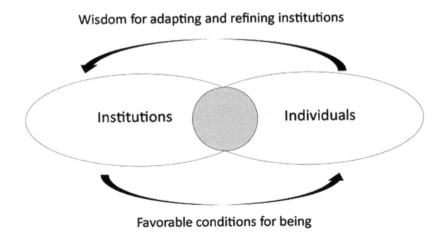

Figure 1. Institutions and Individuals in the Politics of Being

All these successful models actively nourish human values and qualities and build on a different cultural narrative emphasizing our potential for goodness and our relational or "interbeing" nature. The Politics of Being can bring them together into a new coherent vision and agenda for the development of our societies, one that would support our much-needed collective evolution.

SPIRITUAL VALUES AS THE FOUNDATION OF THE POLITICS OF BEING

Cultural development is about cultivating higher values, which lie at the core of our nations' projects as reflected in most national mottos such as France's "Liberty, Equality, Fraternity" or India's "Truth alone triumphs." The 1776 American Declaration of Independence also recognizes "Life, Liberty, and the pursuit of Happiness" as unalienable rights which governments are created to protect. They are the North stars of our nations, which help us collectively thrive.

The seeds of the Politics of Being can be found in new fields of scientific research, as well as social change and political initiatives rooted in some of the highest values which lie at the core of spiritual teachings. They constitute different communities, organized to promote these values as new lenses through which to look at our current challenges or new paradigms to transform our societies. These values include the understanding of interdependence (systemic, integral, and complex thinking), life (as in the regeneration movement), happiness, love or empathy, peace, mindfulness, and mystery. Together with Plato's transcendentals — Truth, Goodness, and Beauty — as well as freedom and abundance, these highest human values constitute the foundations of the Politics of Being.

Science can tell us how to cultivate these values at the individual and collective level, allowing us to identify an agenda for action in all sectors, with clear priorities, as well as many concrete public policies based on existing examples. These can embody the Politics of Being and bring about the cultural, human, social, and environmental regeneration we need.

These values are universal and can unite us all. Each culture also has developed a unique relationship with them, its own vision of the good life, and cultural heritages will keep shaping the evolution of our societies. Nations need to look inside, to reconnect to their own wisdoms. Our collective inner lives should be brought at the center of public debate, through regular psychological assessment and efforts to heal collective traumas, and the disorientation they brought, as a gateway to "being." Unlike economic growth and its single common metrics — Gross Domestic Product — the Politics of Being invites each nation to chart its own path towards fulfillment, to cultivate and share its unique genius to enrich our common humanity.

▍A NEW STORY

In the "having" mode of existence, environmental and social limits tend to be seen as hindrances to our own comfort, which we only acknowledge with regret. In the "being" paradigm, our connection with others and nature (as well as to ourselves) are on the contrary recognized as the foundations for human flourishing. The social and ecological crises are not something to be fixed to keep our ways of life. They are above all symptoms of an inner crisis, a disconnection from our true nature and needs as human beings. Healthy individuals naturally take care of others and nature. We can only all thrive together as one Earth community. And we would be much better. This is the inspiring narrative for our collective transformation — the only one that has enough strength to bring it about.

It goes hand in hand with rediscovering our true spiritual nature and our lives' purpose. The interspiritual movement has recently acknowledged that mystics from all different traditions and cultures have shared a same ultimate spiritual experience, that of oneness or unity with all that is. "To be" is "to inter-be." The spiritual development process of "being more" naturally leads to an increased sense of connectedness with all that is, from which stems prosociality and service, wisdom, and fulfillment.

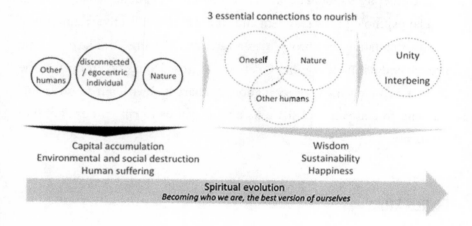

Figure 2. The Inner Path to Sustainability, A Theory of Change

The real question of our times is not about whether or to what extent our societies will collapse. It is whether humanity will finally grow into adulthood. It is the great Earth transition, whose time has come.

▌10 CORE MESSAGES

1. We need a collective shift of consciousness, a cultural evolution of a spiritual nature, to address our current challenges. It is already ongoing,

and we are currently facing an evolutive crisis, which requires individuals and societies to look inward and transform.

2. As a wisdom-based, science-informed approach, a Politics of Being can support this evolution. Its main goal is to support the fulfillment of all beings, that is to say the realization of our truest and highest being. "Being" is a wiser and more adequate development objective than "having;" it applies to the whole Earth community.

3. Cultivating our fundamental "interbeing" or relational nature is instrumental to allow us to live in harmony with one another and the Earth community. Our spiritual nature makes us interconnected at the level of being with everything that is. Only by recognizing their interconnectedness and sustaining the whole can each part thrive.

4. Societies progress as they increasingly honor the highest values, qualities, and ideals, such as freedom, goodness, beauty, truth, understanding, life, happiness, love, peace, etc. These are spiritual qualities in the sense that they reflect an awakened human being or divine perfection. Science and practical initiatives shaped around these universal values can help us design a Politics of Being. Cultural development relates fundamentally to an evolution of our values, which shape our worldviews and institutions.

5. The focus on being and the highest values provide a simple conceptual framework for a Politics of Being, which can integrate all relevant claims and initiatives. As such, it can help unify this vision and strengthen this movement.

6. Our institutions should help cultivate human virtues. They should acknowledge and facilitate the expression of our potential for goodness, cooperation, and intrinsic motivation.

7. Concrete and actionable policy recommendations supporting this agenda already exist in many sectors. A Politics of Being can bring

them together and scale them up, articulating them in a coherent and meaningful narrative.

8. Spiritual teachings and wisdom traditions, through dialogue among them and with science, have much to bring to inspire, help design, and implement a Politics of Being. They are our most valuable common heritage, able to offer a profound understanding of human nature, as well as practical knowledge and tools for inner, and ultimately social, development.

9. Each nation needs to reconnect to its own soul and wisdom to develop its version of a Politics of Being that can support its development and help it bring its unique contribution to the world. Unity in diversity is the key to harmonious coexistence of nations in a globalized world.

10. Healing trauma is, for individuals and societies, the gateway to being. It is fundamental in order for new ways of being and living together to be possible, and for the whole Earth community to flourish.

CHAPTER 15

TRANSFORMING A DEATH ECONOMY INTO A LIFE ECONOMY

JOHN PERKINS

Economic hit men (EHMs) are highly paid professionals who cheat countries around the globe out of trillions of dollars. They funnel money from the World Bank, the US Agency for International Development (USAID), and other foreign "aid" organizations into the coffers of huge corporations and the pockets of a few wealthy families who control the planet's natural resources. Their tools include fraudulent financial reports, rigged elections, payoffs, extortion, sex, and murder. They play a game as old as empire, but one that has taken on new and terrifying dimensions during this time of globalization. (I should know; I was an EHM.)

These words are included in my book, *Confessions of an Economic Hit Man, 3rd Edition: China's EHM Strategy; Ways to Stop the Global Takeover* (February 2023). The book describes the ways we US economic hit men (EHMs) exploited lower-income countries that had resources US corporations wanted, like oil and minerals, and how China's EHMs have learned from our successes and failures and have become even more proficient. The book goes on to explain:

> The current global economic system is promoted by an EHM strategy that took on new and ominous proportions after China entered the fray in the early 2000s. When I decided to update this book to cover the changing relations between China, the US, and the rest of the world, I assumed that I had to address three significant themes. First, competition for global dominance had shifted from the military to the economic. Second, there was a trend toward uniting the world under initiatives like China's New Silk Road (officially the Belt and Road Initiative, or BRI) and American-led global financial structures. And third, the future of life as we know it depends on ending EHM strategies everywhere and transforming a failing degenerative system, known as a death economy, into a regenerative one, known as a life economy. However, as I was working on this new edition, two world-changing events happened that added new perspectives to these themes: the coronavirus pandemic and the Russian invasion of Ukraine.

The pandemic taught us that we are a global community vulnerable to unpredictable crises and that, when necessary, we can change. Russia's invasion catapulted us back to Cold War military policies and fears of a nuclear holocaust. It also showed us the importance of nations uniting against a common challenge.

If we are truly interested in finding a path to a better world, it is imperative that we understand that the two most powerful countries in the world need to cooperate. Together, China and the US comprise nearly half the global economy and cause nearly half the pollution that threatens to destroy life as we know it. Climate change, species extinctions, environmental devastation, income inequality, and most of the other major crises that face us are symptoms of a degenerative death economy. These many crises are problems, but they are not *the* problem. The problem is this death economy that is promoted by strategies that I and other US EHMs perfected which are now being made even more effective by China's EHMs. The book continues:

> My job during the Cold War was to implement the US EHM strategy in Africa, Asia, Latin America, and the Middle East. In our determination to stop Communism, we told the world—and ourselves—that we were ending poverty and encouraging democracy. In fact, we were making the rich and powerful richer and more powerful, causing a climate catastrophe, and increasing human inequality, environmental destruction, and species extinctions. Although we did not fully understand it until 2022, we also were helping to lay the foundations that would encourage a Russian leader to follow in the footsteps of a former ruthless Soviet dictator, Stalin.

It is important to understand that we are all victims of the EHM strategy. Americans, Chinese, Russians, Africans, Asians, Europeans, Latin Americans, and people from the island nations, rich and poor—all living beings—are threatened. We can disagree on political, governmental, religious, and other issues, but we must agree that none of those matter on a dead planet—one where the EHM strategy continues. If we want our children to survive, it is imperative that we come together and end the EHM strategy everywhere. It is essential that China's leaders (and future leaders) apply to the global community their popular Confucian ideal of serving the family; that US leaders (and future leaders) work to unite all the states of America and the world in a concerted effort to evade the crises facing us; and that Russians understand that their safety rests on facilitating cooperation between West and East, not expanding their borders. It is essential that a critical mass of people everywhere join hands to end the EHM strategy and transform the death economy that is driven by a goal of maximizing short-term profits and materialistic consumption, regardless of the social and environmental costs, into a life economy that is driven by a goal of maximizing long-term benefits for all life.

CHAPTER 16

FROM 6TH MASS EXTINCTION TO 6TH MASS EVOLUTION

ALISON GOLDWYN

Imagine ... right now ... everywhere on Earth ... no matter what time zone or season ... there is only one thing that every living being is doing. Breathing.

That notion alone should be stunning when we consider it. But we don't. We're not conscious of this astonishing shared experience and so many others. It's become as rote as New Year's Eves we now take for granted while autopiloting our way through life in what incrementally feels, for many, like a life-sentence. And because we don't take conscience of it, we're diminished as a result of it. Yet, imagine if we did! And imagine not only recognizing it but also celebrating the fact that Consciousness itself is alive and breathing us ... and every living being! Add music to that cosmic mix, and the harmony becomes profoundly rich. For the time being, however, this worldwide symphony sounds more like a cacophony.

In 2020, the world was invited to a "*mask-erade*" party no one wished to attend. A tiny microbe upended and upstaged the greatest kingdoms of wealth, corridors of power, technological marvels, and infrastructures on earth as Humanity no longer played the mighty star on center stage. Some call it The Great Awakening. Others The Great Plague. No matter, The Stage of Life will never be the same.

From pandemic to war, from *"environMental"* breakdown to socio-economic downturn, from racial inequality to geomagnetic instability, from outside in and inside out — earth is quaking, and our species' renewal now beckons — from the insight out. But how to pivot an entire civilization on its healthy axis? More natural disasters? Manmade ones? Disaster and aggression have been impetus for many defining, world-shifting moments. Their traumatic embers scar us, forever etched into the global zeitgeist. Yet, concurrently, the wisdom of the ancients continues its murmur about our connection to All That Is, its voice ever obscured by the noise of Modernity. Strange bedfellows indeed, in perpetual co-existence on a radio dial receiving persistent static interference.

Earth has been poorly marketed. So has Humanity's in-sanity.

Perhaps you're becoming familiar with the role of epigenetics in Health, the language of archetypes, or the missing links about our mysterious human history. Perhaps you're learning about the power of group intention or the importance of breath to deepen self-connection. Perhaps you've become aware of heart-brain coherence and that the "little brain" located in the heart is our actual command center ... or that planetary healing hinges on our species' transformative evolution — at risk of extinction. Perhaps you're wondering if our agitated global body is finally stirring from its comatose state and how that might affect our individual emotional states (or collective nation states). What kind of earthshaking, groundbreaking awakening to anticipate? And might we shape it in a more user-friendly way?

We are all born onto the Stage of Life without conscious choice or a user manual, other than a constricting script that's been passed down by our predecessors over epochs. It allows minimal wiggle room to improvise within societal parameters. A fortunate few burst beyond to forge new horizons with newly scripted storylines. But, for the most part, managing a planetary population is based upon fear & limitation, rather than the power of our "imagiNations." As boundaries now bleed and borders are blurring and thoughts are becoming as cohesive as they are divisive (we share a collective angst and yearning for comfort, yet rage against one another in exasperated attempts to find it), as AI and Transhumanism trickle into our veins, and the veil covering the voice of Consciousness begins to fade ... Humanity's run amok storyline is undergoing a life-changing re-write. What role will we choose to play on this new Life Stage? And who or what will try to upstage us?

We will need to readjust to the notion of boundaries and borders both personally and environmentally as the earth itself now pitches and careens to extremes with inordinately complex conditions that render staggering swaths of the population potential environmental refugees. As it pushes us to our limits, we're pushing back in the process — for better, and also for worse (environmental innovation on the one hand, water wars and fertile land grabs on the other). Who will be the new winners and losers in an unsustainable game of musical chairs when the music stops, and the only chair left is a shrinking earthly spit of habitable land mass – and swelling numbers of Us? Can we accept being not only in each other's midst, but also in each other's faces?

Well, there's always fertile Mars with her gorgeous green pastures, blue skies, and turquoise seas teeming with fascinating life — whoops, wrong planet. Even though we are now discovering remnants of ancient oceans with possible life, imagine the billions of years to evolve another earthly masterpiece of paradise. Or if we could find a user-ready one fast enough, much less transport the bulk of us. So here we swirl ... within a vast cosmos on a blue jewel of incomparable riches, pummeling and plundering it and one another to oblivion.

As we race into space to forge bright new vistas on behalf of damage control and blessed wonder, in certain respects, we're still bringing perpetual toxic thinking, which created this mess of our humanness in the first place. Who owns the air-rights to Earth? Who owns the Moon? The mineral-rich Cosmos? The Outer Space Treaty has loopholes much like the American Constitution, presuming that safeguarding this world is in the hands of Leadership morals (and our better angels). *EnvironMental* health is not merely relegated to Earth's atmosphere. Our unregulated power-plays and destructive competitive strategies are already underway, as individual nations' covert "adventures" put territorial pressure on one another to compete both fiscally and on behalf of national security. It's a metastasizing pattern which holds both the collective and leadership hostage to the centrifugal force of a destructive-competitive system — the dynamics of which are astutely elucidated on John Bunzl's global gov platform Simpol (Simultaneously Policy).

It's easy to assume we're alone in the universe. Our forefathers believed that the Old World was the only world until Magellan and Columbus discovered the New World — and that it was inhabited. To believe that no other intelligent life exists in the cosmos other than our own, simply because we've yet to encounter such, is as hubristic and mystifying as presuming we can fix our broken planet with the same broken minds that (unintentionally or otherwise) created it, to paraphrase Einstein. If we're worried about asteroids obliterating earth, we might wish to consider humanoids first.

Upshifting to a new paradigm can feel like an uphill battle when confronting the mighty undercurrent exerted in this old paradigm upheaval.

We are incredibly innovative with regard to science and technology and have devised some remarkably designed stopgaps to mitigate the worst of our current crises. But there has yet to be a cohesive worldwide rollout in this complex global overhaul. With so much at stake on this planet and untold ripple effects into the cosmic, the great Global Reset depends upon a great shift in mindset — an upshifted mindset — to transition from the precipice of Act 3 Finale to the threshold of an Act We Rally. And a rally is precisely what is needed.

Mother Earth is watching us. Father Time is clocking us. Thus far, it looks rather ominous if you view it from the outside in and the "incite" out. So, what's the point of celebrating yet another New Year's Eve when the forecast looks rather bleak? What's left at this critical inflection point, this pivotal moment of bifurcation?

▌A NEW KIND OF CELEBRATION!

In times of death, destruction, and chaos, the ancients gathered in large numbers — be it to grieve losses or celebrate harvested bounties. Ritual, ceremony, and festivity were key portals to commune with the Gods and appease their anger or offer thanks. They sang. They danced (maybe not hip-hop). They dressed in lavish costumes & headdress and elaborately painted faces. They acted with reverence in asking for forgiveness.

Whether or not the Heavens listened, they themselves heard one another in a sacred form of bonding. Today, we might refer to said Gods as "Higher Consciousness" given that the gods of industry have seemingly forsaken us. But what of the bonding? From *bUsiness* to *indUstry* to *indigenoUs* and *sUstainability*, do you see what I see missing from our collective human experience? Finding a deeper meaning for being human, and a soulful appreciation and expression of our biosphere connection ... this is our birthright and also our missing link.

Much like President Truman's Marshall Plan for rebuilding in post WWII, there comes a dramatic new call, a Marshall Plan for the Environment to drastically step-up momentum. But the roots of Climate Change and nearly all our global crises emanate from a still deeper common root system that desperately needs pruning: Changing the Emotional Climate. With a disintegrating, disenchanted, ever disengaged society in which competition overrides collaboration ... corruption infiltrates competition ... and a media-compass focuses on doomsday messaging ... we've lost our north star. Where is there a mirror-image reflecting the dazzling face of our global selfie from its "good" side, in real time? There may be glimmers here and there, but until this becomes the predominant energetic of enough of us, the current driver of society will drive us to the edge rather than toward well-being.

Not everyone can travel to Space like William Shatner — nor astronaut Edgar Mitchell who experienced an Overview Effect which forever shifted his perspective about the world around him and within him. This power-packed term, coined by Space Philosopher Frank White, holds immeasurable possibility for accelerating profound connectivity. If only we can turn the compass inward to propel us forward collectively and conscientiously — on a magnanimous, majestic, world-scale arena.

In 1987, I began party-planning the unfathomable: an interstellar Party for the Planet honoring Every Living Being in a music-driven celebration about us all — broadcast live worldwide! Co-starring Earth & Space in an edutainment spectacular of epic scope and depth, the stage would be everywhere, and the stars would be every sentient being.

Originally intended as a millennium event spanning multiple global venues featuring locals and luminaries and nature's beauty, the concept was intriguing yet daunting to the many media titans I broached.

By the time 9/11 ushered in two turbulent decades, including an Arab Spring, Brexit, an unprecedented U.S. President, cyber security threats, fake news, AI and the inevitable questioning of reality itself, a feverish worldwide clip accelerated to a frenzied dance. And when that tiny microbe shoved humanity from the spotlight in 2020, it highlighted longstanding frailties that brought us to our very knees. The familiar dance steps had become crippling missteps.

In a sweeping stroke, the roaring engine of human acceleration halted across the world. Everyone everywhere was upended by a shared shock. Imposed isolation unified us and also divided. For a heartbeat, the Developed World felt the heartbreak of an Underdeveloped World that's been living an oppressive existence on a daily basis. Thanks to technology, for the very first time in history, an entire civilization experienced itself devoid of invincibility, and filled with utter fragility and vulnerability — simultaneously.

The impact of viewing the pathos, creativity, and even humorous absurdity on social media as each one grappled to make sense of this destabilizing human experience ... was inestimable. So was the trauma. Coupled with Climate Crisis and Russia-Ukraine war, it has left an overheated Emotional Climate whose trail of PTSD sprawls across the world. Food chain and supply disruptions. Economic hardships. Social Inequality eruptions. All punctuate a precipitous turning point and the need to process it with restorative, regenerative measures never seen before. After all, it's not a guarantee our species is "meant to be."

The tumult has exacerbated our hunger for a sense of community and belonging and also for asserting individual identity and assuring national sovereignty — all with ferocity and velocity. Individualism, Nationalism,

Globalism: three blind mice unaware that they're actually a part of rather than apart from a very complicated common organism. Parts of the world are flooded with conferences and rock concerts. Other parts remain in Covid restrictions and lockdowns. Rockets launch into space as missiles launch onto war-ravaged landscapes. The face of education is changing, and creativity is going mainstream. Heightened states of depression and exhilaration characterize a rising Renaissance as well as Dark Ages ... and amidst it all, a familiar word reemerges: Story.

We need a new story. And new stories are nothing new. History repeats itself with innumerable "fresh" versions guised in various wardrobe changes under different Directors on our spiraling Life Stage. So, what's different this time? Perhaps it's that this seismic birth on earth (the *"b'earth contractions"* of which are accelerating and intensifying) is being witnessed and experienced by everyone in real time, that we're poised to both midwife and birth it consciously (and hopefully, conscientiously), and that time is running out.

The Climate is drastically changing. So is the Emotional Climate in relation. Learning to dance this tricky tango is imperative so we step less on each other's toes. Thus far, we remain dramatically uncoordinated — Covid vaccine staggered rollouts were a stunning example. Once-upon-a-dance-step, a privileged few seemed exempt from the fallout of reckless behavior. Less and less now, as the effects are encroaching and ever widespread. It will take some fancy footwork to retrieve our footing, and living on Mars (currently at least) is not the solution. Do we want to march through this in regimented fashion? Or dance through it in an upshifting new rhythm?

While the lights dim on center stage and the future looks grim, there is much afoot backstage (and stage right & stage left) with phenomenal innovations ready to save the planet. But what's stalling the colossal roll-out? And what's to stop us from falling back into habitually destructive patterns? Genuine change is not a sprint. It's a marathon which demands vigilance, diligence, endurance, practice — and tolerance. To truly generate sustainable renewal, humans need to be able to safely liberate their authentic (caring) nature and impulse to healthily create in supportive ways. Our collective needs heaping doses of hope, TLC, and nourishing engagement — as well as a mighty mirror-image to reinforce this vision ongoing. From leadership to citizenship to species and biosphere, it's a paradigm-shifting lesson in the ultimate relationship rebuilding.

We have mega-events to coalesce us within mega-niches: Sports (e.g., Olympics, World Cup), Entertainment (e.g., Academy Awards, Grammys), Environment & SDGs (e.g., Earth Day, Global Citizen), Culture (e.g., Chinese New Year, Carnival in Rio). Yet, we remain as fractured and splintered as ever. It's a consternation how concerned we are about alien encounters and foreign life forms when our species itself is alienated from self and other in the ultimate example of a "foreign relations" blunder.

Why has there never been a commanding celebratory experience to coalesce us based on spellbinding creativity and our very existence? Will manmade or natural catastrophe define humanity's greatest legacy? How to extricate ourselves from this mess of our humanness and transition us — upshift us — to a more universally appealing tempo that's transformative, health-inducing, awe-inspiring, and uplifting?

With environmental powerhouses like Christiana Figueres, Jane Goodall, and Al Gore speaking of the need for hope ... with philanthropic titans (even Jeff Bezos) echoing this approach ... with longstanding Wisdom Leaders like Ervin Laszlo espousing profoundly essential truths ... and with many fresh voices joining established ones in a growing crescendo led by Youth ... perhaps the collective chrysalis is cracking, our voracious caterpillar has eaten everything in sight, is finally getting "sick of itself," and is ready to butterfly!

Everyone has a birthday. It's an earthly human experience many celebrate with a birthday party. However, we've never celebrated our collective birth — our birth on earth — with a *"B'earthday"* Party; one which includes Mother (Earth) and the entire biosphere of comrades living amongst us. Maybe the Marshall Plan for the Environment needs a Party Plan for the Planet!

Welcome to *Synchronistory*®, a new word for a new world!

The impact Arts and Culture have on mass-scale social change cannot be underestimated. It is evidenced in historic events like Woodstock, Live Aid, and more recently, Global Citizen. Music is the motivator, moving the masses through the healing power of sound. You love Rock? Opera? Jazz? R & B? You love Hip-Hop? Waltz? Samba? Ballet? Imagine making history in synchronicity with an exhilarating, morale-boosting edutainment spectacular spanning the planet, one that showcases the best of us, the ingenuity of us, the *miraculoUs*! We can still thrill to power, competition, drive, and ambition, yet do so with a winning new disposition of purposeful, compassionate, collaborative rebuilding.

Synchronistory® will rock the planet while stirring the soul, so it's game-on rather than game-over.

Releasing compounded tensions and traumas from our toxic collective drama has never been more imperative. And there has never been a more vital time to prime the planet for party time with some *serioUs* fun — something we've never before done. Sync's epic, stylish, enthrallingly dynamic musiCall to Action, Inner Action, and Interaction invites a 6th Mass Evolution we can all upshift to!

We're running on empty. From a nuclear world to a new clear world ... the Human Condition's operating system now needs to run on Love.

NOTES & REFERENCES

▌CHAPTER 7

1. Einstein, A., & Freud, S. (1933). *Why War? An International Series of Open Letters.* Paris: International Institute of Intellectual Cooperation League of Nations. See also The UNESCO Courier (May 1985): https://en.unesco.org/courier/may-1985/why-war-letter-albert-einstein-sigmund-freud

2. De Zayas, A. (2021). *Building a Just World Order.* Atlanta, GA: Clarity Press. Available at https://www.claritypress.com/product/building-a-just-world-order/

3. https://www.ohchr.org/en/special-procedures/ie-international-order and https://www.ohchr.org/en/special-procedures/ie-international-order/mr-alfred-maurice-de-zayas-former-independent-expert-2012-2018

4. De Zayas, A. (2022). *Countering Mainstream Narratives: Fake News, Fake Law, Fake Freedom.* Atlanta, GA: Clarity Press. Available at https://www.claritypress.com/product/countering-mainstream-narratives-fake-news-fake-law-fake-freedomcountering-the-mainstream-narratives-fake-news-fake-law-fake-freedom/

5. https://paradoxoftheday.com/war-is-peace-freedom-is-slavery-ignorance-is-strength/

6. De Zayas, A. (2011). *Völkermord als Staatsgeheimnis: Vom Wissen über die "Endlösung der Judenfrage" im Dritten Reich* (Genocide as a State Secret: Knowledge of the "Final Solution of the Jewish Question" in the Third Reich). Munich: Olzog Verlag.

7. UN Human Rights Committee (HRC), *General comment no. 34, Article 19, Freedoms of opinion and expression,* 12 September 2011, CCPR/C/GC/34, available at https://www.refworld.org/docid/4ed34b562.html: "49. Laws that

penalize the expression of opinions about historical facts are incompatible with the obligations that the Covenant imposes on States parties in relation to the respect for freedom of opinion and expression. (So called "memory-laws", see communication No., No. 550/93, Faurisson v. France. See also concluding observations on Hungary (CCPR/C/HUN/CO/5) paragraph 19.) The Covenant does not permit general prohibition of expressions of an erroneous opinion or an incorrect interpretation of past events." See also De Zayas, A., & Martín, Á. (2012). Freedom of Opinion and Freedom of Expression: Some Reflections on General Comment No. 34 of the UN Human Rights Committee. *Netherlands International Law Review*, 59(3):425–454. https://doi.org/10.1017/S0165070X12000289

8. UN Human Rights Council, *Report of the Independent Expert on the promotion of a democratic and equitable international order, Alfred-Maurice de Zayas*, 1 July 2013, A/HRC/24/38, para. 37, available at https://www.ohchr.org/sites/default/files/Documents/Issues/IntOrder/A-HRC-24-38_en.pdf

9. UN Commission on Human Rights, *Human Rights Resolution 2005/66: Right to the Truth*, 20 April 2005, E/CN.4/RES/2005/66, available at: https://www.refworld.org/docid/45377c7d0.html

10. UN Human Rights Office of the High Commissioner, Special Rapporteur on truth, justice and reparation, https://www.ohchr.org/en/special-procedures/sr-truth-justice-reparation-and-non-recurrence

11. UN Human Rights Office of the High Commissioner, Special Rapporteur on freedom of opinion and expression, *Report on Artificial Intelligence technologies and implications for freedom of expression and the information environment*, 29 August 2018, A/73/348, available at https://www.ohchr.org/en/calls-for-input/report-artificial-intelligence-technologies-and-implications-freedom-expression-and

12. https://thegrayzone.com/

13. See UN General Assembly Resolutions 76/161 and 76/191 (10 January 2022), and UN Human Rights Council Resolution 46/5 (23 March 2021), available at https://www.un.org/en/ga/76/resolutions.shtml and https://www.ohchr.org/en/hr-bodies/hrc/regular-sessions/session46/res-dec-stat

14. See my 2014 report to the UN General Assembly, A/69/272, paras. 63–77, available at https://ap.ohchr.org/documents/alldocs.aspx?doc_id=24160

15. De Zayas, A. (2023). *The Human Rights Industry*. Atlanta, GA: Clarity Press. Available at https://www.claritypress.com/product/human-rights-industry

16. UN Human Rights Office of the High Commissioner, About International Solidarity and human rights, https://www.ohchr.org/en/special-procedures/ie-international-solidarity/about-international-solidarity-and-human-rights

17. Eleanor Lives! A Plan for Humanity: www.eleanorlives.org

▌CHAPTER 9

18. McNeill, J.R., & Engelke, P. (2016). The Great Acceleration. An Environmental History of the Anthropocene since 1945. Cambridge, MA: Belknap Press.

19. Steffen, W., et.al. (2015). Planetary boundaries: Guiding human development on a changing planet. *Science*, 347(6223):736. https://www.science.org/doi/10.1126/science.1259855

20. WWF (2020). *Living Planet Report 2020 - Bending the Curve of Biodiversity Loss*. Almond, R.E.A., Grooten M. and Petersen, T. (Eds). Gland, Switzerland: WWF. https://www.worldwildlife.org/publications/living-planet-report-2020

21. Kurzweil, R. (2006). *The Singularity Is Near: When Humans Transcend Biology*. New York, NY: Penguin Books.

22. Meadows, D. H., Meadows, D. L., Randers, J., & Behrens, W. W. (1972). *The Limits to Growth; A Report for the Club of Rome's Project on the Predicament of Mankind*. Universe Books.

23. Laszlo, E. (2022). *The Upshift: The Path to Healing and Evolution on Planet Earth*. Cardiff, CA: Waterside Productions.

24. Vernadsky, W. I. (1945). The Biosphere and the Noösphere. *American Scientist*, 33(1). https://monoskop.org/images/5/59/Vernadsky_WI_1945_The_Biosphere_and_the_Noosphere.pdf

25. Teilhard de Chardin, P. (1961). *The Phenomenon of Man*. New York: Harper Torchbooks (Harper & Row).

26. Sri Aurobindo (1971). *The Supramental Manifestation and Other Writings.* Pondicherry, India: Sri Aurobindo Ashram Trust.

27. Hubbard, B. M. (1998, 2015). *Conscious Evolution: Awakening the Power of Our Social Potential.* Novato, CA: New World Library.

28. Tsiolkovsky, K. (2004). *Selected Works of Konstantin E. Tsiolkovsky.* University Press of the Pacific.

29. Kardashev, N. S. (1964). Transmission of Information by Extraterrestrial Civilizations. Soviet Astronomy, 8(2):217. https://www.adsabs.harvard.edu/full/1964SvA.....8..217K

30. Laszlo, E. (1989). *Inner Limits of Mankind: Heretical Reflections on Today's Values, Culture and Politics.* London: Oneworld Publications.

31. Fullerton, J. (2015). *Regenerative Capitalism: How Universal Principles And Patterns Will Shape Our New Economy.* Stonington, CT: Capital Institute. https://capitalinstitute.org/wp-content/uploads/2015/04/2015-Regenerative-Capitalism-4-20-15-final.pdf

32. Roberts, L. (1992). Ensuring The Best Of All Possible Worlds: Environmental Regulation of the Solar System. *6 New York University Environmental Law Journal.*

33. Vernadsky, V. I. (1997). *Scientific Thought as a Planetary Phenomenon.* Translated from Russian by B.A. Starostin. Moscow: Nongovernmental Ecological V. I. Vernadsky Foundation.

34. Teilhard de Chardin, Pierre (1946). A Great Event Foreshadowed: The Planetization of Mankind (La planétisation humaine). *Cahiers du Monde Nouveau.* A Great Event Foreshadowed: The Planetization of Mankind - Pierre Teilhard de Chardin (organism.earth)

35. Turchin, V. F., & Joslyn, C. (1989). *The Cybernetic Manifesto.* Principia Cybernetica Web. http://pespmc1.vub.ac.be/MANIFESTO.html

36. Frank, A., Grinspoon, D., & Walker, S. (2022). Intelligence as a planetary scale process. *International Journal of Astrobiology,* 21(2):47–61. https://doi.org/10.1017/S147355042100029X

37. Luksha, P., et. al. (2018). *Educational Ecosystems for Societal Transformation.* Global Education Futures Report. The Netherlands: GEF. https://www.globaledufutures.org/educationecosystem

▌CHAPTER 11

38. Smitsman, A. (2019). *Into the Heart of Systems Change*. Doctoral Dissertation, International Centre for Integrated assessment and Sustainable development (ICIS), Maastricht University, the Netherlands. https://dx.doi.org/10.13140/RG.2.2.28450.25280

39. Smitsman, A., & Currivan, J. (2019). Systemic transformation into the birth canal. *Systems Research and Behavioral Science*, 36(4):604–613. https://doi.org/10.1002/sres.2573

40. Smitsman, A. (2022). Applying the Cosmic Architecture of Consciousness for a New World Paradigm. *The New Paradigm in Cosmology*. The New Paradigm Symposia Series, Book 2. New York: SelectBooks.

41. Bohm, D. (1980). *Wholeness and the Implicate Order*. London: Routledge.

42. Smitsman, A. (2020). The Power and Importance of our Evolutionary Coherence. *Medium.com*. https://anneloessmitsman.medium.com/part-1-the-power-of-our-evolutionary-coherence-8033810029cb

43. Currivan, J. (2017). *The Cosmic Hologram: In-formation at the Center of Creation*. Rochester, VT; Toronto, Canada: Inner Traditions/Bear & Company.

44. Garisto, D. (2022). The Universe Is Not Locally Real, and the Physics Nobel Prize Winners Proved It. *Scientific American*. Accessed on 10 December 2022 via: https://bit.ly/3kVp3Y4

45. Arkani-Hamed, N. (2017). The Doom of Spacetime: Why It Must Dissolve Into More Fundamental Structures [Video]. *PSW Science*. https://bit.ly/2SbsI5Y

46. EARTHwise Centre. EARTHwise Constitution for a Planetary Civilization. www.earthwisecentre.org/constitution

▌CHAPTER 12

47. Atkinson, R. (2022). A New Story of Wholeness: An Experiential Guide for Connecting the Human Family. Fort Lauderdale: Light on Light

Press; Atkinson, R. (2017). The Story of Our Time: From Duality to Interconnectedness to Oneness. Fort Lauderdale: Sacred Stories Publishing; and Laszlo, E. (1989). The Inner Limits of Mankind: Heretical Reflections on Today's Values. Culture, and Politics. Oxford: Oneworld Publications, 65-7:120–28.

ROADMAPS TO THE GREAT UPSHIFT

PART TWO

UPSHIFTING OURSELVES

ROADMAP CLUSTER III

UPSHIFTING OUR HEALING

- *Keynote*: The Great Upshift in Healing
- Healing the Wounds of Separation: Soil, Soul, and Society
- Healing the World from the Ground Up
- Consciousness-Revolution: Upshift in the Neurosciences
- The Global Psychedelic Upshift and Holotropic Breathwork

CHAPTER 17

KEYNOTE

THE GREAT UPSHIFT IN HEALING

MARIA SAGI

The same as all the contributors to this remarkable roadmap compendium, my intention is to provide a practicable roadmap for the upshift of the human family to a more peaceful and sustainable mode of acting and being. I am a practicing natural healer, and as I accepted the invitation to provide such a roadmap, I asked myself, "How can healing, in particular natural healing, contribute to the upshift we need? What does holistic healing have to offer in regard to facilitating and promoting the Great Upshift? Does this form of healing contribute effectively to the wiser living on the planet?" The ensuing pages convey the answer I can offer to this question.

I begin with the basics. We know that we are at a critical juncture of our tenure on Earth. This realization is supported by the contributions to this book. I approach it from the angle of health and well-being. We are more and more "unwell" on the planet, and this means that we need more and more to heal: to become healthier, lest we encounter challenges we can no longer meet.

We need healing — but what kind of healing? The answer must be based on our understanding of what made us unwell, on what went wrong in the life and evolution of humanity. The answer is complex, and finding it is difficult if we aspire to comprehend specific details. But when all is said and done, in its essence, the answer is not difficult to find. Whatever went wrong has gone wrong because we diverged from the way of life and evolution in the biosphere. We have entered pathways that exceed the limits of sustainable life and development on the planet. We have created an artificial environment that satisfies short-term aspirations but fails to assure humanity's presence in the biosphere. At stake is not only our individual health and well-being, but also the persistence of our species on this planet.

Sustainability is the key issue, as we are beginning to realize at last. We perceive the seriousness of the problems of the environment as they appear in regard to climate, because these problems are highly visible — they affect our day-to-day existence. There are scores of other problems entailed by our divorce from the ways of nature, however, and these are less evident and, thus, do not sufficiently engage our attention. Yet, they affect and often threaten the social, economic, and political dimensions of human life.

We need to come back to a healthier, more sustainable way of living our life — we need to heal in a natural way, both individually and collectively. We must change the path of our evolution. We cannot continue by taking arbitrary paths of evolution guided only by a search for power and profit. We need to return to embrace the norms of healthy life. We need to recover our natural viability. As Ervin Laszlo proclaims in his books, *we must make our evolution conscious.*

Turning for guidance to the processes of evolution in nature is a survival imperative of our day. But this does not mean that we must abandon other ways of healing — forego the search for finding effective cures to specific ills. The requirement is not to reject the miracles of modern medicine, only to create a firm and sustainable basis for employing them. We must not continue to distance ourselves from the ways of nature, but turn to them for healing and guidance. We must become a viable species in the system of life on Earth.

I am convinced that healing by nature is the kind of healing we need. Nature is generous: it offers myriad ways to "keep body and soul together." It is up to us to find and follow the best and most applicable of these ways.

We were born as members of a viable species, capable of thriving on the planet, but became corrupted in our short-sighted search for the immediate satisfaction of self-centered aspirations. We have acted without sufficient regard for the consequences — for others, for humanity, for the planet, and for ourselves.

The challenge to the contemporary healing arts is to access and consciously recognize the goals and practices of healthy and sustainable life on the planet. How do we discover these goals and practices?

Upshift is only possible if people's thinking shifts to the global level. Nature around us is a system in which every element is connected to every other, and all elements are in cooperation with and complement each other. We individual humans are part of this system, yet we behave as if we were not. We seek to control the system, not become part of it. People are depressed, stressed in mind, and functionally disordered in body. People's feeling of separation has led to a critical juncture in human life.

Mainstream academic medicine does not live up to the challenge of our condition. Doctors center their attention on curing maladies, not on preventing them. Health-care is deteriorating, while individual disease treatment is progressing. The bulk of the population is suffering, living under unhealthy and often life-threatening conditions.

We need an upshift in our view of health and disease. Maintaining the human population in good health must be the priority objective of the healing arts. *Mens sana in corpore sano* ("a healthy mind in a healthy body") is an age-old wisdom. It is true today. And it is true that if our body is not healthy, we cannot upshift to a higher level of consciousness.

Modern medicine has amazing accomplishments. In case of major malfunctions, the methods of modern medicine are useful and necessary, but in many cases, they are a treatment of last resort. When other methods are available, we should not resort to last resorts, but look for less drastic and less risky alternatives. Alternatives to Western medical practices are available; traditional healers have known them for thousands of years. Today, people are rediscovering them, as interest in natural and other alternative forms of medicine spreads and intensifies.

The principal complement to the biochemical and surgical procedures of Western medicine is natural information medicine. This medicine is likely to have originated in the East, but it has not remained confined to the East. Time and time again, great healers in both East and West have practiced its tenets. Its fundamental premise is different from that of Western medicine.

Instead of correcting for a malfunction by biochemical means or surgical intervention, natural medicine seeks to enable the body itself to correct for the malfunction. Resorting to the use of this method is indicated when the biochemical treatment of mainstream medicine fails or overshoots the mark. This often happens because the body is not a biochemical machine: more goes on in the organism than chains of chemical reactions. Such reactions do go on — hundreds of thousands every second — but they are surface manifestations of underlying processes. The chemical reactions that occur on the level of cells, tissues, and organs are the end results of a long chain of causes and effects that are not initiated by chemical processes.

The organism operates on several levels at the same time. It needs a constant input of nature-based information to function. Such remedies, whether they are homeopathic, Ayurvedic, or geometric, or use acupuncture and acu-massage, provide the necessary cure.

Natural information-based medicine never treats the symptom alone, but attempts to remedy the cause of the symptoms. It treats malfunctions in the organism (i.e., disease) not only in a biochemical or surgical way, as classical Western medicine does, but also in a way that allows the information operating in the system to maintain the biochemical structure of the organism. It operates under the assumption that the living organism is a self-sufficient, self-healing whole, capable of correcting and healing its occasional functional disorders. If the malfunction has not yet manifested in the body, it is easier to overcome its physical pathologies by correcting the information that is the operating basis of the system. Sickness does not start with a headache, but with a disturbance in the system of information — with the abnormal functioning of cell membranes and of ion- and electron-exchange in the organism. Sometimes, the symptoms only show up after a long time. They appear only in the phase of dysfunction in the organism, the phase in which the metabolic alterations are detectable in the laboratory. In the further phase of the malfunction, these alterations reach a condition that is detectable by X-ray, ultrasound, CT, and MRI. When this stage has been reached, disharmony in the organism has already had a long history, and health can most likely be reestablished only by surgical and artificial means.

Natural information medicine activates the body's self-healing mechanisms. The healer changes the information in the malfunctioning parts and, thus, helps the body trigger its self-healing processes. This medicine views not only the physical body, but also considers the patient's emotions, mind-sets, relationships, and existential circumstances. It uses numerous methods, such as homeopathy, psionic medicine, low-dose medicine,

Körbler's "New Homeopathy," various bioenergetics methods, and radionics — among others.

How does natural information-based healing work in practice? It has two important aspects:

1. *Holism*: Everything should be treated as part of a whole. Parts of the organism cannot be treated separately, only as part of the whole organism.

2. *Informational Implementation*: Information in healing is in-formation in the sense intended by David Bohm when he wrote "information" as "in-formation" (with a hyphen). The healing in-formation we use is a subtle-energy in-forming impulse that acts on the body of the patient even without the conscious intent of the patient. The body cannot be fully healed by material, i.e., biochemical, means, only by addressing the information that governs the biochemical system. Information, however, is part of a universal information-field. The traditional cultures have intuited this.

It is nearly impossible to account for all of the remedies and the healing traditions of the cultures of China, India, Egypt, Mexico, and others, but they all share the attribute of being based on information and conveying a holistic view of the world. They link the healing of the physical body with the healing of the soul and spirit. Ancient cultures accepted the reality of subtle energies and used the bioenergetic processes that take place both inside and around the physical body in their healing. Although they go by different names, the subtle energies and related spiritual factors are the same across cultures and times.

The manifestation of cosmic energy was discussed in yin-yang theory in Taoism and early Chinese natural philosophy. The basic thesis stipulates that any one part in the world can only be understood in its relation to the whole of which it is a part.

Yin-yang theory is based on the unity of two polar opposites and is a useful way of representing processes of change in nature. This system of thought is also reflected in Chinese medicine, according to which the harmony between the yin (the passive, receptive, lunar) and the yang (the active, creative, solar) is achieved in humans in a particular way: through the flow of chi, the fundamental life force. Its main method, acupuncture — the practice of which dates back thousands of years — is more akin to art than science.

Essentially, the goal of acupuncture is to restore the balance of energy flow within an energy system; the physical carriers of this flow can actually be measured with today's technology. By massaging the various acupuncture points, or by inserting needles into these points, or by drawing geometrical symbols at these points on the skin as in the practice of New Homeopathy, we can restore the functional balance of the diseased organism. One can only marvel at this system of medicine, which expresses with such perfection the subtle energetic fabric of the living organism and its role in the functioning of the physical body. This is what we read in the books of China's Yellow Emperor: The state of the world is defined by the fluctuation and variation of Yin and Yang forces ... under normal conditions, these forces maintain balance in the world as well as in the human body. This was intuitively known by the Chinese healers. Chinese doctors were paid to keep their patients healthy and well. If the patient got sick, the doctor would not be paid until he or she got well again.

In the sections that follow, I return to the contemporary practices of healing and summarize the method of querying the body, and understanding how the response of the body can serve to diagnose health problems and identify the cure.

The method of information-based healing and therapy I developed (the Sagi method) makes use of both the Körbler New Homeopathy method and the Psionic method.

Erich Körbler built his method, the New Homeopathy, on the principles of Chinese medicine. He diagnosed his patients' conditions by observing the oscillations of his specially designed dowsing rod, the "bioindicator." The movements of the rod are automatic, not under the control of the person using it. The rod is the only instrument as far as we know that exhibits the relevant movements. The only prerequisites on the part of the user are to have a good working knowledge of the Körbler vector system as well as medical science. This is required to be able to assess the meaning of the movements.

The Körbler method works through the electromagnetic (EM) field. With the help of a bioindicator, the electromagnetic radiation emanating from the body of the patient can be measured. Geometric forms function as "antennas" to pick up information in the patient's EM field. Each geometrical form possesses a corresponding geometric code for restoring the energy balance of the organism. These symbols affect the body and can correct flawed information. They can also produce healthier conditions in the body.

The advantage of this healing method (information medicine) is that it is also a preventive treatment. Using the symbols of the vector system, we can correct a malfunction already at the informational level. This is how the traditional Chinese insight acquires fresh validity: it gives priority to prevention over curing.

My informational healing transcends the classical confines of space and time. It is nonlocal healing, as it relies on information transmitted by, or through, the healer to the patient. It works as long as the patient is willing to receive it. And it acts regardless of the patient's physical distance from the healer.

In diagnosis and treatment, the healer seeks to recognize and interpret how the patient's individual imprint in the information field differs from the imprint that is typical for the species and represents the norm for it. The difference indicates a malfunction that may then manifest as a disease. This means that, besides the conventional healing method, the healer can establish a space- and time-transcending diagnosis to understand the cause of the illness. The process is essentially the same in every form of nonlocal healing.

The diagnosis can be created by the "tuning" of the healer to the quantum information field. This tuning resembles the work of a transmitter joined to a receiver. Such a system in today's world receives broadcasts transmitted through the ether. We need an antenna so that the apparatus can transduce the information in a usable form. In nonlocal healing, the "antenna" functions when one is in an altered state of consciousness. We are connected to the quantum information field whether we know it or not, but in a normal wakeful state, the reception of everyday information overrides the information regarding the state of the patient himself and herself. In an altered state, the healer is able to receive information regarding his or her own condition from the field.

The healer needs to attune to the frequency of the patient and focus on the pertinent information. He or she scans the patient's imprint in the field, which in the case of a malady exhibits abnormal features.

For tuning one's "antenna," there are as many approaches as there are healing methods. The healer can make use of any device or "witness" for effecting his or her tuning. A witness can be a photo of the patient, a writing sample, an audio recording, a lock of hair, a sample of blood or saliva, and so on. Every sample facilitates the process of calling up information from the quantum field. If the patient is a close acquaintance of the healer, there is no need for a witness — the antenna transmits information directly.

In the information-based healing method, the healer evaluates the information gleaned from the patient's imprint in the field. Everyone has his or her own system, so different modes of diagnosis and healing are possible. After making the diagnosis, the healer can recommend a therapy for overcoming the malfunction.

The information we receive in an altered state of consciousness indicates the physical condition of the patient at the given time, and also the nature of the problem. The diagnosis can be as detailed and thorough as in a personal examination. One can find out if it is a temporary illness or a chronic problem that originated earlier, what the causes are, and to what extent it is influenced by harmful conditions (e.g., electrosmog and/ or different types of earth radiation). After having made the diagnosis, we can determine if it is necessary to change the patient's milieu, and one can select the optimum way to meet this requirement.

Of course, therapy can be based on other diagnostic systems as well. The healer can recommend a variety of treatments — specific allopathic remedies, diet, phytotherapy, homeopathic remedies, and so on. The healer can also recommend methods to influence how the information is acquired by the patient. He or she can restore a normal healthy state of the patient's organism by inserting healing information into his or her imprint in the quantum field. It is not necessary for the patient to be consciously aware of the transmission of information in either direction. In most cases, it is not even necessary that the patient knows when and that the healing takes place. The main thing is that he or she should welcome the healing. A negative attitude can block the reception of the healing information.

When the transmission of information is accomplished, it affects the entire condition of the patient, including the problem areas. The effect can be measured in a follow-up diagnosis either through conventional or information-based methods. The patient feels better, the pains that have thus far tormented him or her disappear or are lessened, and the healing process begins. This is the consequence of treatment, and it is what happens in a significant number of cases.

The corrected information enters the quantum information field, and, as a result, the individual's imprint in the field begins to match the norm: the healthy human imprint. The autonomic nervous system reads the corrected information and adjusts the functioning of the organism accordingly.

The healing recounted on these pages signifies an upshift in contemporary healing practices, upshifting both the practices and the view of health they inspire. It contributes to keeping healthy the human population of the planet — not only curing the existing ills, but also preventing their occurrence. It is a return to traditional practices, now in a new form. This transformation is an organic part of the great upshift that will allow us to live wiser on the planet.

CHAPTER 18

HEALING THE WOUNDS OF SEPARATION: SOIL, SOUL, AND SOCIETY

SATISH KUMAR

M ost of our present problems are a consequence of our separational
worldview. We see nature and humans as separate, soul and body
as separate, matter and spirit as separate, and subject and object as separate, and within human community, we see separation and division in the
name of race, religion, nationality, and political philosophy. This worldview is based on outdated Newtonian physics which considers nature as
a machine and the Earth as a dead rock. The Cartesian dualism of mind
over matter has also contributed to the separational paradigm. Now we are
in the age of the new science of entanglement, interdependence, Gaia, and
quantum physics, where everything exists in relationship with one another
and where Earth is a living organism.

The new path to a better world is to heal the wounds of division, disconnection, and separation. We need to see the unity and interrelatedness
between nature, spirit, and humankind; we need a trinity representing
the unity of life, the Trinity of Soil, Soul, and Society, a trinity of a new

paradigm, a trinity of relational worldview, a trinity to upshift our consciousness, a trinity to launch a new movement of connectedness to make peace with the Earth, peace with the self, and peace among people of diverse cultures and backgrounds. Peace within and peace without. Inner peace and outer peace.

Many historical movements in the world have three key words that express their spirit. During the French Revolution, for example, the key words were *liberté, égalité, fraternité,* and in the American Declaration of Independence, we find the words *life, liberty and the pursuit of happiness.* 'Liberté, égalité, fraternité' is a very nice trinity, but it is very human: human liberty, human fraternity, human equality. In the same way, in the American Declaration of Independence, life is primarily human life, liberty is human liberty, and happiness is human happiness. These words represent an anthropocentric worldview. We have come to think that somehow human beings are separate and yet at the center of the universe. It is as if humans are the most important species and Earth's other species are all there to serve humankind. This is not only a human-centered worldview but it also sees humans as apart from the rest of nature.

But in the age of Gaia, this worldview is out of date. Especially once we realize that we are utterly dependent on and connected with other species. We need to recognize that humans are not the rulers of the world; they are not here to do what they like. It is our responsibility to take care of the other species because we are all made of each other, we are not separate, we are all related, and we are members of one Earth community. The animals, birds, forests, oceans, and mountains are our ancestors. We all have come from a single source, a single origin.

So, we need a new trinity to replace those human-centered trinities (even the trinity adopted by the New Age movement, 'mind, body, spirit,' refers to the human mind, human body, and human spirit). We need a new trinity that is holistic and inclusive, a trinity that embraces the well-being of the entire planet Earth and not just the well-being of the human species. We need a philosophy, a science, a religion, and a legal system that will recognize the intrinsic value of all living beings, not just the well-being of human beings.

For this reason, I propose a new trinity. At the top of this new trinity, I put the word 'Soil,' which represents the entire natural world. Without soil, there is no food, and without food, there is no life, no trees, no forests. Food and forests are transformed soil. Soil represents life on Earth. In our human-centered worldview, in our educational systems, in our study of science and technology, we have come to think that soil simply means dirt, and that dirt is dirty. But dirt is not dirty: dirt is the source of life. Without dirt, there is no life.

Soil, therefore, represents all natural life. And it is a fact that we are related to and dependent on the soil. Some people may think that food comes from the supermarket; most of us don't grow food these days. If somebody grows food, we think: "Oh poor man, peasant, laborer; he is not educated, so he has to grow food." If you are educated, then you don't grow food. Growing food in the Industrial Age has no dignity. You sit behind your computer, and your food comes from faraway places. You don't want to grow food because growing food is seen as a sign of backwardness. If you are advanced, educated, rich, and smart, then you manufacture cars, computers, or some other gadgets, or you become a banker, a lawyer, or a civil servant. Production of food is increasingly left to robots, computers, and other machines.

Growing food has become a sign of underdevelopment. The word 'peasant' has become a term of insult. We need to change that. We need to say that we must touch the soil; we must put our hands into the soil. How many times do we touch our mobile phone every day? Maybe 100 times? How many times do we touch the soil? Hardly ever! We need to give dignity to peasants, to those who grow food, to farmers and gardeners.

Soil is so important, yet we have forgotten it. Yes, we humans are important too, but the human species is only one of the 7.8 million species on Earth. We are not the kings. We are not an imperial power, and the Earth is not a human colony. At the moment, we behave as if we can do to Earth what we like. We do things which cause global warming and change the climate, we poison the soil, we destroy the rainforests, we overfish the oceans and fill them with plastic, and we interfere with seeds through genetic engineering. We treat animals cruelly in factory farms. These are acts of war with Nature! We engage in such a war because we see ourselves as separate from Nature. This human behavior must change urgently to move towards a better world, a peaceful world. We need to realize that we are Nature, that we are all an integral part of this healthy web of life maintained by soil in particular and by nature in general. We are nature; therefore, what we do to nature, we do to ourselves.

We need to be humble; to be human is to be humble. The Latin word humus means soil. 'Human,' 'humility,' and 'humus' come from the same root. Human beings are literally soil beings. There is no separation between humans and humus. The soil is so important yet humble. When humans lose humility, they are no longer true humans. Seeing humans as separate and above soil, above Nature, is a sign of arrogance.

Once, the Buddha was sitting in meditation, with his right hand above the palm of the left hand, and his son, Rahul, came to him and asked: "Father, you teach compassion, forgiveness, love and forbearance — from where did you learn all these wonderful qualities? You are a world teacher, but who is your teacher?" The Buddha lifted his right hand in the *bhūmiśpara mudra*, which means 'touch the Earth posture,' and he touched the Earth. Then he said: "I learned my forgiveness, compassion, friendship, kindness and all the other wonderful qualities of love, beauty, unity and generosity from the Earth."

Do you know where the Buddha was enlightened? Sitting under a tree. My mother used to say that the Buddha got enlightenment because he was sitting under a tree!

A tree has intrinsic value. That is, a tree is good not because it gives us food, wood, shade, or aesthetic pleasure. No, the tree is good in and of itself, even if nobody goes and looks at it, even if nobody ever says: "Wow, look at those beautiful cherry blossoms!" Even if no one ever sees it, the tree will still blossom. Trees represent the divine grace appearing on the Earth. Trees, animals, plants, rocks, mountains, rivers, worms, butterflies, honeybees — all creatures upon this Earth have intrinsic value. They have the right to be as they are, who they are, and what they are. We talk about human rights, and that's fine. But Nature also has rights. The trees have a right to exist. We have no right to cut them down without proper purpose. When we understand this, when we recognize the rights of the trees, the rights of Nature, then we are truly ecologists and have understood the paramount importance of the word 'soil.' Recognizing the integrity and the sanctity of the soil is the first essential step towards a better, sustainable, and regenerative world. This is a step towards making peace with the Earth.

The second word in this new trinity is 'Soul,' which sounds similar to 'soil.' Soil has soul. Trees have soul. Everything is soulful, yet it is something we cannot see. The body we can touch, hug, kiss, and admire, but in order to touch soul, we have to close our eyes. Soul is something we can only experience. Trees, animals, worms, and humans — all have a soul. Soil is the outer landscape, and soul is the inner landscape.

We need to take care of the soul, as we take care of the body. But we can only take care of the soul when we slow down. No computer. No car. No shopping. Just sit in your room with tea and flowers: elegantly simple, without clutter. Go into a room which is peaceful; take no mobile phone. Take time for yourself. Meditate on the fact that you represent the totality of the universe. There is nothing in the universe that is not in you, and there is nothing in you that is not in the universe. The universe is the macrocosm, and you are the microcosm. You are earth, air, fire, water, imagination, creativity, consciousness, time, and space — you have all these elements in your genes and in your cells. Your soul is billions of years old. You have been recycled and recycled, again and again. You are a beautiful example of the total recycling principle of the universe.

So, if you want to take care of the universe, you start with yourself. Care of the soul is the way to self-realization. Meditation is for self-realization. Mindful gardening is a form of meditation. When you are cooking mindfully, you are also in meditation because you are not just cooking to feed yourself or your family, you are cooking for self-realization: taking care of yourself, being at ease with yourself, being happy with yourself, and being fulfilled in yourself is the way to self-realization. Whoever I am, I am. Self-realization will make you at ease with yourself. Everything you truly need and want is within you; courage, compassion, creativity, and consciousness are all within you. You are capable of solving every problem in the world with your inner wisdom. Wisdom is a soul quality, as are generosity, love and friendship, unity, and beauty. We are all gifted with these qualities. They are all there to be cultivated and to be manifested.

You will realize that all you need is already here: the air, fire, food, water, trees, soil, sun, and sky. Everything is here. What more do you want? If you want more possessions and more clutter, it is because you have lost touch with your soul. That's why your soul is hungry. That hunger will not be satisfied by computers, cars, or mobile phones. To nourish the soul, you need to slow down and take care of your soul. Without a happy soul, you are the poorest of the poor. Spiritual poverty is the greatest poverty, greater than any physical poverty. As you take care of the soil, you take care of the soul. Your outer body is soil, and your inner being is soul. When you take care of both, body and soul, you experience a sense of the sacred, you gain self-realization, and you achieve true well-being.

Caring for the soul has nothing to do with our ego. This is why we have the third word of our trinity: "Society." First and foremost, we are members of the Earth community. Then, we are members of the human community. This sense of belonging to the human community liberates you from Ego!

I walked from India to America without money. When I came to the border between India and Pakistan — where three wars have been fought — I was joined by 35 people who had come to say goodbye. One of them said: "Here are some packets of food. At least take some food with you." I said: "Thank you, but no thank you. I'm going for peace. And peace begins with trust, trust in human community. These packets of food are not packets of food; they are packets of mistrust. What would I tell my Pakistani hosts? That I did not trust them to feed me?"

My friend began to cry. I said: "Why are you crying, my friend?" She replied: "Satish, this might be our last meeting. I may never see you again. You are going to Muslim countries, Christian countries, capitalist countries, communist countries, mountains, forests, deserts, snow. You have no money, no food. You are walking. How are you going to survive?" At that moment, I said: "My friend, from today, I'm not afraid of death. If I die while walking for peace, then that is the best kind of death I can have. And I'm not afraid of hunger. If I don't get food, I'll say this is my opportunity to fast."

Then we entered Pakistan, and to my astonishment, there was someone waiting for us. He said: "Are you the two men coming to Pakistan for peace?" I was surprised. "How do you know?" I asked. He said: "I read about you. And I thought that if you are coming for peace, then I should welcome you. This war between India and Pakistan is complete nonsense. We are all members of one human family."

At that moment, I realized the fundamental unity of the human family. If we come here as Indians, then we will meet Pakistanis. If we come here as Hindus, then we will meet Muslims. But if we come here as human beings, then we meet only human beings. This way, I was able to rise above my narrow identity and identify myself instead with the whole of human society.

Mahatma Gandhi said that there is enough in the world for everybody's need but not enough for anybody's greed. At the moment, one percent of the greedy population is driving the economy while 99 percent of the people are suffering. This one percent of the population wants to be the superpower and dominate the world. For them, there is no such thing as society. But for peace, justice, and happiness, we need to embrace the whole of society. We need to solve the social problems of poverty and war with imagination, creativity, and forgiveness. All human problems can be solved by negotiation, by friendship, by letting go of ego, and by going into eco. Eco means home; eco means relationships. Let us make a shift from ego to eco, from self-interest to mutual interest, the common interest of the whole human society.

If we can have a holistic trinity of Soil, Soul, and Society, if we can understand the interdependence of all living beings and understand that all living creatures — from trees to worms to humans — depend on each other and we are all gifted with human spirit, then we are healed: we can live in peace and harmony with ourselves, with other people, and with Nature. That is why I present to you the new trinity of Soil, Soul, and Society.

▌A MEDITATION ON THE UNITY OF LIFE

Let us bring both our palms together and bow to sacred life, sacred soil, sacred Earth, sacred universe.

We see all Being in us, and ourselves in all beings.

We see the whole universe in ourselves and ourselves in the whole universe.

Each one of us is a microcosm of the macrocosm.

Cosmos is our country,

The planet Earth is our common home,

Nature is our nationality,

And love is our religion.

All living beings are sustained by the same breath of life.

Thus, we are all connected, we are all related, we are interbeings.

We all share a single origin.

Unity and diversity dance together.

All our thriving is mutual.

When separation and divisions end, suffering ceases.

We go beyond right and wrong, beyond good and bad.

We bow to the unity of life. We bow to the diversity of forms.

We bow to the sacred, to life, to the Earth, to the universe.

Breathe in. Breathe out.

Smile, relax, and let go.

Let go of all expectations, attachments, and anxieties.

Let go of all worries, fears, and anger.

Let go of ego.

Let us move from ego to eco.

Breath in. Breath out.

Smile. Relax. Let go.

We are at home. I am at home. We are at home.

CHAPTER 19

HEALING THE WORLD FROM THE GROUND UP

LYNNE MCTAGGART

Since the millennium, commentators of every variety have been trying to get a handle on the collective significance of the continuous crises besetting us in modern times — banking crises, war and terrorist crises, sovereign-debt crises, climate-change crises, energy crises, food crises, ecological crises — man-made and otherwise.

But the crises we face on many fronts are symptomatic of a deeper problem, with more potential repercussions than those of any single cataclysmic event. They are simply a measure of the vast disparity between our definition of ourselves and our truest essence. For hundreds of years, we have acted against nature by ignoring our essential connectedness and defining ourselves as separate from our world.

We have reached the point where we can no longer live according to this false view of who we really are. What can end the story we have been told up until now about who we are and how we are supposed to live? Because in this ending lies the only path to a better future.

A mosaic of influences — religious, political, economic, scientific, and philosophical — writes the story that we live by. Nevertheless, most of the big ideas we have about the universe and what it is to be human derive from three revolutions, the Scientific Revolution or the Age of Enlightenment, and the two Industrial Revolutions of the eighteenth and nineteenth centuries, which transformed the cultural and socioeconomic conditions of the West into our modern developed world.

These movements largely created the modern sense of our own individuality by drastically altering our vision of the universe from a harmonious, benevolent, and interconnected whole to an amalgam of a load of separate and unrelated things competing with each other for survival.

In 1687, with the publication of the *Philosophiae Naturalis Principia Mathematica*, Isaac Newton, the father of modern physics, described a universe in which all matter was thought to move according to certain fixed laws within three-dimensional time and geometrical space. Newton's laws of motion and gravity depict the universe essentially as machine — a vast clockwork of separate parts that could always be relied upon to follow predictable behavior.

Once Newtonian laws demonstrated that the trajectory of virtually everything, from single objects to the motion of the planets, could be reduced to a mathematical equation, the world came to be viewed as dependably mechanistic. Newtonian laws also demonstrated that things exist independently from each other, complete in themselves, with their own inviolate boundaries. We ended with the hairs on our skin, at which point the rest of the universe began.

Undoubtedly, the scientific discovery with the most pervasive hand in our current worldview is Charles Darwin's theory of evolution through natural selection.

When assembling his ideas for *On the Origin of Species*, the young Darwin was profoundly influenced by the concerns of the Reverend Thomas Robert Malthus about population explosion and limited natural resources.[1] Darwin concluded that, since there wasn't enough to go around, life must evolve through what he termed a "struggle for existence."

Darwin was at pains to note that his catch phrase 'struggle for existence' was not literal but highly elastic — encompassing everything from the search of tree roots for water to the reliance of a pack of animals on each other (It was actually British philosopher Herbert Spencer who first coined the term "survival of the fittest.").

As an inadvertent consequence, Darwin unleashed upon the world a metaphor that came to represent the human experience: *Life as war*. An individual or population thrives only at another one's expense.

Almost immediately, the narrower meaning of the metaphor stuck, offering a scientific framework for all the various burgeoning social and economic movements of the day. Most subsequent interpretations of Darwin's work, even in his lifetime, promoted a vision of all aspects of life as a battle over scarce resources, in which only the toughest and most single-minded survived.

The metaphorical representation of life as a race to the finish line has been used as intellectual justification for most aspects of modern industrialized society, which regards competition as society's perfect shakedown mechanism, separating out the economically, politically, and socially weak from the strong.

The winners have a right to "winner take all" because the race as a whole would benefit from it.

Many psychologists argue that competitiveness is hardwired within us, a natural biological urge as inherent as our basic urge to survive. After we stop fighting over food, water, shelter, and mates, the theory goes, we begin competing over more ephemeral prizes: power, status, and, most recently, fame.

Consequently, for more than three hundred years, our worldview has been shaped by a story that describes isolated beings competing for survival on a lonely planet in an indifferent universe. Life, as defined by modern science, is essentially predatory, self-serving, and solitary.

Every modern recipe in our lives has been drawn from our interpretation of life as an individual and solitary struggle, with every-man-for-himself competition an inherent part of the business of living. Our entire Western economic model is built on the notion that competition in a free-market economy is essential to drive excellence and prosperity.

In our relationships, we extol our inherent right to individual happiness and self-expression above all else. We educate our young by encouraging them to compete and excel over their peers.

The currency of most modern, two-cars-in-every-garage neighborhoods is comparison and one-upmanship.

The world, as Woody Allen once put it, "is one big cafeteria."

The individualistic, winner-take-all zeitgeist of modern times is to blame for many of the crises we presently face in our society, particularly the excesses of the corporate sector, with its insistence on a bigger and better profit every year, at any cost.

Although our Newtonian vantage point has afforded us technological mastery over our lives, the ongoing difficulties of our global economic model, the current ecological crises, the threatened shortages of water and food, and the exhaustion of petroleum sources all expose the extreme limitations of this mindset, which now threatens our planet with extinction.

On a personal level, it has left most of us with a distinctly hollow feeling, as though something profound — our very humanity — has been trampled over, in our daily wrestle with the world.

We need some new rules to live by. We need another way to "be."

An entirely new scientific story is emerging that challenges many of our basic Newtonian and Darwinian assumptions, including our most basic premise: the sense of things as separate entities in competition for survival. The latest evidence from quantum physics offers the extraordinary possibility that all of life exists in a dynamic relationship of cooperation.

Quantum physicists now recognize that the universe is not a collection of separate things jostling around in empty space. All matter exists in a vast quantum web of connection, and a living thing at its most elemental is an energy system involved in a constant transfer of information with its environment.

Rather than a cluster of individual, self-contained atoms and molecules, objects and living beings are now more properly understood as dynamic and protean *processes*, in which parts of one thing and parts of another continuously trade places.

This revolution is not confined to physics. Extraordinary new discoveries in biology and the social sciences have profoundly altered our view of the relationship between living things and their environment. Frontier biologists, psychologists, and sociologists have all found evidence that individuals are far less individual than we thought they were.

Between the smallest particles of our being, between our bodies and their environments, between ourselves and all of the people with whom we are in contact, between every member of every societal cluster, there is a *Bond* — a connection so integral and profound that there is no longer a clear demarcation between the end of one thing and the beginning of another. The world essentially operates, not through the activity of individual things, but in the connection between them — in a sense, *within the space between things.*

The most essential aspect of life is not the isolated thing, whether a sub-atomic particle or full-fledged living being. It is the relationship itself: the inseparable, irreducible *Bond*. This connection — the space in between — holds the key to the life of every organism, from subatomic particles to large-scale societies, and also the key to our viable future.

These discoveries hold not only vast implications about how we choose to define ourselves, but also vast implications about how we ought to live our lives. They suggest that all our societal creations, invested as they are in competition and individuality, run counter to our most fundamental being — that a drive for cooperation and partnership, not dominance, is fundamental to the physics of life and the biological makeup of all living things. They imply that most of us in the developed world are not living in harmony with our true nature. That we are constantly affecting and being affected by all matter in a constant and ever evolving Bond demands a drastic change in the way we relate to ourselves and all other living things.

Although most of us are taught that the single most important impulse we have is to survive at all costs, as the latest science demonstrates, our urge for relationship is more fundamental still. Rather than a will to power, the essential impulse of all life is *a will to connect.*

Deep connection, rather than competition, is the quality most essential to human nature: we were never meant to live a life of isolation and self-serving survival. Human beings need partnership just to survive; we experience the greatest stress and the most serious illnesses when we are isolated from others and from a sense of connection.

An enormous body of research, as detailed in my book *The Bond*,[2] reveals that the root emotions of stress and ultimately illness are a sense of isolation and (appearingly most toxic of all) our current tendency to pit ourselves against each other.

A group of researchers at Brigham Young University pooled and analyzed data from 148 studies that compare human interaction with health outcomes over an average of seven years. Their stark conclusion: *relationships of any sort — good or bad — improve your odds of survival by 50 percent.* Isolation was equivalent to smoking fifteen cigarettes a day or being an alcoholic, and twice as harmful as obesity.[3]

Social psychologists at the UK's University of Exeter have shown that membership in social groups of every variety is extraordinarily strengthening — one of nature's best medicines. Exeter University's ground-breaking research shows that the most important predictor of health — even more than diet and exercise — is the number of groups to which you belong, particularly if you have strong relationships within them.[4] The higher your group membership in voluntary social organizations such as religious groups or unions, the lower your risk of death from all causes.[5]

"As a rough rule of thumb," wrote Harvard political scientist Robert D. Putnam in his book, *Bowling Alone*, which exposed the breakdown of community life in America, "if you belong to no groups but decide to join one, you cut your risk of dying over the next year in half."[6]

The need to move beyond the boundaries of ourselves as individuals and to bond with a group is so primordial and necessary to a human being that it remains the key determinant of whether we remain healthy or get ill, even whether we live or die.

Virtually all developed countries are founded on a culture of individualism and individual gain. For hundreds of years, we have followed a false trail of individual satisfaction as our primary motivation, at great cost. As individualism rises, the indices of every major aspect of life satisfaction, from health care and education to life span and urban safety, fall further among every member of the population, rich and poor.

With every step away from the Bond, our natural birthright, we take a further step toward separation and alienation, and away from what is best and truest about ourselves. We create further economic crises, further political struggle, more conflict, more calamitous ecological disaster. We erect higher and higher walls between ourselves and the rest of the world.

We live now with the uneasy feeling that something profound in our lives is missing, a longing we cannot quite define. We are experiencing a disengagement from our birthright, our need to live in holism. We're left with something far worse than a simple case of unfairness, the vague sense of an important connection that has been broken: the evidence, every-where we look, of unrequited humanity.

We stand at the crucial point in our evolution where we must make a choice. We are one of the most important generations in the history of humanity. With all the calamities in our midst, our choices will affect our children's children — and indeed the world for all time.

When considering all the crises we now face on so many fronts, the sheer enormity of the problems now before us in every sector of our lives, we feel both frustrated by the inability of our leaders to solve them and powerless to fix anything ourselves. Most of us throw up our hands and cry, *"What can I do? What can any one person do to change anything?"*

This fear grows out of the mistaken notion that the crises in our midst can only be addressed from the top down. But the change that is neces-sary — the one that will truly solve most problems in our individual lives, our society, and indeed our world — is not just a change of policy, a new law, a new president, or a tighter regulation, *but a fundamental change of heart.*

The change required now must come from the bottom up — from ordi-nary individuals making individual changes that ultimately cause a pos-itive contagion of change in their neighborhoods and workplaces, which grows and spreads to their town or city, their state or county, their country, and even further.

This change starts with you and me, in the fundamental way that we engage with the world.

What we must realize is the incredible power that you — and each of us — already hold to make major change in the world. As Margaret Mead observed, virtually every major historical movement has started with a small group resolving to do things differently.

It was the strategy adopted by Mohandas Gandhi, when initiating his non-violent resistance to British rule that ended up creating an independent India. It was the strategy behind the Prague Spring that freed Czechoslovakia from Soviet Communism without a single shot being fired. It was the strategy adopted by Martin Luther King that birthed the US civil rights movement, ignited by a single decision: Rosa Parks' simple refusal to sit at the back of the bus.

All of these movements began with the recognition that corrupt, unfair, and unworkable systems prevail *only because we allow them to do so.*

As Gandhi put it: "I believe that no government can exist for a single moment without the cooperation of the people, willing or forced, and if people suddenly withdraw their cooperation in every detail, the government will come to a standstill."

One of the most powerful mechanisms, I have discovered, for making deep and lasting change is a small group of people doing intention together — what I call a 'Power of Eight®' group. The group-intention experience itself causes big changes in people: changing individual consciousness, removing a sense of separation and individuality, and placing members of the group in what can only be described as a state of ecstatic unity.

After running thousands of Power of Eight® groups, I have observed this same group dynamic, a dynamic so powerful and life-transforming that it enabled individual miracles to take place. I have recorded hundreds, if not thousands, of these instantaneous miracles in participants' lives.

They healed long-standing serious health conditions. They mended estranged relationships. They discovered a renewed life purpose or cast off workaday jobs in favor of a career that was more adventurous or fulfilling. A few of them even transformed right in front of me.

And there was no shaman or guru present, no complex healing process involved — in fact, no previous experience was necessary. The inciting instrument for all of this was simply the gathering of these people into a group.

There are tens of thousands of Power of Eight® groups at the moment, and I am now enlisting them to create nothing less than a vast community of changemakers, a grassroots movement of individual Power of Eight® groups, banding together to create a closer and better community and society, making tiny local changes that spiral into a vast contagion of change.

I am offering tools to help them create radical change in their communities to make them vibrant, sharing, and connected villages, towns, and cities, with alternatives to unfair institutions and ways to lift their local economy and create close connection through larger projects they carry out together.

The groups are discovering that intention alone and in a group isn't just for healing yourselves. It also works to heal communities. In the process, they are learning the greatest gift of all: how powerful a small group can be, how deep the love they receive from it, how influential its changes. The future is in our hands — and in the hands we join in our groups.

CHAPTER 20

CONSCIOUSNESS-REVOLUTION: UPSHIFT IN THE NEUROSCIENCES

NITAMO FEDERICO MONTECUCCO

Humanity is at a critical point in its history, at a "paradigm shift." It could generate a huge leap in individual and planetary consciousness, the most significant evolution since the beginning of history towards a more humane, peaceful, and sustainable global civilization.

Scientific and technological discoveries could allow us to make this evolutionary leap in consciousness today; however, this leap is having difficulties taking the flight!!

The root causes of these difficulties can be identified in the nature of the "old paradigm," which is still deeply conditioning our society (dictatorial governments, ecologically irresponsible multinationals, aggressive religions, etc.) and ourselves (beliefs, self-control, fears, pains, and repressed angers), closing our hearts and obscuring our global awareness.

To understand the state of the art regarding the furthering of the evolution of human consciousness, we need to understand some fundamental tenets.

▌MOLECULES OF EMOTION AND CONSCIOUSNESS

Each cell is a living unit with a "systemic consciousness" which owns the same "molecules of emotions and consciousness" discovered by Candace Pert, that we have in our brain and endocrine system. So, we can literally say that we experience the same basic emotions and sensations as the first cells do!

As 100,000 billion cells assemble and evolve into an extremely more complex multicellular animal consciousness, these molecules of emotion and consciousness are organized in the brain into the seven major "emotional systems" discovered by Jaack Panksepp, with whom we have directly collaborated, as defined neuroanatomical structures in the brain.[7,8]

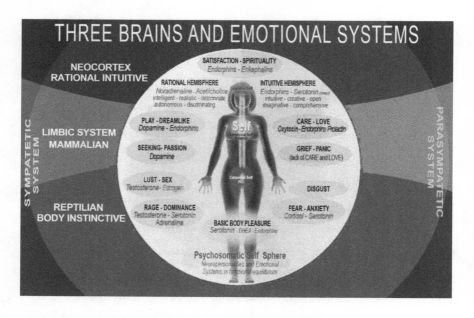

Figure 1. Three Brains and Emotional Systems

Reptiles (See lower part of Figure 1) develop only the BODY PLEASURE system linked to serotonin, the emotional-instinctive systems of RAGE-POWER and SEX to testosterone, and of FEAR linked to cortisol. For this reason, they do not develop family and social relationships.

Mammals evolved the emotional system of CARE-LOVENESS linked to oxytocin and the PLAY-SOCIALIZATION system linked to dopamine and endorphin. This makes it possible to create the first forms of family and animal society.

Panksepp points out that the "emotional systems" are the "ways of expression of the self" and that if they are disharmonious, inhibited, or blocked, the self progressively loses awareness, up to psychiatric illness where the person is literally "beside himself."

▌THE BEGINNING OF HUMANITY: RATIONALITY, INTUITION AND FREE WILL

The Nobel Prize laureate Sir John Eccles points out in the book *The Evolution of the Brain and the Creation of the Self* [9] that, since its beginnings in the Paleolithic, the evolutionary leap from primates to *Homo* occurs with the synchronic development of the neocortex together with the higher RATIONAL and INTUITIVE mental systems.

Nobel laureate Gerald Edelman defines the thalamus as *Core Consciousness* as it allows the synchronization of the whole brain functions and information.

The *thalamus* is a somato-sensory region located in the center of the "mammal-emotional brain": the "heart" of the "limbic system" (See Figure 2).

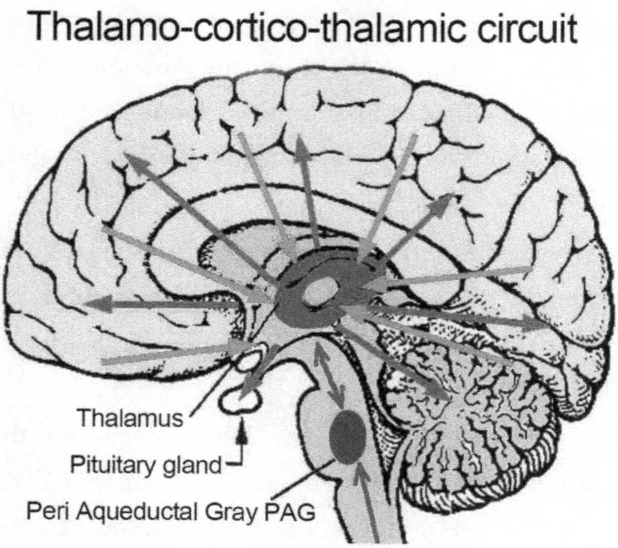

Thalamo-cortico-thalamic circuit

Figure 2. Thalamo-cortico-thalamic circuit

Edelman calls *Dynamic Network of Consciousness* this fundamental thalamo-cortico-thalamic circuit which allows to create the first "Self-Awareness" neurocircuit.[10]

▌THE NEOLITHIC REVOLUTION

With the "Neolithic Revolution," the complete neocortical and consciousness development allowed human beings to understand the laws of nature, learning how to manage fire, to develop cultivation and animal husbandry, thus creating the first forms of settled societies based on agriculture and pastoralism.

With much less effort than before, the Earth turned into an almost infinite source of nourishment enabling everyone the possibility of living in harmony with the environment.

The archaeological research conducted by Marija Gimbutas,[11] James Mellaart,[12] and Nikólaos Pláton[13] and supported by scholars like Riane Eisler,[14] show that from 9,000 to 4,000 B.C., the major European and Middle Eastern Neolithic settlements — from Italy, Greece, Syria, Palestine to the Mesopotamian Fertile Crescent — lived and progressed for centuries and in some cases for millennia in a state of relative economic prosperity, social peace, and natural spirituality.

This was the first primaeval but concrete "unitary paradigm" of a possible human and sustainable civilization.

▌THE SPIRIT OF GRATITUDE AND LOVE FOR THE EARTH

Excavations have shown that Neolithic spirituality was born from the loving kindness and veneration of "Nature," from the mystery of the birth of "Life," from the profound sense of gratitude and devotion to the "Earth" and for the "Feminine" from which every human and living being originates and by which they are nourished and sustained. This was a form of spirituality not so much linked to the matriarchal myth of the "Great Goddess," but rather a simple, "impersonal," and spontaneous feeling of gratitude and reverence towards life and nature as "Mother Earth" or sometimes as a "Great Spirit."

The finds show simple artistic works of love and respect for the "Feminine," which perhaps personified the Earth, and was represented with terracotta statuettes of women in different shapes and positions, from purely maternal ones to those richly dressed or in solemn and spiritual poses. There was equality between women and men in holding political or spiritual offices.

Despite the presence of different social classes, no excessive economic inequalities were highlighted.

THE UNITARY PARADIGM: THE FIRST FORM OF A PEACEFUL AND SUSTAINABLE CIVILIZATION

This profound perception, based on love for life and respect for nature and for every living being aspiring to Unity with Existence, is the root of the systemic and ecological vision of the "unitary paradigm."

We certainly don't want to idealize these Neolithic societies as the perfect golden age, since most probably each one of them experienced some forms of violence, conflicts, and injustices, but certainly the excavations, particularly in Crete, show that an ecological, peaceful, and sustainable civilization had developed in the Neolithic. This was a culture based on the loving recognition of the worth of the Self, the "soul" of every living being — not a utopia, but a sustainable reality that could have developed, improved, and evolved in any part of the world.

It was precisely in that prosperous Neolithic period that the great evolutionary distortion of the "dichotomous paradigm" happened.

THE GREAT EVOLUTIONARY DISTORTION: THE PROTOINDOEUROPEAN INVASIONS AND THE "DIVISION PARADIGM"

Archaeologists and historians show that the flourishing and peaceful Neolithic period was progressively destroyed by the invasions of the "Protoindoeuropeans," populations of nomadic shepherds, hunters, and gatherers, coming from the vast area of central Asia.[15] The invasions coincided with horse domestication. Their rational intelligence, but "with little heart," led them to use metals, first copper and then bronze and iron, in a warlike sense, to forge swords, spears, and war daggers, capable of killing better. This could be identified as the beginning of the "techno-reptilian" culture that uses the concrete mind for selfish and material goals.

From their original region, the Protoindoeuropeans in a period of 2-300 years, expanded by successive waves, invading all the cultures of the time: in Siberia as "Afanasievo," in Ponto-Caspian steppes as "Yamnaya," in Greece as "Achei" and "Danai," in Anatolia as "Hittites," in Mesopotamia as "Irani," and in India as "Aryans."

Their aggressive nature generated looting, brutal massacres, people impaled alive, women raped, people reduced to slavery, and entire buildings and forms of art irretrievably burned or destroyed.

DYĒUS: THE "GOD THE FATHER OF HEAVEN" SUBJUGATES "MOTHER EARTH"

It is essential to note that the Protoindoeuropeans adored Dyēus, the "God the Father of Heaven," omnipotent and dominant over everything, who characterized the rigid structure of their pyramidal and patriarchal social model where women were considered inferior. Only men had the right to become kings or priests. The principles of Neolithic spirituality were radically inverted: it is Dyēus, the Father God of Heaven who fertilizes Mother Earth with lightning and rain. The Earth Mother becomes over time a secondary Goddess, a submissive wife. Kindness and art were not considered useful and primary.

In their successive invasions, the Protoindoeuropeans imposed their religion with extreme force. The name of their god Dyēus conditioned and contaminated all subsequent cultures: such as Zeus Patēr in Greece, Dyáuṣ Pitṛè and Deva in Indian culture, Djous Patēr in Rome, up to the current "God the Father" or "God of Heaven" of the Judeo-Christian tradition.

A NEUROPSYCHOSOMATIC VIEW OF THE CLASH OF PARADIGMS

These dramatic historical events represent the evident roots of the "dichotomous paradigm" which separated the human being and nature, which divided man and woman, which created conflicts among peoples, which, not recognizing the deep soul of each living being, spawned the beginning of ecological devastation.

Using a neuropsychosomatic approach, we observe that all the characteristics of the ancient holistic, systemic "unitary paradigm," are precisely the same ones of the serotonin-oxytocin CARE system of the "mammal-limbic-affective" brain, and of a dopamine-endorphin PLAY and FANTASY System oriented towards socialization, play, beauty, and art. From these systems derives a clear "human-feminine" use of rational intelligence oriented towards collective well-being. These systems help to create a tendentially mutual equal society, based on respect for the individuality of every person and every creature as part of the "great cycle of life." *The unitary paradigm is an expression of unitary self-awareness and neuropsychosomatic integrity.*

The pyramidal "dichotomous paradigm" linked to devotion to the male divinity was instead strongly characterized by the sense of domination, always associated with values and behavior of adrenaline-testosterone RAGE-POWER system activated by "reptilian-instinctive," that generates aggression and territorialism and the rational-noradrenaline use of technologies (primarily metallurgy) oriented towards war and dominance. The dichotomous paradigm is expression of the neuropsychosomatic fragmentation of being.

A "TECHNO-REPTILIAN" APPROACH

These logics have generated a strongly patriarchal kind of society, governed by rigid "royal-divine laws," the transgression of which is punished violently or with the death penalty. There is no real recognition of loving kindness or of the value of the "soul," of the Self, the basis of respect and dignity of every human and living being — a system that in fact generated and still generates serious forms of social and economic injustice and eco-systemic disasters.

Several research studies show that testosterone-adrenalin-noradrenalin aggression inhibits the systems of loving kindness, the pleasure of living, and self-awareness.

▌THE HISTORICAL EFFECTS OF THE DICHOTOMOUS PYRAMIDAL PARADIGM

These violent invasions brought about a radical change in human history. It is believed that millions of people fled their conquered and devastated lands, others submitted, and still others armed themselves and lost the quality of peace and harmonious contact with nature. The female statu-ettes, the ancient forms of joyful art, and the evidence of peaceful cultures almost completely disappeared; instead, the first fortifications and images of wars and weapons appeared.

The invasions unleashed a profound defense reaction, which generated millennia of history of wars, of civilizations with a hierarchical-military organization, based on fear, dominance and divisions between races and cultures.

Many genetic studies, including the population genetic maps of Luigi Luca Cavalli-Sforza and Alberto Piazza have lent support to the theory of Protoindoeuropean invasions.[16]

Today, almost all the organizational structures of governments, reli-gions, companies, and families are rooted in the ancient pyramidal struc-ture of power.

The "imperialist" policies of the great nations, the "expansionism" of religions, the numerous wars that still afflict our planet, the violations of human rights and the treatment of women, the "conquest" of the markets by multinationals, the "predatory" use of raw materials, and the environmental "devastation" and "wild" industrial pollution unequivocally testify to the dominance of the dichotomous paradigm over the unitary and loving paradigm in our contemporary civilization.

▌THE GENETIC EFFECTS OF THE DICHOTOMOUS PARADIGM

The dichotomous paradigm generates the neuropsychosomatic fragmentation of being — the root of pain and traumatic dissociation.

Epigenetic research of children born after the famine caused by the 1944–45 war, in which 18,000 Dutch people died, shows dramatic pathological effects (depression, diabetes, metabolic syndrome, schizophrenia). Numerous studies show that there is a *"transgenerational epigenetic"* transmission of the stress and fear experienced by worrying mothers to their children up to the second generation.[17]

▌OBSTACLES TO THE CHILD'S NEUROCOGNITIVE DEVELOPMENT

The mothers' "transepigenetic transmission" of stress-fear could alter the neurocognitive development of children with dramatic pathological effects after birth, and profoundly damage their psychosomatic health, generating reduced development of the superior affective-cognitive maturation.[18]

Maternal stress-fear inhibits the harmonious and loving development of social and familial relationships, which allow the neocortical brain and the limbic system to control the more aggressive and egoic impulses of the reptilian brain, in the name of the highest human and affective values. According to Henri Laborit,[19] director of *Agressologie*, Konrad Lorenz,[20] Reich,[21] MacLean,[22] and Van der Kolk,[23] the activation of the system of fear and physical, emotional, and mental pain generates anxiety, unconscious fears, and "inhibition of action" and damages personal dignity.

THE NEUROPSYCHOSOMATIC EFFECTS OF THE DICHOTOMOUS PARADIGM

A considerable number of scientific research studies (See Figure 3) show that fear activates the "stress axis" which lowers serotonin, oxytocin, dopamine, and endorphins, "closes the heart," freezes lovingness, self-awareness, and the pleasure of existing, and stimulates the production of stress hormones cortisol, adrenaline, and noradrenaline.

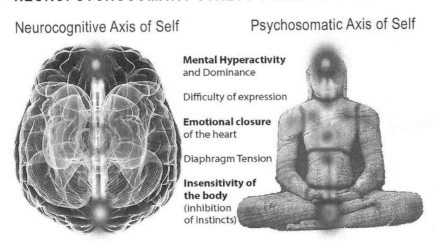

Figure 3. Neuropsychosomatic Stress Collective Blocks

Stress neuro-muscular tensions are generated in all parts of the body, from which the main psychosomatic disorders arise: nervousness, insomnia, sadness, low self-esteem, shyness, anxiety, digestive and sexual disorders, and joint pain. This creates a state of neuropsychosomatic fragmentation, low self-awareness, and high self-control.

In highly reactive people, stress could activate the testosterone anger response.

As can be seen in Figure 4, the electroencephalographic research carried out in our Institute clearly shows that stress and depression inhibit cerebral coherence-synchronization which manifests as a progressive loss of self-awareness and psychosomatic unity and health.

While personal growth and meditation improve brain coherence and synchronization, then, what can we do to foster the evolution of global consciousness?

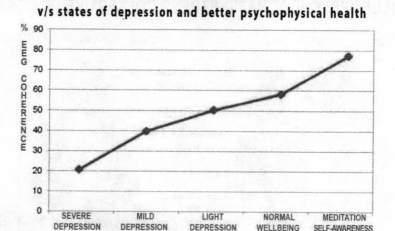

Figure 4. Correspondence between self-consciousness EEG coherence vs states of depression and better psychophysical health

▌THE NEUROSCIENCE REVOLUTION

Global Consciousness Practices

Neuroscience not only helps us to understand the roots of evolutionary obstacles but can also help us overcome them.

Given that the main damage of the old paradigm is the fragmentation of being, since 1988, our Institute (in accordance with the WHO guidelines and life skills, and the UN 2030 Agenda and UNESCO goals) has developed the "Psychosomatic Mindfulness Protocol" (PMP), a global humanistic approach to human evolution that integrates the scientifically proven most effective practices of mindfulness meditation (self-awareness) with those of body, emotional, and psychological awareness.

In *PubMed*, one of the most important scientific search engines, there are more than 25,000 articles on "meditation" or "mindfulness." In recent decades, the number of research and scientific publications proving the effectiveness of meditation and mindfulness has increased exponentially. This shows that millions of people are starting to meditate with efficacy!

These studies show that self-awareness practices reduce stress, anxiety, depression, and aggression and improve loving-kindness, empathy, and collaboration.

But meditation mainly works on the more conscious part.

Our approach highlights that developing self-awareness without first freeing the person from their unconscious emotional conditioning and psychosomatic blocks is like pushing the accelerator on a car with the handbrake activated. For these reasons, we have developed the "Psychosomatic Bodyscan," a practice that allows people to become aware of their unconscious bodily, emotional, and psychological blocks.

Then, we begin loosening bodily blocks with "*energy exercises*" (such as *tai ci, qui gong, kum nye* and *yoga* practices) and other active meditations (*evolution*, *three sounds*, *oxygen*) and "emotional" blocks with practices to release inhibited emotions (particularly pain, fear, and anger with our active practices: *power* and *tree brains*) and "emotional intelligence" exercises to learn how to express and manage them consciously. Finally, with psychotherapy, we free obsolete beliefs and "old paradigm" negative mental conditioning.

Each body, emotional, and cognitive practice is experienced in a space of self-awareness, so that every energy released from blocks becomes part of the individual's resources and the person's creative potential.

Neuropsychosomatic Unity

We have worked with more than thirty thousand people for over one million hours of personal growth. Our research is published in *Mindfulness*[24] and in books and is taught in various universities and conferences. It shows that using the PMP protocol decreases stress anxiety and depression, increases serotonin, oxytocin, dopamine, and endorphins, and develops a state of high self-awareness and feeling of neuropsychosomatic unity (See Figure 5).

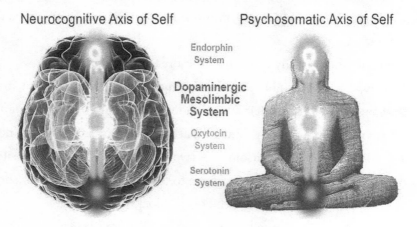

NEUROPSYCHOSOMATIC HEALTH AND SELF AWARENESS

Neurocognitive Axis of Self   Psychosomatic Axis of Self

Endorphin
System

Dopaminergic
Mesolimbic
System

Oxytocin
System

Serotonin
System

Figure 5. Neurosychosomatic Health and Self Awareness

Our neuroscientific research on brain synchronization shows evident efficacy of our PMP protocol in transforming stress associated with low coherent EEG waves (See left of Figure 6) into higher self-awareness and the sense of unity associated with highly coherent EEG waves (See right of Figure 6). This improved EEG coherence associated with a sense of unity and connection also happens between couples and among groups.

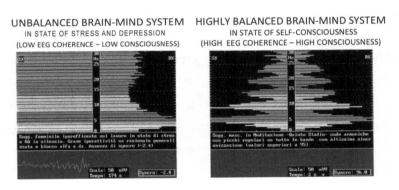

Figure 6. Unbalanced Brain-Mind System, Highly Balanced Brain-Mind System

We have also created a "Gaia Project" for transdisciplinary education in self-awareness and global well-being of humanity and the Planet, which has reached over fifty thousand people, children, and adults, throughout Italy, Palestine, France, Spain, and the US. We use meditations and medical and psychotherapy practices from all major traditions of the world. Our Institute does not insist on copyright for its practices! All our protocol practices are freely available on the Internet.

▌EVOLUTIONARY CONCLUSIONS

To conclude, there is a constant increase worldwide in the number of "cultural creatives" — in the exponential diffusion of meditation and mindfulness practices, considering the huge development of peace, ecology, and human rights movements, in the volume of neuroscience research on self-awareness, and in the development of personal growth and psychotherapy practices. We can state that we have arrived at a turning point today!

The two paradigms are in each person's mind, but now we have developed scientific knowledge, cultural foundations, educational programs, and r-evolutionary practices, so as to able to free ourselves from negative conditionings and awaken our global consciousness.

We are all already actively and creatively participating in the birth of the new paradigm. If we continue to work with love and enthusiasm, we will certainly witness the evolution of a more conscious and peaceful planetary civilization, in harmony with the planet, of which we are parts and co-creators.

CHAPTER 21

THE GLOBAL PSYCHEDELIC UPSHIFT AND HOLOTROPIC BREATHWORK

STANISLAV GROF

A lbert Hofmann's discovery of the psychoactive substance LSD-25 became a sensation overnight in the scientific world. What is not generally known is that it was not the psychedelic effect of LSD that caused the sensation. Anthropologists and historians had known for a long time that many ancient and native cultures used plants with psychedelic effects in their ritual and spiritual lives and for healing, and by the time of Albert's discovery, chemists had already isolated the active principles from some of these plants.

It was the incredible intensity of the effects of LSD-25 that was sensational; this remarkable substance is effective in minute quantities — millionths of a gram, known as micrograms or gammas. For comparison, about 100mg of mescaline are needed for an effective session. Approximately the same intensity can be achieved with 100 mcg of LSD-25, about one-thousandth of that dose. It was therefore conceivable that the human body could be producing a similar substance ("toxin X") and that serious mental diseases and psychoses might actually be chemical aberrations.

In that case, psychoses could be treated by an appropriate antidote, a substance that would neutralize their effects. This substance would have been a test-tube solution for schizophrenia, the Holy Grail of psychiatry. In the early stages of LSD research, psychedelics were referred to as hallucinogens, psychotomimetic substances or delirogens, and the states induced by them were called "experimental psychoses." It took psychotherapeutically oriented clinicians to overcome this preconception. The discovery of LSD and the hunt for "toxin X" started what had been called a "golden era of psychopharmacology." Although these biochemical theories of schizophrenia were eventually refuted and abandoned, LSD remained at the center of attention for researchers. Never before had a single substance held so many promises in such a wide variety of fields.

For psychopharmacologists and neurophysiologists, the discovery of LSD meant the beginning of this promising era of research of synaptic transmitters and chemical antagonisms. For historians and art critics, the LSD experiments provided extraordinary new insights into the psychology and psychopathology of art. This was particularly true for paintings and sculptures of various so-called "primitive" cultures, psychiatric patients, and outsider art (l'art brut), as well as modern movements such as abstractionism, impressionism, expressionism, cubism, pointillism, surrealism, fantastic realism, and dadaism.

For professional painters who participated in LSD research, the psychedelic session often marked a radical change in their artistic expression. Their imagination became much richer, colors more vivid, and style considerably freer. They could also often reach into the deep recesses of their unconscious psyche and tap archetypal sources of inspiration. On occasion, people who had never painted before were able to produce extraordinary pieces of art.

LSD experimentation also produced fascinating observations that were of great interest to spiritual teachers and scholars of comparative religion. The mystical experiences frequently observed in LSD sessions offered a radically new understanding of a wide variety of phenomena from the spiritual domain, including shamanism, rites of passage and ancient mysteries of death and rebirth, Eastern religions and philosophies, and mystical traditions of the world. The fact that LSD and other psychedelic substances could trigger a broad range of spiritual experiences became the subject of heated scientific discussions. These debates revolved around the fascinating problem concerning the nature and value of this "instant" or "chemical mysticism."

LSD was also highly recommended as an extraordinary unconventional teaching device that would make it possible for psychiatrists, psychologists, medical students, and nurses to spend several hours in a world resembling that of their patients. As a result of this experience, they would be able to understand them better, communicate with them more effectively, and be more successful in their treatment.

Psychedelic research seemed to be on its way to fulfilling its initial promises. Psychopharmacologists, psychologists, psychiatrists, and spiritual teachers, inspired by this sense of a golden era, were building the foundation of a future Science of Consciousness. Physicians and psychiatrists wrote articles about surprising improvements in previously incurable patients. Because of these uses for a wide range of disciplines, LSD became known as Albert Hofmann's "Wonder Child."

Unfortunately, substances that had been used for millennia in non-Western and preindustrial countries as sacraments for healing were profaned and eventually prohibited in Western civilization. Many members of the younger generation used psychedelics of unknown origin in haphazard, recreational ways. Hippies with unusual hairstyles and clothing met in fields and parks for huge be-ins and love-ins. There were frequent anti-war protests that provoked conflicts with the police. The most famous confrontation happened between Harvard University and Timothy Leary, Richard Alpert, and Ralph Metzner, who experimented with psychedelics with their students.

In the late 1960s, Maimon Cohen and his colleague researchers from the State University of New York in Buffalo, NY, observed structural changes in chromosomes of children whose mothers had taken LSD during pregnancy. However, structural changes in chromosomes had been previously observed in experiments with commonly used drugs, such as aspirin, caffeine, and tetracyclic antibiotics. Sensation-hunting journalists blew this unimportant article out of proportion, into a mass hysteria that mothers who have taken LSD could have malformed children.

The misguided political and administrative sanctions in the 1960s against psychedelics were effective only against law-obeying scientists but famously failed to stop the street use of psychedelic substances. Draconian legal sanctions and deceptive and mendacious anti-drug propaganda actually motivated the rebellious young generation to experiment with these substances. Initially, LSD seemed to have such fantastic potential that people called it Hofmann's Wonder Child as we have seen. But after its criminalization, Albert renamed LSD "*My* Problem Child."

During my last visit at Albert Hofmann's house four weeks before his death in 2006, we talked at some length about his favorite subject — the Eleusinian Mysteries of Death and Rebirth. These mysteries conducted in the Eleusinian sanctuary near Athens took place regularly and without interruption every five years for a period of almost 2,000 years. The secret of the Eleusinian mysteries was the sacred potion, *kykeon*, capable of inducing visions of the afterlife so powerful that the initiates lost the fear of death. They realized that they were immortal souls temporarily in mortal bodies, which radically changed their life.

In the Telesterion, the giant initiation hall of Eleusis, at its cult´s height, more than 3,000 neophytes at a time experienced powerful psychospiritual transformation. The cultural importance of these mysteries for the ancient world and their role in the history of European civilization has yet to be acknowledged. It becomes evident when we realize that among the initiates of these mysteries were many famous and illustrious figures of antiquity, including the philosophers Plato, Aristotle, and Epictetus, the playwrights Euripides and Sophocles, the poet Pindaros, and the politician and military leader Alcibiades.

Ancient Greece was a remarkable culture. Greeks were outstanding in many disciplines — science, medicine, architecture, painting, sculpture, ceramics, poetry, music, theatre, tragedy, and others. Because the use of psychedelics increases creativity, the cultural influence of the sacred psychedelic potion, *kykeon*, that the initiates in the Eleusinian mysteries used for almost two millennia is a very intriguing question. These rites were observed regularly from c. 1600 BC until 392 AD. They did not simply cease to attract the attention of the antique world. The ceremonial activities in Eleusis were brutally interrupted when the Christian Emperor Theodosius interdicted participation in the mysteries and all other pagan cults. Shortly afterward, in 395 AD, the invading Goths destroyed the sanctuary.

During my last visit to Albert's house, we talked the whole afternoon about ancient Greece and Eleusis. Albert believed that it would be possible that his "Wonder Child" LSD and psilocybin, the alkaloid he isolated from the "magic mushrooms" of the Mazatecs, could be integrated into modern society. These medicines could heal diseases, resolve violence, foster ecological responsibility, support international peace, and enhance a more universal and mystical spirituality.

As Albert described the great potential of psychedelics used in the right set and setting, he saw the beautiful vision of a New Eleusis. Having worked many years with psychedelics, I have seen many hundreds of people who experienced the deep transformation that Albert talked about. However, to talk about the vision of a new "New Eleusis" in the four decades of the Dark Age of psychedelics, when even research and therapy with these medicines were illegal, seemed like a silly utopian fantasy.

None of us, who participated in Albert's dreams of a New Eleusis imagined that we would experience within our lifetime a major renaissance of psychedelic research on a global level. This amazing situation resulted largely from the effort, energy, and determination of Rick Doblin and his remarkable team at the Multidisciplinary Association for Psychedelic Studies (MAPS). I saw firsthand how this was happening when we witnessed Rick Doblin introduce MDMA and cannabis as therapeutic medicines to Israel.

We brought to Israel a team of our holotropic breathwork facilitators to help Rick assemble volunteers for his research. We ran a large breathwork workshop in Tel-Aviv, and I gave lectures and seminars in Jerusalem and Safed. While working in Israel for these four weeks, Rick had hardly an hour when he was not negotiating with psychiatrists, psychologists, chemists, pharmacologists, clergy, medical doctors, biologists, and politicians. He also arranged a large dinner for Raphael Mechoulam, known as the Israeli Albert Hofmann, who isolated THC from cannabis. Thanks to his heroic efforts over many years, Rick Doblin achieved what seemed to be impossible — assembling researchers from various countries and sufficient funds to conduct studies which confirmed the positive results of psychedelic medicines.

Psychedelic therapists had responded differently to psychedelic prohibition, ignorant propaganda, and draconic legislation. Some of them resigned themselves to the situation. They returned reluctantly to routine psychiatric practice that now seemed lifeless and dull after they had experienced the excitement of the new therapeutic perspectives. Other therapists, convinced of the value of psychedelic medicines, decided not to deprive their clients of the benefits offered by these substances. They continued their work underground or found legal loopholes that allowed them to continue their work legally or semi-legally.

Others, aware of the limitations of verbal therapy, decided to use non-drug experiential approaches developed within humanistic psychology such as Fritz Perls' Gestalt or various Neo-Reichian approaches. In this situation, Christina and I developed an exciting alternative therapy which offered an effective non-drug method of inducing holotropic states of consciousness. This approach was not as powerful as psychedelics, but surprisingly close. Holotropic breathwork became rapidly popular, beginning at Esalen where it was born.

The fame of holotropic breathwork was enhanced by the magic of Big Sur and Esalen, nestled on one side by the mountains of Ventana Wilderness and on the other by the magnificent Pacific Ocean, vibrant with gray whales, dolphins, seals, and sea otters. This territory once belonged to the native American people, the Esselens, after whom the Esalen Institute was named. Everyone who comes there feels that it is a sacred space and power spot.

I would like to thank Michael Murphy, who opened this amazing property to hundreds of thousands of people, many of whom experienced transformation and healing. Michael Murphy and Dick Price, cofounders of Esalen, created a unique human laboratory that functions as one of the cutting edges of consciousness evolution. Jeoffrey Kripal called it a

"Religion of No Religion." Our holotropic breathwork and transpersonal psychology workshops at Esalen helped to revive and maintain the spirit of the 1960s during the prohibition era of psychedelics.

Soon came invitations from other countries, and Christina and I traveled around the world – France, Italy, Germany, Switzerland, Czech Republic, England, Scandinavian countries, Russia, Ukraine, India, Japan, Mexico, and the countries of South America. We conducted holotropic breathwork workshops, training modules, lectures, and seminars. People who learned our breathwork know the basic principles of working with holotropic states of consciousness, knowledge which can be applied to support psychedelic experiences, spiritual emergencies, shamanic practices, and deep meditation in retreats.

Thanks to the immense effort of Rick Doblin and his MAPS team, the psychedelic world has dramatically changed. As a result, many people now realize that LSD had been Hofmann's "Wonder Child" all along, but it was brought up in a dysfunctional family. Suddenly, physicians, psychiatrists, and legislators recognized that psychedelics are remarkable medicines. For some disorders that previously did not respond to treatment, psychedelics are now methods of choice — MDMA for Post-Traumatic Stress Disorder (PTSD); psilocybin for depression and anxiety especially in cancer patients; ibogaine for addiction; and cannabis and THC for pain, nausea and vomiting, anorexia, epilepsy, and asthma.

During the four decades of criminalization of psychedelics, psychiatrists, psychologists, and other mental health professionals did not have any possibility of working with psychedelic medicines. The global renaissance of psychedelics will potentially bring these medicines to many patients, yet there is currently a shortage of fully trained therapists. Psychedelics are very powerful, sacred tools of healing and transformation and need to be used with great respect, care, and expertise. Psychedelic sitters and therapists need profound theoretical and practical training and personal experience.

In the Grof Legacy Training we teach our technique of holotropic breathing under the brand name Grof® Breathwork.[25] People who go through our breathwork training learn the basic principles of working with holotropic states of consciousness. As it becomes legally possible, they can then easily augment this knowledge with information about specific psychedelic medicines they might be working with — MDMA, psilocybin, LSD, mescaline, ayahuasca, 5-methoxy DMT, or ketamine. Extensive training about the proper set and setting of psychedelic sessions and the supervision of ethical and moral respect and integrity of psychedelic therapists will be crucial for the success of this new psychedelic renaissance.

We are not yet on the path to a New Eleusis. But with intelligent regulations, it might be possible to expand psychedelic medicines from therapy with patients with a specific diagnosis to other purposes for which we know it can be very promising — spiritual awakening, creative breakthroughs, and expression in painting, music, sculpture, architecture, and film. It could eventually include rites of passage for teenagers. One of the ultimate hopes is to create centers where people could experience healing sessions with pure substances, a proper set and setting, and expert guidance. These would all help enable the global rebirth that Albert dreamed about.

NOTES & REFERENCES

▌CHAPTER 19

1. Malthus T.R. (1798). *An Essay on the Principle of Population as it Affects the Future Improvement of Society*. London: J. Johnson; reprint, Oxford World's Classics. http://www.esp.org/books/malthus/population/malthus.pdf
2. McTaggart, L. (2011). *The Bond: Connecting through the Space Between Us*. New York, NY: Free Press/Simon & Schuster.
3. Holt-Lunstad, J., et.al. (2010). Social Relationships and Mortality Risk: A Meta-analytic Review. *PLoS Medicine*, 7(7):e1000316. https://doi.org/10.1371/journal.pmed.1000316
4. Hawton, A., et. al. (2011). The Impact of Social Isolation on the Health Status and Health-related Quality of Life of Older People. *Quality of Life Research*, 20(1):57–67. https://doi.org/10.1007/s11136-010-9717-2
5. Kawachi, I., et al. (1997). Social capital, income inequality, and mortality. *American Journal of Public Health*, 87(9):1491–8.
6. Putnam, R. D. (2000). *Bowling Alone: The Collapse and Revival of American Community*. New York: Simon & Schuster.; and Putnam, R. D. (2001). Social Capital: Measurement and Consequences. *Isuma: Canadian Journal of Policy Research*, 2(1):41–51. https://www.oecd.org/innovation/research/1825848.pdf

▌CHAPTER 20

7. Panksepp, J. (1998). Affective Neuroscience: The Foundations of Human and Animal Emotions. New York: Oxford University Press.

8. Panksepp, J., & Biven, L., (2012). *The Archaeology of Mind: Neuroevolutionary Origins of Human Emotions*. Norton Series on Interpersonal Neurobiology. New York: W. W. Norton & Company.

9. Eccles, J., (1989), *Evolution of the Brain: Creation of the Self*. London/New York: Routledge.

10. Edelman, G. M., (2004). *Wider Than the Sky: The Phenomenal Gift of Consciousness*. New Haven/London: Yale University Press.

11. Gimbutas, M. (1956). *The Prehistory of Eastern Europe. Part I: Mesolithic, Neolithic and Copper Age Cultures in Russia and the Baltic Area*. American School of Prehistoric Research, Peabody Museum, Harvard University, Bulletin No. 20. Cambridge, MA: Peabody Museum.

12. Mellaart, J. (1967). *Çatal Höyük: A Neolithic Town in Anatolia*. London: Thames & Hudson Ltd.

13. Platōn, N. (1971). *Zakros: The Discovery of a Lost Palace of Ancient Crete*. New York: Charles Scribner's Sons.

14. Eisler, R. (1987). *The Chalice and the Blade: Our History, Our Future*. New York: Harper & Row.

15. Mallory, J. P. (1991). *In Search of the Indo-Europeans: Language, Archaeology and Myth*. London: Thames & Hudson.

16. Cavalli-Sforza, L. L. (1997). Genes, Peoples, and Languages. *Proceedings of the National Academy of Sciences of the United States of America*, 94(15):7719–7724. https://www.pnas.org/doi/epdf/10.1073/pnas.94.15.7719

17. Jablonka, E., & Raz, G. (2009), Transgenerational Epigenetic Inheritance: Prevalence, Mechanisms, and Implications for the Study of Heredity and Evolution. *The Quarterly Review of Biology*, 84(2):131–176. https://doi.org/10.1086/598822

18. Schore, A. N. (2003). *Affect Dysregulation and Disorders of the Self*. New York/London: W. W. Norton & Company.

19. Laborit, H. (1979). *L'inibition de l'action: Biologie, physiologie, psychologie, sociologie*. Paris/New York: Masson.

20. Lorenz, K. (1966). *On Aggression*. New York, NY: Harcourt, Brace and World; First Edition.

21. Reich, W. (1945). *Character Analysis: Principles and Technique for Psychoanalysts in Practice and in Training.* (Trans. by T. P. Wolfe.) (2nd ed.). New York, NY: Orgone Institute Press.

22. MacLean, P. D. (1990). *The Triune Brain in Evolution: Role in Paleocerebral Functions.* New York, NY: Plenum.

23. Van der Kolk, B. A. (2014). *The Body Keeps the Score: Brain, Mind, and Body in the Healing of Trauma.* New York: Viking Penguin.

24. Scafuto, F., Ghiroldi, S., Montecucco, N. F., Presaghi, F., & Iani, L. (2022). The mindfulness-based Gaia program reduces internalizing problems in high-school adolescents: A cluster randomized controlled trial. *Mindfulness, 13*(7): 1804–1815. https://doi.org/10.1007/s12671-022-01920-9; and Ghiroldi, S., Scafuto, F., Montecucco, N.F., et al. (2020). Effectiveness of a School-Based Mindfulness Intervention on Children's Internalizing and Externalizing Problems: the Gaia Project. *Mindfulness,* 11:2589–2603. https://doi.org/10.1007/s12671-020-01473-9

▌CHAPTER 21

25. *The Way of the Psychonaut* (Documentary film about Stan Grof's life and work) www.thewayofthepsychonaut.com; and Grof, S. (2019). *The Way of the Psychonaut: Encyclopedia for Inner Journeys (Volume One; Volume Two).* Santa Cruz, CA: Multidisciplinary Association for Psychedelic Studies.

ROADMAP CLUSTER IV

UPSHIFTING OUR THINKING

CHAPTER 22

KEYNOTE

THE UPSHIFT TO SYNTONY IN THOUGHT AND ACTION

ALEXANDER LASZLO

And would it have been worth it, after all …

Would it have been worth while,

To have bitten off the matter with a smile,

To have squeezed the universe into a ball

To roll it toward some overwhelming question…

—T.S. Eliot, *The Love Song of J. Alfred Prufrock*

I like to think of business as the science of accomplishment, though perhaps it is better thought of as an art-science. If it is true that it provides a
path for value exchange in service of accomplishing means and ends, then
the critical issue is that of the values being exchanged. Getting clear on
the values that drive our quest for accomplishment will tell us everything

about the path it involves — both in terms of the tracks it leaves and where those tracks are leading us, as well as what it's like to be on this path right here, right now. Is it comfortable? Is it meaningful? Is it worthwhile?

At least the last of those questions is "businessy." Calculating worth, even in terms of time investments, is very much a matter of business. But if we see our role in the business world as simply that of "being busy" with our business, then our identity takes on a sterile or more value-neutral role. In Swedish, if someone is involved with business as the artscience of accomplishment, they are said to engage in *näringsliv*. Näringsliv translates to "nourishment for life." How different is it to partake in that sort of identity than just to be a "busyness person." In Spanish, it's even worse. In Spanish, business is *negocio* — neg (as in the opposite of) + ocio (leisure). You're just supposed to not be idle, and you qualify as a captain of industry.

But imagine if business — as the artscience of accomplishment — were really and truly about *nourishment for life*. It could lead to an entire re-branding of our species. In fact, the evolutionary upshift in consciousness calls for nothing less than this. It is the imperative of our time, for the artscience of accomplishment might actually be able to bring an evolutionary value-add to not only our species, writ large, but also to the business of life, writ larger.

We have been flying the flag of *Homo sapiens sapiens* for long enough. It is time to evolve beyond the strategically wise, the rationally refined, the intellectually erudite, and the technologically talented. Our patterns of being and becoming now need to align with the brand identity of nature and the cosmos in and all around us — with patterns and processes that continually create conditions conducive to life. This will mean positioning ourselves — our species — as a creative force in the world, contributing to the increased vitality and robustness of the ecosystem in which we operate.

In his brilliant essay on the rise of an ecological era and with hat tip to the work and insights of Thomas Berry, musician and composer Sam Guarnaccia suggests that we may be ushering in a new collective identity, a new being: the Ecozoan. According to him, "an Ecozoan is a person who is leaning in to the Ecozoic — open to an intimate presence to, and an integral and creative understanding of the natural world, and is moving into a new kind of wholeness, belonging, and exuberant participation seldom experienced in the modern period ... Everyone who breathes air, drinks water, takes in nourishment from the land, marvels at the moon, sun, and stars, and is conscious of being energized by wondrous processes that evolved over billions of years is an Ecozoan."[1] Could this be our new brand? If so, are we open for business *näringsliv*?

One thing is certain: *Homo sapiens sapiens* is a species bound for extinction. And actually, this is cause for celebration. The universal human emerging to take its place — whether to be known as an Ecozoan, as *Homo Universalis* (as Barbara Marx Hubbard would have it, and Leonardo da Vinci, before her), as *Homo sensorium* from the popular Netflix™ television series "Sense8," or as some form of *Homo sapiens cosmicus* — is stepping up to the plate. And it is us!

Provided... provided we prove capable of manifesting both our mundane individuality and our sacred connectivity as part and whole at one and the same time. This is the upshift imperative. It is up to us to be this new species, to curate our own emergence through holistic and reverence-rich relationships — with all that manifests the patterns of being and becoming that continually create, nourish, and evolve life.

How can we do this? It's actually not rocket science. In fact, it is the artscience of *näringsliv*. To begin with, we can actually make ourselves available to the warp and weft of cosmic emergence — the information stream from the deep dimension of the universe. Do you have to be a yogi or a fakir or a shaman to do this? No, not at all (it certainly wouldn't hurt if you were, though!). It is both the simplest and most natural thing in the world and, at the same time, requires focus, attention, and above all, practice. Animals and plants do it without a second thought — and that's actually part of the problem of *Homo sapiens sapiens:* we spend too much time giving all sorts of second and third thoughts to how we should express things rather than just making ourselves available to *being expressed.*

So that's where we must begin — learning not just to be "the busybody minds of business" and making ourselves available to the upshift in consciousness. The admonition becomes: *Don't just do something; sit there!* We start with that, with helping our minds to take a break. Easier said than done, but absolutely essential to the upshift movement. We're constantly cluttering our consciousness with an internal stream of commentary about what is going on in our lives, moment by moment. But as soon as we reflect on what is going on, or think about it in any way, we are no longer in tune, no longer living in the moment. We are thinking about what just happened, distilling it into words, and freezing the moment so that we can reflect on it. This lands us just behind the present, always catching up to it, thinking about everything that just happened, as it is just happening.

If you can turn off what psychologists call "the monkey mind" — that part of your consciousness that keeps up the constant chatter in your head, commenting on everything — then you start to make yourself more available to the information flows from the deep cosmos, from Akasha Dimension. Essentially, there are the three steps to an ecology of spirit/mind/consciousness (with a nod to Gregory Bateson): 1) quieting the monkey-mind, 2) releasing into the moment (without the need to "do anything" with it, just being present — fully present), and 3) allowing your perceptions to flow with whatever arises in your field of awareness. This is the practice. This is the way. Three simple steps that take a lifetime to cultivate. The end result is greater flow with what's going on in your life, greater coherence with yourself, with others, with nature, even with your ancestors and those who will come after you, and fundamentally, with the deep dimension of being and becoming that is the interconnected holo-tropic cosmos arising in, through, and all around you.[2]

A re-branded species going about its business in this way nourishes life. And, not surprisingly, life nourishes it right back! Now there's a principle of value exchange that can truly undergird a new upshifted science of accom-plishment!! To focus on this path, it helps to follow certain fuzzy guiding principles, ones that are:

- *Future Creating.* This does not mean ignoring the past or disavowing tradition and heritage. Quite the contrary, it involves creating a coher-ent and integral path from past to future. But the point is that the destination is arrived at through innovation, not through seeking to recapture some glorious golden past of business success. Neither is it oriented to affirming or maintaining the *status quo*. Strategy is set with an evolutionary eye.

- *Life Affirming.* This means that both the products and the processes of the organization are non-destructive of life and the ecosystem services upon which they depend. Näringsliv does not engage in utilitarian strategies that sacrifice the interests of a few for those of the many (or vice-versa, as is more common in actual practice). This ethic applies to dealings with both external as well as internal stakeholders.

- *Opportunity Increasing.* To the extent that business strategy creates more opportunity to have more opportunities, it can be said to be opportunity increasing. This builds on such seminal work as that of Swedish oncologist Karl-Henrik Robèrt and *The Natural Step*[3] frame-work he developed. Rather than just leveling off both the demands on the natural environment created by business practices and the rate at which ecosystem services are being diminished in the hope of stabilizing human activity within sustainable parameters of the planet's carrying capacity, the idea is to operate in such a way as to create an ever more robust and supportive environment.

Truly, these fuzzy guiding principles are such a "natural step" that nature has been operating along their lines since time immemorial. For instance, studies in macro-cellular biology have discovered that if you place two living heart cells next to each other — not touching, but just a short distance apart — they will very quickly begin to beat in unison.[4] They start off each contracting, pulsing, at their own rhythm, and very soon, they are doing it at the same time, even though they aren't touching! But if there are disturbances in the environment, such as electric impulses or swirls of ionized water flowing around them, they won't sync up.

Understanding that things — stars, atoms, you, and me — continually flow into existence through the information binding action of the Akasha Dimension that embeds all of existence creates the space of allowance in which we live and breathe — this natural step in the flow and pulse of co-emergent interbeing. The fuzzy guiding principles and the three steps toward an upshifted mind are just guideposts and support structures to help us along the way. The key thing is to "get out of our own way" so that what we do, who we are, and how we are can be correlated with holotropic patterns of coherent cosmic emergence. How directly this happens is a function of how well and how deeply we access the Akasha Dimension.

Alfonso Montuori[5] helps us to understand why an upshift in business mindset, skillset, and heartset suggests competencies closer to those of the jazz player than the orchestral musician: "Everything an artist produces, how s/he shapes the silence, and our interpretation of it, is a product of a historical period, which both enriches and constrains" (p. 145). Business that makes a difference in this world tends more often than not to explore opportunities to create new patterns and processes as they appear, rather than to focus *only* on what they already know to sustain a pattern or process in existence. Gordon Rowland[6] reinforces this point by suggesting how this stylistic difference in musical metaphor relates to ways businesspeople tend to work together. He notes that "teams resembling jazz ensembles are more capable of meeting today's challenges than teams resembling orchestras" (p. 19). According to Rowland, we are living in a world that more and more demands the ability to work flexibly and loosely together in ways that combine rational thought, technical skill, creativity, intuition, and empathy. Rather than "following the score" that is handed to us, the challenges of an evolutionary upshift in the business world ask us to improvise around a basic theme of life, and the nourishment of it.

The upshift imperative in business calls for new vision, a new ethos, and new leadership skills. Take, for example, the new shared leadership that project-based work teams display. To illustrate this, the following set of images from a televised corporate advertisement serves to describe the shift well. The commercial begins with a classical music quintet performing a beautiful piece of chamber music. The black of the tuxes, gowns, and music stands of the two violinists, violist, cellist, and flautist create a nice contrast with the all-white space in which they play. And they play beautifully, weaving their melodies together in a harmony of classical counterpoint. Then, all of a sudden, a basketball sails in from off stage, bouncing once, and landing right in the cellist's lap! The startled cellist stops playing immediately, as do the other musicians who all stare incredulously at the basketball. The cellist looks at his companions, shrugs once, gets up, and begins dribbling the ball. The other musicians glance at each other briefly, put down their instruments, and get up to join the now former cellist. They all move off to the right, their instruments and stands quickly forgotten and fading out of view. Soon, the five of them are passing the basketball back and forth in ways that would have made the Harlem Globe Trotters green with envy. As when they were playing music, their motions seem to flow in a graceful harmony of interdependence and partnership. Then, just as they are really getting into it, a trapeze bar swings in from off stage and almost hits the former flautist in the head, but at the last minute, she reaches up and grabs it. The others stop to look at her, the one with the basketball just letting it drop and roll off. She looks back at her partners, shrugs once, and begins to swing. As she does, the others move with her as one, the scene fading out as the commercial ends.

This little story illustrates the phenomenon of "syntony" within a group — an idea central to an upshifted consciousness among emerging Ecozoans. Syntony, in essence, means to tune in and consciously align one-self with the evolutionary flows of one's milieu.[7] All five "players" acted in unison, although each did their own thing, and when something in their environment changed, they neither ignored nor reacted against it, but instead immediately adapted to it. They didn't have to stop for long discussions to weigh out the pros and cons of one course of action or another, to analyze, plan, or argue the strengths and weaknesses, opportunities, and threats of one option over another, and they didn't have to go off to training seminars to learn how to deal with change. They learned together, "on the job" as it were, and in dynamic interaction with each other and their environment.

Wouldn't it be wonderful if the world of business were able to cope with uncertainty and change like this group did? Actually, it wouldn't. The people in that story demonstrated the essence of *syntony* — of harmonizing with, and tuning to, each other — but they did so only *among themselves*. In other words, they were an internally coherent system, but not a supercoherent system that *also* manifested coherence with the system of which they were a part. They were totally out of syntony with their environment. Whenever they were challenged by a change in their environment, they simply shrugged and adapted *to* it. In short, they reacted. Where were they going with this pattern of adapting to anything that came their way? While they may have been very much in syntony with each other — fluidly co-creating consonant patterns of behavior among themselves — they did not go the extra step required of true systems of syntony: they did not co-create *with* their evolving environment in holotropic consonance and fulfilment of the evolutionary requisite of supercoherence.

The next stage in the evolution of our species is upon us. That is to say, if we can upshift our consciousness so as to seize the (r)evolutionary opportunity on our doorstep. Re-branding our species, re-storying our relationship to life, re-membering our role as nourishers of life and the systems that augment and support it — these are part of the great upshift awaiting our conscious participation.

CHAPTER 23

EVOLUTIONARY ARC TO PRODUCTIVE DIALOGUE

ALLAN LESLIE COMBS

A small farming village in China once suffered from a drought. Concerned over this situation, the town's people invited a rain-maker to move into the village. He came to the village, quietly proceeding to live his life like anyone else. He conducted no special ceremonies and performed no magic rituals, but simply went about his business, cutting wood, carrying water, and so on. The town's people were growing impatient with him when it finally began to rain. Leaves turned green, and crops grew again. Curious as to how this good fortune had come about, a local Taoist philosopher was consulted. He explained without hesitation that the drought had been triggered by discord among the residents of the village. The presence of the rainmaker had brought a sense of harmony to the village again, and since rain is part of the natural order, it was not too long before it returned.

The story tells us two things about community. First, a gentle solution to a difficult problem can spread like a soft fragrance, uplifting an entire community. Second, such an approach may even penetrate the natural world around us. In modern, even scientific, terms, we might suspect that the rainmaker was the source of a morphic field,[8] bringing harmony to both the human world and the world of nature.

We citizens of the modern world tend still to think in terms of concepts introduced hundreds of years ago during the Enlightenment. For instance, causation was then believed to be the result of interactions between independent physical objects. Newton was baffled by gravity, since physical objects were believed to interact through the agency of hooks, barbs, and the like. Today, we take it for granted that the physical world, and its laws and principles, are governed by non-physical forces such as gravity and electromagnetism, and that the laws of nature have not changed since that time. Whether this is true or not remains to be seen, but there is reason to suspect, for example, that even physical "constants," such as the temperatures at which physical elements melt or vaporize, change slowly over time.[8] Moreover, we are told almost daily that the deep quantum structure of the cosmos is "entangled" in ways Enlightenment philosophers could not have imagined, yielding a wholistic or integrated universe quite different than the assemblage of objects that comprised the conceptual cosmos of the Enlightenment. Indeed, things are looking more and more like the visions of ancient Eastern sages and Western mystics such as Meister Eckhart, Hildegard of Bingen, and Nicholas of Cusa.

All this aside, however, our human world today is connected by networks of information that bring us each within electronic earshot of nearly anyone we might choose to connect with, anywhere in the world. There is a parlor game called *Six Degrees of Kevin Bacon*, based on the now out-of-date idea that anyone in Hollywood can be tracked in six steps to the actor Kevin Bacon. In fact, in the real world, six person-to-person steps will get you to almost anyone, anywhere. This is especially true if we include the relatively few individuals who know a large number of others. For example, click the email address list on your computer. How large is it? My own desktop computer presently holds about 2,500 names and addresses, and who knows how many others are connected to them?

Such networks are reminiscent of huge spiderwebs, across which a small vibration at one location sends a wave throughout the entire network, diminishing in amplitude with distance but never disappearing. Bear in mind through all this, our moment-to-moment actions and decisions are often inspired by the tiniest of thoughts and impulses. Putting all this in plain language, it means that we have a more profound and extensive influence on others, and the worlds they inhabit, than you might think. Simply living a good life, expressing the values you hold dear, and as the Dalai Lama says so often, being kind to others, is more than enough for living a good life.

WHAT MORE SHALL WE DO?

It is unrealistic to think that the major world powers — governments, corporations, religions, and educational institutions — will take the growing ecological and social crises seriously enough to deal with them forcefully until they have become overwhelming. This is because they are designed for stability, rather than for creative resilience in a rapidly changing world. I hope I am wrong about this, but in the meantime, I believe informed and thoughtful voices may widen an awareness of the urgency in our times, and that such voices can also offer creative suggestions for solutions.

Many creative individuals throughout the world are working both individually and in groups to explore solutions to the problems that plague us. Yet, they often do not know of each other because the dominant sources of news, and the institutions that support them, are dedicated to stability, and thrive on conflict. "Blood sells" is the common adage of newspapers. In the meantime, many people and groups doing good work are isolated by separate issues and language, not recognizing that they are partners in seeking answers for a world that has moved beyond traditional values, agendas, and goals.

The growing presence of such creative persons and groups seems to me to be a source of optimism. Their greatest potential, however, will come only in the sharing of ideas and plans in conversations that connect individuals into groups and groups into larger groups, ultimately creating spreading networks of shared values and efforts that bind together. This emergent joining of communities over wide ranges of geography and topics of interest has the potential of breaking through the surface of conventional institutions and media, while at the same time taking on a powerful self-organizing dynamic of its own. Such a dynamic could bring significant numbers of people together in what may be our best hope for preserving that which is most valuable from the past, and at the same time midwifing the emergence of a life-affirming third millennium civilization.

▮ SUGGESTIONS FOR CONVERSATIONS

The following list of guidelines for conversations was originally proposed by Robert Theobald[9] after much reflection on the styles of conversations that might be helpful in getting process started. They are predicated on the belief that we do not have final answers, and so would be best advised to carefully listen to each other. They also rest on the observation that large scale fix-it programs have not worked well, so we need to seek solutions from people who are genuinely involved in particular situations and who can offer concrete creative solutions from their own experience.

- Stress the opportunities in a situation rather than the problems. The opportunities in situations usually have to be discovered rather than being obvious. Creative thinking is required to see what can go right rather than wrong.

- Encourage generative thinking. Generative thinking supports individuals and groups in moving toward more open and creative thought and activity.

- See healthy relationships as essential to effective activity. The time put into really knowing the people with whom one works pays handsome dividends in the quality of collaboration.

- Acknowledge the importance of spirituality. We are spiritual beings. Denying this reality in the ways we live impoverishes not only ourselves but those around us and our work. We need more than logic to make sense of the varied and unpredictable developments which develop around us all the time.

- Recognize the importance of using values as a compass which guides our choices. My own short listing is honesty, compassion, responsibility, humility, love, faith, cooperation, and a respect for mystery.

- Move beyond dichotomized thinking. We need to see that "both-and" language is important and only possible after we have moved out of industrial-era systems [One aspect of this notion is to seek "win-win" rather than the usual "win-lose" solutions typical of traditional business and managerial strategies.].

- Understand that reality is not fully objective or given but is born largely from the beliefs and boundaries we co-create with those around us. Although we need boundaries and beliefs to function, we need to realize they also limit us. So, we are mindful to not take them too seriously, and welcome opportunities to co-create more functional new realities, boundaries, and beliefs.

- Acknowledge and empower competence based on knowledge, skills, abilities, wisdom, perspectives, and experience, rather than accepting the dominance of coercive power [Effective decision making must move beyond "experts," "managers," and hierarchical dominance structures.].
- Be aware of our patterns of behavior and recognize that strengths, especially when overplayed, carry weaknesses with them.
- Learn that we can make progress together to the extent we show maturity by controlling our ego needs and growing beyond them.
- Recognize that people operate in their perceived self-interest because they must screen reality through their own senses and the "stories" and "myths" they have learned. We should also understand that this does not mean that people will necessarily see their "self-interest" narrowly or selfishly, because they will be aware, to a greater or lesser extent, of community values, nature's requirements, system feedback patterns and the implications of mystery.
- Learn that people will inevitably see the world very differently and that individual views and reactions will therefore be highly diverse — the world can only operate successfully if we find the validity within various viewpoints. Careful and active listening is a core requirement for effectiveness.
- Discover that our ability to see, think, and respond together depends largely on how consciously and creatively we use our diversity to learn from the disturbances and changes we face, for they can show us the opportunities of our time.
- Support the emergence of new systems which will enable us to continue to grow without damaging the ecological patterns on which we depend for survival.

▌WHAT GOOD CAN CONVERSATIONS DO?

When two people enter into conversation a larger dynamic comes into being, one that embraces but is larger than both of them taken separately. When three people become involved the dynamic grows further, and as more join in, it continues to change, taking on the dynamic properties of a creative system. Information is exchanged, ideas are born, and cognitive vistas arise that extend beyond the reach of the separate individuals who make up the group. When these individuals also communicate in other such groups, they become conduits for connecting these groups, carrying information from one conversation to another, and almost unwittingly guide the separate discussions toward common languages and values. If this process continues far enough, conversational loops form, and feedback dynamics become a reality.[10] The strength of the effect grows exponentially in a powerful autopoietic organizational dynamic involving the exchange of ideas. Human nature being what it is, however, ideas soon lead to action. So, if the powerful dynamics of sharing creative ideas are once set in motion, they will inevitably give birth to the next vital step of planning and initiating transformative activities.

As for forms of conversations, I personally feel that nothing substitutes for the old-fashioned face-to-face variety. This kind seems essential for deep listening and understanding other people's viewpoints, and for overcoming differences which separate us. I believe we cannot do without it. Nevertheless, much useful information can be exchanged in slower conversations that take place over great distances, using electronic connections such as e-mail and the world-wide-web. Some observers speculate that the world-wide-web itself may take on dynamic self-organizing properties of its own in time.[11] My own view, however, is that much of the work of bringing people into dialogue at a distance has already begun by email, first in the form of the early bit-net, and today more powerfully through the world-wide-web. The inexpensive, virtually instantaneous, and above all easy conversations that e-mail makes possible overcome distance and national barriers without effort and seem to bring the extra benefit of equality among conversants. A friendly and intelligent letter that arrives in one's inbox is most often answered in the same spirit. One has surprisingly little inclination to make value judgments based on whether the letter comes from someone of one's own background, or whether that person resides at the proper type of business, academic institution, or the like. From its very beginning, this democratic aspect of e-mail made it an important vehicle for connecting people of many backgrounds and geographical locations in productive conversations. It holds similar promise for conversations about the wiser living we need to upshift to a sustainable and peaceful world.

CHAPTER 24

UPSHIFTING THE BUSINESS MINDSET

STEVE RODGERS

The secret of change is to focus all of your energy, not on fighting the old, but on building the new. — Socrates

The word "business" is often used to refer to the activities and practices of commerce and industry, but its etymology and deeper meaning reveal a much more complex and nuanced concept. The Old English word "*bisignes*" means "a state of being occupied or engaged in," and being "occupied" or "engaged" in something implies a sense of purpose and intentionality. It suggests that the concept of business is not just about making money or conducting transactions but about a way of *being* in the world.

As human beings, we are driven by a need to engage with the world and make a positive impact. As a way of engaging with the world, a business can be seen as a reflection of this fundamental human drive. It can be understood as a way of fulfilling our purpose and mission and of making a positive impact on the world.

With this expanded understanding of the word and the idea of "business," we are better equipped to recognize that every human being is engaged in the act of "doing business" and that this is intrinsically tied to our purpose and mission here as a human being.

I often emphasize in my coaching and consulting that *everyone* is a leader. Whether we are a business leader, an entrepreneur, or an employee — we are all the CEO of our own life. We all have a choice in deciding how we will operate and what we will build and create with our time and energy. Therefore, you are engaged in doing business, and you are a business leader — no matter how that manifests in your life experience.

▌THE ROLE OF BUSINESS IN BUILDING THE PATH TO WISER LIVING

Throughout history, business has played a crucial role in shaping our world. From the earliest forms of trade and commerce to today's globalized economy, businesses have been drivers of progress and change. However, as the world faces increasingly complex and pressing problems, such as climate degradation, economic inequality, and political polarization, the question arises: amidst the current chaos and challenges, what is the role of business in finding and building a path to a better world?

One view is that the primary role of business is to generate profit and to create wealth. In this paradigm, businesses should focus solely on maximizing shareholder value and efficiency. However, this narrow perspective on the role of business ignores the fact that businesses are also powerful social and economic institutions that have the potential to shape society in positive ways.

The role of business in finding and building a path to a better world is multifaceted. Companies have the potential to create not only economic value but also social and environmental value. They are responsible for considering their actions' impact on society as a whole and striving to create positive change through job creation, promoting economic growth, investing in education and training, promoting sustainable practices, protecting the environment, and much more. By doing so, they can help to build a better, more just, and sustainable world for all.

As a former Warren Buffett CEO, one of the great highlights of working with his companies over the years is knowing that he pledged to give away over 99% of his wealth. And he went on to try and get other people to join him in making the same pledge.

> Were we to use more than 1% of my claim checks (Berkshire Hathaway stock certificates) on ourselves, neither our happiness nor our well-being would be enhanced. In contrast, that remaining 99% can have a huge effect on the health and welfare of others. — Warren Buffett

Individuals like Mr. Buffett have set a positive example by taking the wealth they have generated and investing it back into humanity. Now imagine if we lived in a world where most or all individuals who have had the good fortune, intelligence, and hard work to attain success are similarly committed to raising the rest of us up with them.

The young activist Greta Thunberg has recently become a voice for the younger generations and the urgent need for immediate changes in how we do business and live our lives: "You say that you love your children above everything else. And yet you are stealing their future in front of their very eyes."

Greta reminds us to think about our children and grandchildren and the future world they will live in. The decisions we make today will directly impact their lives and the planet they will inherit. We must consider the long-term consequences of our actions and make choices that will create a better future for them.

In my work coaching and consulting with entrepreneurs, business leaders, and a wide variety of companies, I have met and worked with people from all walks of life who are increasingly waking up to a greater purpose that can be accomplished through their business endeavors. I see a shift happening in the collective consciousness of humanity, and that brings me great hope, but there are still great challenges to overcome.

▌HOW WE DO BUSINESS IS A REFLECTION OF OUR STATE OF CONSCIOUSNESS

The way we do business is a reflection of our state of consciousness. Our approach to business reflects our beliefs, values, and attitudes, manifesting our inner state of being.

In a materialistic worldview, the primary focus of business is profit and material gain. In this view, business is seen as a means to an end, with the ultimate goal being acquiring wealth and power. However, this materialistic approach to business is based on the belief that material wealth is the key to happiness and fulfillment. This belief is limiting, as it ignores the fact that true satisfaction and joy come from deeper, intangible sources.

As we evolve spiritually and morally, our understanding of the world and our place in it deepens. This leads to a shift in our values, beliefs, and, ultimately, our approach to business. As a result, our business practices become more aligned with our inner state of being and our understanding of the interconnectedness of all things.

A more spiritual or "upshifted" approach to business recognizes that true wealth and fulfillment come from a deeper understanding of the nature of reality and our place in it. In this view, business is seen as a way to serve and contribute to the greater good.

▌UPSHIFTING THE BUSINESS MINDSET

In the 20th and 21st centuries, businesses became increasingly profit-driven at the expense of the environment, human health, and the human spirit. It is essential to recognize the negative impact of these practices and to work towards a more conscious and responsible approach to business that prioritizes the well-being of our societies, our people, and our Earth environment over short-term financial gain.

There are many ways in which businesses can change their mindset, philosophy, and practices to "do well by doing good" in the world and to contribute to a better society for everyone. The phrase "doing well by doing good" refers to the idea that a business can achieve financial success while positively impacting society and the environment.

For a business to do this, it must operate with a deeper consciousness and intention behind every aspect and every individual in the company. This means the business must have a clear sense of purpose and values that are reflected in all aspects of its operations. This includes its products and services, its supply chain, its treatment of employees, and its impact on the environment. This "upshifted" company also recognizes its success is intimately connected to the well-being of *all* stakeholders, including shareholders, employees, customers, and the communities in which it operates.

When a business and its leadership "walks the talk" and lives in alignment with their values, it helps to create a positive culture within the organization, and it also helps to build trust with customers, shareholders, and other stakeholders.

Studies show the ever-growing importance of socially responsible companies. For example, one study found that ninety percent of consumers feel trust and loyalty to socially accountable companies over companies that aren't, and 92 percent of consumers seek out products that support a good cause.

CHANGES IN WHAT WE VALUE AND HOW WE EXCHANGE IT

Service is the rent we pay for being. It is life's very purpose, not something you do in your spare time. — Marian Wright Edelman

Upshifting one's mindset and way of operating in the realm of business is changing one's perspective and approach to align with the inevitable future of business.

One example of a new way is found in B Corporations. This is a legal structure that lets the world know exactly where you and your company's intention lie. B Corps are for-profit companies certified by the non-profit organization B Lab to meet rigorous social and environmental performance standards, accountability, and transparency.

The B Corp certification is a way for companies to demonstrate their commitment to creating a positive impact on society and the environment and to be held accountable for meeting those commitments. To become certified, a company must pass a rigorous assessment of its social and environmental performance and amend its legal governing documents to include language committing to consider the impact of its decisions on all stakeholders, including workers, customers, suppliers, the community, and the environment.

Examples of B Corps include Patagonia, Ben & Jerry's, Allbirds, Bombas, Warby Parker, and Eileen Fisher. These companies are known for their commitment to sustainability and ethical business practices and have been recognized for their leadership in using business as a force for good.

Business is a fundamental aspect of human society as it concerns how we create and exchange value. Value can be defined as the worth or usefulness of something, and in business, it is the exchange of goods and services that creates value. How we create and exchange value has evolved, is currently rapidly changing, and will continue to transform as human consciousness evolves to be more holistic and aware of our interconnectedness with the earth, nature, and other human beings.

Historically, the primary focus of business has been on economic value, which is the exchange of goods and services for money. However, as society becomes more aware of the impact of business on the environment, culture, and individuals, we are beginning to see a shift toward a more holistic view of value. This holistic view of value includes economic, humanistic, social, environmental, and spiritual values.

In the very near future, we may live in a world where value is placed much more on the things that truly enrich and uplift ourselves individually and collectively. This shift in values would be reflected in the business sphere, and it would be those entrepreneurs, companies, products, and services that can deliver higher value in a holistic, sustainable, and integral manner that will thrive.

▎HOW BUSINESSES OPERATE IN A NEW CONSCIOUSNESS PARADIGM

Here is a short list of practical things a business or entrepreneur can do to change their paradigms and mindsets from old, outdated ways of looking at profit and success to new, more conscious, and holistic perspectives and actions:

- *Adopt a long-term perspective*: Rather than focusing solely on short-term profits, businesses can adopt a long-term perspective and prioritize sustainable growth and long-term value creation for all stakeholders.

- *Prioritize social and environmental impact*: Businesses benefit by prioritizing social and environmental impact and making conscious decisions to minimize negative and maximize positive impact. This can be achieved by implementing responsible practices such as using renewable energy, reducing waste and emissions, and incorporating sustainable materials and production methods.

- *Prioritize ethical behavior*: Businesses should prioritize ethical behavior and social responsibility in their operations. This can include engaging in fair trade, ethically sourcing materials and products, and valuing high ethical standards in all employees from top to bottom.

- *Create a positive culture*: Businesses can create a positive culture within the organization that prioritizes creativity, collaboration, and open communication. This can foster employee engagement and satisfaction.

- *Invest in education and training*: Successful businesses invest in education and training for employees to help them adapt to new technologies, paradigms, and ethical behavior.

- *Collaborate and partner with other organizations*: Businesses that collaborate with other organizations, including other businesses, non-profits, and government, to address societal needs and challenges and create shared value generate exponentially more goodness and positivity.

- *Measure and track progress*: Measuring and tracking progress in terms of sustainability, social impact, and ethical behavior can inform decision-making and improve performance over time. I teach others to do this through the 4 B's — Body, Being, Bonds, and Business.

- *Communicate transparently*: Businesses that communicate transparently about their operations, performance, and impact build trust and credibility with customers, employees, and other stakeholders.

Keep in mind, this list is just an initial outline, and there is much more that goes into an "upshifted" approach to business.

▌A TIME FOR ACTION

The question now before us is: what will you do with the roadmaps in this book to help you live wiser on the planet? You must first answer that question for yourself — internally in your mind, your heart, and your soul.

I have shared some concepts, some ideas, and some insights. I've pointed out a particular direction that has transformed my life and many other entrepreneurs and business leaders with whom I have worked over the past few decades. But all these nice-sounding concepts are meaningless if they are not put into practice and engaged with through your own experience.

It is not all that difficult. But it does require self-honesty and the willingness to know your deepest principles and to align your life and professional work with them. I promise you that, if you do, it will not hinder your professional success. Implementing these changes will supercharge your creativity and impact in the world in ways you cannot imagine from your current state of consciousness.

As stated at the beginning, the world of business does not just play a secondary role in the Upshift into a better world; the truth is that business is the primary expression of our creativity and where we choose to put the focus of our time and energy as well as how we exchange goods and services of value. Therefore, it is absolutely essential that the way we do business and the consciousness behind all of our choices and actions are aligned with the world in which we wish to live. The rapid changes occurring in our world and within human beings mean that very soon, it will only be those businesses which are operating ethically and with a deeper purpose that will survive and thrive.

I look forward to working with today's and tomorrow's business leaders to help the business world evolve to the next level of "doing well by doing good." I hope you will join us!

CHAPTER 25

SHIFTING TO A RESONATING WORLD: THE GREAT UPSHIFT FOR BUSINESS

DAVID TALMOR

The Informed Path to wiser living speaks to alignment of our approaches and activities as humans with the approaches and activities of the world around us. Upshift for Business guides business toward operating within the context of the Resonating World. Business owners gain an initial understanding of Upshift for Business with an understanding of how the world works,[12] which is energies.[13]

Our understanding of how the world works is based on the views of Nikola Tesla and Albert Einstein. Nikola Tesla said, "If you wish to find the secrets of the universe think in terms of energy, frequency, and vibration,"[14] and translated this into understanding of the connections between people when he said, "To know each other we must reach beyond the sphere of our sense perceptions."[15] Albert Einstein emphasized the importance of energies when he said, "Concerning matter, we have been all wrong. What we have called matter is energy, whose vibration has been so lowered as to be perceptible to the senses. There is no matter."[16] He is purported to have brought this to human-actionable terms: "Everything is energy, and that's all there is to it. Match the frequency of the reality you want, and you cannot help but get that reality. It can be no other way. This is not philosophy. This is physics."[17] At the same time, Einstein made clear his disdain for commercial considerations: "I was originally supposed to become an engineer but the thought of having to expend my creative energy on things that make practical everyday life even more refined, with a loathsome capital gain as the goal, was unbearable to me."[18] Everything is energy, and one of the inherent characteristics of energies is resonating, and from this it follows, as the light follows the dark, that it's a Resonating~World.

It is worth a brief moment to start to absorb what this means. As we look around and see a things-world, in which the physical is everything and we think that the world is as we see/hear/smell/touch/taste it, we can start to overlay a sensing of the energies-world onto this and a recognition of what an energies-world feels like. When we sense an energies-world everything is flowing, everything comes from the energies that proceeded it and will continue with the energies that will follow it, and we sense into the past and the future within the flows we sense now. Based on this Resonating~World understanding,[19] we can see and sense everything differently — individuals,[20] couples,[21] communities,[22] the natural world, etc. — and for our purposes, we will focus on how this perspective allows us to understand business differently.

As mentioned above, the first key aspect of an energies-world is that everything in it is resonating, and the second key aspect is that every "thing" (collection of energies) has a Natural Frequency[23] at which it vibrates. This is very important — every thing/system has its inherent Natural Frequency but is subject to vibrations of everything around it which are, for that object, Forced Frequencies[24] which disturb it from its Natural Frequency. A system is functioning best when it is at its authentic Natural Frequency, and there is great value in recognizing and addressing Forced Frequencies that may affect a system. In fact, for people, the disruption of Natural Frequencies by Forced Frequencies has been described by one of the leading experts on this topic as the biggest cause of stress on the planet: "The lack of alignment to our deepest self is the biggest unrecognized stress on Earth."[25]

Now, let's talk business. How do Nikola Tesla's and Albert Einstein's views relate to business? The first answer is obvious — this is the way the world works, and business is of the world, so business is completely part of this and affected by this and should be viewed from this perspective. To put it in energies terms: everything is connected, and the energies of business resonate with the energies of everything else, either as a Natural Frequency that aligns with and supports the functioning of the world or as a Forced Frequency that disturbs the world's Natural Frequency. Similarly, a business owner and a business each have a Natural Frequency that may be disrupted by Forced Frequencies. This is not a socio-political position but rather an approach that clarifies the reality of how the world in which we live works and provides tools for relating to business and how it functions.

The Upshift Movement[26] advocates that people relate to the world with a vision of "wiser living," and Upshift for Business[27] advocates that business owners relate to the world with a vision of "wiser working." The Upshift for Business model combines the principles of Upshift[28] and Resonating~Business[29] and applies them to business. The process starts with the owner of the business ensuring that the owner's Natural Frequencies are clearly sensed — what is the owner's vision for his/her role and the business' role for themselves, for their community, and for the world? The process then expands to the business to align the company's frequencies with those of the owner as well as to examine alignment with the employees, customers, suppliers, and the world around it.

Understanding energies is of course an important aspect of Upshift for Business. Learning to identify and distinguish between Natural Frequencies, which make up the essence of a business/person/etc., and Forced Frequencies, which are distracting and often damaging energies, is basic to creating an Upshift for Business environment. With practice, a person can distinguish between the various shades of gray that make up the noise of Forced Frequencies and identify the bright yellow energies of Natural Frequency which are also the energies of Upshift. Upshift is about thinking cleaner, thinking wider, thinking higher, breaking away from the little things and the limitations and the noises, and envisioning and acting according to the principle "be the change you wish to see in the world."[30] Or as the verse in the Bible says: go find yourself, find the right environment for you and the place in life that you feel is right for you, and follow your spirit to the place that it will lead you to.[31] We add here that you should bring your business with you.

With these understandings, we can bring real change and impact to business owners, to businesses, and to the world. This informed path can be completely incorporated into our thinking about business and how business functions in the world. Techniques that may be used to actualize Upshift for Business include the following.

As described above, undertake a process that Upshifts the business owner and the business. The radiating energies of the Upshift for Business process start personally with the energies of the owner of the business, in which the owner's Natural Frequency is distinguished from the Forced Frequency by which the owner may actually live much of his or her life. This "wiser living" for the owner then flows to "wiser working" for the business. This approach also corrects an artificial creation that is the basis of business, that there is a separate independent entity of business apart from the personal. Perhaps the falseness of this assumption was expressed most dramatically, if not most pleasantly, in one of the most famous business-oriented books (made into one of the most famous business-oriented movies) of all time: "Tom, don't let anybody kid you. It's all personal, every bit of business. Every piece of s--- every man has to eat every day of his life is personal. They call it business. OK. But it's personal as hell."[32] Upshift for Business takes this personal-business continuum in a very positive direction, of incorporating and even flourishing the personal aspects of what we've come to consider as "business," starting with the owner of a business. The idea and process of Upshift for a person are laid out in *The Upshift* by Ervin Laszlo.[28]

Ask the business what-if question — if the business weren't about money, what would it be about? The answer to this question points toward the Natural Frequency/Essence of the business. In fact, the process of answering this question helps to release the mind from some of its locked-in understandings and open it toward how Upshift for Business can be expressed. The definition of Business Purpose[33] is often overlooked, framed in terms of market positioning/branding, or laid out as financial objectives or competitive strategy. Upshift for Business takes the definition of business in a different direction by focusing on a business within the context of the larger world around it. This can perhaps be understood most easily by thinking in terms of an individual — while many individuals are interested in making money this does not mean that they see making money as their purpose in life. That is, even within the context of work, an individual defines goals in life other than making money and which making money might serve, and an individual may define the purpose of life altogether differently in terms not related to money.

Within the Upshift for Business approach, this is extended to the business — what is the business' role in the world? For example, it is a very large shift for a business to move its definition of itself from Corporate

Capitalism to Profitable Peopleism — both definitions provide for the role of money in the purpose of the business but differ greatly in whether the company exists to make money or whether the company makes money while undertaking its goal of advancing matters of people such as its employees, customers, neighbors, etc. The Upshift for Business process serves to expand upon the Upshift of the owner of the business, of everyone whom the business touches, and of the world as a whole.

Bring the Essence/Noise conversation into the company culture, which brings Upshift focus into all aspects of the business. Language is an incredibly powerful tool in any situation, and the language of Upshift for Business is a very important aspect of undertaking the process, including use of a vocabulary that reflects the energies aspects of business. As above, thinking at a personal level can be a good foundation for thinking at a business level. In things we hear/see/feel during our daily lives, which part of it is the Noise that is continuously all around us, and which part of it is Essential authentic energy that we should relate to as such? The Essence-Noise sensor is one we develop just as any other sensor we may have or want to put in place, and with practice, distinguishing between Essence and Noise can become an integral part of our thought/feeling process. Once this occurs within ourselves on a personal level, we can then utilize this sensor related to business. This becomes part of the Upshift for Business process, with the Upshifting meaning that the business knows how to identify and act on the Essential and at the same to identify and properly relate to the Noise that is continuously present.

There are many additional aspects of the Informed Path philosophy that may be integrated into the Upshift for Business approach. The Informed Path describes the critical importance of many energies-oriented processes such as the Butterfly Effect, radiating emotions such as love, human consciousness, life and death, forest bathing, the "aesthetic experience" and sensory experience, the biosphere, an all-pervading intelligence, evolution, "the Force" and attractors, and the ultimate oneness of the World — all of these speak to the Resonating~World and may be adapted for inclusion in the Upshift for Business approach.

The presentation and operation of Upshift for Business will be fully supported with appropriate technology starting with its website[27] and extending through the tools used to demonstrate, implement, and operate the approach. Application and adaptation of techniques such as healing/yoga/ etc. for a business environment will also be included.

In this spirit, we summarize Upshift for Business by saying that in addition to being about business, it's about the world and about ourselves and about really essential things. It's about the future that we are all constantly creating whether we choose to think about it or not. It turns out that combining Upshift with Resonating~Business can be a beautiful way to help us align with the Resonating~World in which we live.

CHAPTER 26

A COCKTAIL OF YOGA AND AI

SUNIL MALHOTRA

To harness the full human potential in a unique partnership with Artificial Intelligence ("AI"), we need an 'intuitive reasoning' approach, a kind of spiritual, whole-brain, holistic, and systemic view. In a world of growing strife, fear, anxiety, polarization, and conflict, we need simple and practical solutions for people to manage themselves and the ever-increasing instability all around. Add to these a new rabbit out of the hat — AI. With ChatGPT hijacking attention towards the end of 2022, AI is being deconstructed every which way; one camp speaks of it as existential threat and destroyer of jobs and the other as AI being the next step in the evolution of humanity.

Likewise, other exponential technologies including augmented and virtual reality (AR, VR), digital biology and biotech, medicine, nanotech, digital fabrication, robotics, and autonomous vehicles, among others, are hurtling on their own trajectory, leaving most people dazed and confused. An already unintelligible world is becoming even more difficult for people to relate to and to navigate.

Yet, all of this ignores deeper and more fundamental issues — *Has our quest for more led to less understanding of ourselves? Is it lack of understanding of ourselves that is having us make more out of what is than there is? Are we being driven by fear of the unknown?*

Part of the reason for our anxiety and consequent inability to deal with uncertainty is our inadequate understanding of our own mind-body-spirit system. And as for the world outside, it is safe to say that it has already gone out of human control.

Our anxiety does not come from thinking about the future but from wanting to control it. — Kahlil Gibran

▌THE CHATGPT HOOPLA

The sudden yet expected "open" arrival of GPT technology in November of 2022 destroyed the myth that humans have any degree of control on the speed and scale of technological proliferation. Barely one month in, the Large Language Model based artificial intelligence, ChatGPT, boasted of 100 million users worldwide and threatened to disrupt almost every domain from education to medicine to law to politics to technology to everything else. By April of 2023, people were running scared; several AI experts and business leaders called for an immediate stop to further development of AI. Their reaction is not surprising given that humans are not good at accepting sudden change, much less handling its effects. The reaction is a biological response of the amygdala, an organ responsible for the human fight-or-flight response, which has barely evolved since the hunter-gatherer times.[34] It is our survival meter. The petitioners seemed powerless in containing the potential spread of a runaway AI, having been caught unawares by a contemporary version of Frankenstein's 'monster.' In a hilarious twist of irony, the violators became their own victims.

Simon Biggs, a professor of interdisciplinary arts at the University of Edinburgh, foretells, "AI will function to augment human capabilities. The problem is not with AI but with humans. As a species we are aggressive, competitive and lazy. We are also empathic, community minded and (sometimes) self-sacrificing. We have many other attributes. These will all be amplified. Given historical precedent, one would have to assume it will be our worst qualities that are augmented. My expectation is that in 2030 AI will be in routine use to fight wars and kill people, far more effectively than we can currently kill. ... We cannot expect our AI systems to be ethical on our behalf – they won't be, as they will be designed to kill efficiently, not thoughtfully."

The hype around the ethical implications of GPT and the frenzied call by US business and technology leaders to *'shut down AI'* are harbingers of the age we have stepped into, an age of anxiety and uncertainty.

▌UPSHIFTING THE COLLECTIVE MIND

Back in 1999, in *The Consciousness Revolution: A Transatlantic Dialogue: Two Days with Stanislav Grof, Ervin Laszlo, and Peter Russell*, Ervin Laszlo, two-time nominee of the Nobel Peace Prize, and systems philosopher, had already observed:

> We, as individuals, are not prisoners of our own cranium and locked in our skin, but are intimately tied in with one another, and possibly with all life on this planet. So that when there is a situation like we have at present, where a real danger is facing all of us,

there is something which, though most people are not aware of it consciously, is penetrating their mind, putting up warning signs, focusing on change, providing impetus.

There may be forces operating in this world beyond the usual economic and political and social forces. The fact is that there are time-lags built into the dynamics of our world, and they are considerable. We would have had to change yesterday, so to speak, to head off the crisis tomorrow. But if there is something in our collective unconscious which can diffuse into our individual consciousness, then the situation becomes more hopeful.

Well-nigh quarter of a century later, we are still exploring the possibility of a more evolved collective consciousness, while the narrative remains one of gloom and doom. Global warming, political uncertainty, the Russia Ukraine war, the China Taiwan standoff, the relentless COVID-19 pandemic, the economic meltdown ... we could go on. The systemic fragility of the present times is exacerbated by new technologies, geopolitical instability, the climate crisis, and an outmoded economic paradigm. All these are deeply intertwined, making each more and more difficult to solve.

What preoccupies us most of our waking life is just trying to process the stream of stimuli being thrown at us, now coming at a pace that is mind-boggling (pun unintended), leaving us little time or energy to understand our own selves. The times are not going to slow down, and trying furiously to keep up with everything around is an exercise in futility.

The bodymind instrument, attracted by sense objects, is designed to go outward via the senses — eyes see forms, ears hear sounds, skin feels touch, tongue tastes flavors, and the nose smells fragrances — whose inputs are processed by our minds to give us the experiences we keep having throughout our lives. Yoga and allied practices, such as meditation, come out on top for their promise of deep relaxation, combating anxiety, treating depression, fighting mood swings, boosting immunity, and whatnot. These powers apart, the true purpose of Yoga (and meditation) has always been spiritual. Call it God realization, enlightenment, self realization, or whatever else. Yoga, therefore, qualifies as the system of choice for the inner journey, and for the much needed understanding of who we are and our place in relation to everything else in Nature.

The dominant worldview wants us to believe that winning the competition for money, possessions, social position, power, and fame is enough to make us happy. However, as we were told in the Economics 101 class, all worldly gain is governed by the first law of economics, the inescapable law of diminishing marginal utility.

Ervin Laszlo explains:

[We must] become aware of a deeper evolutionary drive (expressed in various ways in Eastern philosophies as evolution itself; as the dao, as development, as going towards a sacred level of existence). I believe that all of us have this mystic drive or tendency which I call an attractor — to use systems language, an attractor toward coherence — which is the key to coherence within these with ourselves and with the world around us, and what we are trying to do by bringing artificial intelligence and yoga together is to introduce a new connection between them, and between them and life; our human existence aims at making things more coherent, more understandable.

Our internal workings are well within reach; the serenity prayer comes to our aid here, "… grant me the serenity to accept the things I cannot change, the courage to change the things I can, and the wisdom to know the difference."

▌YOGA AND AI?

The biggest similarity between Yoga and AI is that both are barely under-stood, and often misunderstood. The former spreads its roots in the mysti-cal past; the latter tenuously lays claim on the future of scientific endeavor. Yoga is a misunderstood discipline, and artificial intelligence is a some-what muddled fantasy. Never have these been on the same page, much less in the same book.

Both Yoga and AI have been kept out of reach. For most, the priesthood of AI experts keeps it as unintelligible as the mysticism cornered by Yoga gurus; shrouding them in mystery helps these select few to exploit them for their own gain. They can both, however, be put to the service of human-ity by democratizing and demystifying them. As different as the two may seem, there is a thread that ties them together in ways that makes both more understandable and useful in our daily lives and work.

AI has brought humanity to the brink of a dramatic shift that has chal-lenged the very basis of humanity's perch at the pinnacle of evolution. Our position as nature's ultimate achievement may soon be displaced by the far greater intelligence of AI. Beyond the obvious constraints of duality, of whether humans will be subjugated by AI or will it be the converse, the question changes to: *"Is there a third way — can we craft a strategy to coexist as friends and coevolve as partners with AI?"*

This is where Yoga can make the big difference. The technology of Yoga teaches us how to go inside and integrate with the source of our being. Yoga is already accepted, even in the West, as a holistic mindbody fitness practice for individuals. We need to discard the misconception that Yoga involves a quest only for personal growth and freedom without a concern for the larger social welfare; it may well serve as the next collective evolu-tion to harmonize humanity and a planet functioning as a single organism.

Going beyond our familiar — and largely superficial — understanding, Yoga is a technology, a system encompassing *philosophies, principles, and practices* to discipline, control (yoke), and still the mind.

But where is the need to still the mind? And to what effect? If we wanted to bridge the inner being with the external world, in a kind of whole-brain thinking that combines rational, Western scientific thought with intuitive spiritual understanding, Yoga would be the ideal candidate. Bridging these opposing dimensions — internal and external, West and East, science and mysticism, individual and collective, technology and consciousness, left and right brain, among other tensions — needs a new understanding.

Yoga and AI working together can dramatically improve the quality of daily living; you can leverage both 'technologies' in resolving the inside-outside dichotomy. Yoga teaches us to observe all repetitive thought patterns by which we have been programmed, to spontaneously manifest an unprecedented level of neural coherence.

WTF — WHAT'S THE FUTURE?

We have stepped upon the ledge of a perception revolution. According to the late James Lovelock, "New beings will emerge from existing artificial intelligence systems. They will think 10,000 times faster than we do and they will regard us as we now regard plants … These hyper-intelligent beings will be as dependent on the health of the planet as we are. They will need the planetary cooling system of Gaia to defend them from the increasing heat of the sun as much as we do. And Gaia depends on organic life. We will be partners in this project." "It is crucial," Lovelock argued, "that the intelligence of Earth survives and prospers."[35]

As individuals take charge of their own destiny, instead of relying on traditional institutions to contain existential problems, systems like Yoga become essential. The fiasco of the Western narrative, abject failure of global business and political leadership, and rejection of greed-driven extractive practices have unleashed massive energy across societies, calling for urgent change. India's resilience, spiritual traditions, diversity, innate innovation culture, advanced scientific (even if undocumented) history, etc. can help point to a new direction and offer tools and techniques for value-based life and commerce.

Several Westerners as well as the most successful people in other parts of the world have shown how spirituality not only matters, but also is the only quest worth our while. The most visible and direct understanding of spirituality is the undeniable connectedness of everything we see around us. Conventional religion is sought after for improving one's lot in worldly terms or other-worldly outcomes. Yoga is meant for spiritual seekers, meaning for the higher religion of God realization. If one does not like the word God, it could simply be seen as the search for oneSelf.

"Western Science is approaching a paradigm shift of unprecedented proportions, one that will change our concepts of reality and of human nature, bridge the gap between ancient wisdom and modern science, and reconcile the differences between Eastern spirituality and Western prag-matism," wrote Stanislav Grof in *Beyond the Brain*.

In order to understand ourselves and our connection with the cosmic order, we must use practices that give us confidence and comfort. In its full glory, Yoga is a comprehensive system. The most authoritative text on the subject, *The Yoga Sutras*, was compiled in the early centuries CE, by the sage Patanjali in India who synthesised and organised knowledge about yoga from much older traditions. Patanjali's Yoga Sutras shows one path, meditation (Rāja Yoga), to the ultimate knowledge of the Self through a

spiritual practice that strives to seamlessly "join" the Self and the world —
the spirit and the mind-body — into one single consciousness.

Best known for its reference to Ashtānga, eight elements or limbs of practice, culminating in Samādhi (Self realization), Yoga addresses preparatory
as well as realizations steps — the popular breath control (Prānayāma),
postures (Āsana), and meditation (Dhyāna) taught in 'gym yoga' are sand-
wiched between. The eightfold path of Patanjali's Yoga consists of a set of
prescriptions for a morally disciplined and purposeful life. The second
verse of Patanjali's Yoga Sutras simply states *"yogas chitta vritti nirodha,"*
which translates to *"complete quietness and peace of the mind is Yoga"* — in
other words, getting rid of the modifications of the mind. By cultivating a
particular kind of awareness of the Self, a person can immediately recognize the egoic stuff such as self-centred emotions, impulses, motivations,
and thoughts.

> We now see that all the various forms of cosmic energy, such as
> matter, thought, force, intelligence and so forth, are simply the
> manifestations of that cosmic intelligence, or, as we shall call it
> henceforth, the Supreme Lord. Everything that you see, feel, or
> hear, the whole universe, is His creation, or to be a little more
> accurate, is His projection; or to be still more accurate, is the Lord
> Himself. It is He who is shining as the sun and the stars, He is the
> mother earth.... He is the speech that is uttered, He is the man who
> is talking. He is the audience that is here ... It is all He. — Swami
> Vivekananda (1896)

Karan Singh shared this mind-bending proposition:

> There has been a theory for many years which Nobel Laureate
> George Wald discussed with me to the effect that ours is a "mind

breeding universe" and that the whole object of evolution was to create a being who could become aware of the greater consciousness. In other words, a being through which the universe could look into itself. This is an interesting thesis and Artificial Intelligence has become a major factor in the next step of our evolution. However, as with many such innovations, it is a double-edged weapon, misused it can become a real threat to the human race, as the late Stephen Hawking, Bill Gates and Elon Musk have all warned.

That Nature needs to understand herself for which it uses the mechanism of evolution can have startling implications for AI. We seem blindsided by our anthropomorphic view of everything, taking for granted that the superiority of our species will remain unchallenged forever. We are convinced that AI is going to 'obey' our commands since it is we who have created these 'machines.' Unlike traditional software, AI is no longer dependent on programming by human engineers. It learns mostly by continuous observation, creating artificial neural networks, branching them, and pruning them for more coherent connections. Since AI learns by simply watching the world and the humans around it, much like children do, it will reflect the global human mind with all its imagined & imaginative capabilities, and even the mind of Nature in all her diversity.

In the words of Garry Kasparov,[36] among the world's longest reigning chess grandmasters:

> Unlike in the past, when machines replaced farm animals, manual labor, now they are coming after people with college degrees and political influence. And as someone who fought machines and lost, I am here to tell you this is excellent, excellent news. Eventually, every profession will have to feel these pressures or else

it will mean humanity has ceased to make progress. We don't get to choose when and where technological progress stops. We cannot slow down. In fact, we have to speed up. Our technology excels at removing difficulties and uncertainties from our lives, and so we must seek out ever more difficult, ever more uncertain challenges.

Machines have calculations. We have understanding.
Machines have instructions. We have purpose.
Machines have objectivity. We have passion.

We should not worry about what our machines can do today. Instead, we should worry about what they still cannot do today, because we will need the help of the new, intelligent machines to turn our grandest dreams into reality.

"We must learn to reawaken and keep ourselves awake," Henry David Thoreau wrote, in contemplating what it really means to be awake, adding: "Only one in a million is awake enough for effective intellectual exertion, only one in a hundred million to a poetic or divine life."

CHAPTER 27

A THOUGHT EXPERIMENT

MICHAEL CHARLES TOBIAS

The question before us, the fate of humanity, calls for representing by a set of numbers and subsets that cannot be reconciled. As with all existing unanswerables, we ponder the societal implications of individual behavior, noting that historically there has never been a friendly mob, yet people, alone or in small conversation, can proffer quiet, lovely, and non-violent paradigms. This paradox bedevils norms and projections, polls and statistical extrapolations, the chimeric core of science and engineering, and the demise of a natural life.

As with all environmental fate, use and reuse of materials, cycling conditions and ecological flux, have never allowed for a status quo, either in geological or biological timeframes. In the case of our eight billion and counting dyspeptic souls, our history is but one of countless metrics that would behoove us to consider seriously — the relations of mass and energy and the nature of photons, another. But ultimately, we are referring to the present time. All that has come before us happens with the perennial throw-weight of this instant. We must answer to ourselves, and recognize that in posing the questions, we are entrusting our conceptual restlessness to a biosphere where other species' lives hang utterly in the balance of our choices. Tens of thousands of viral and bacterial species vie with us for dominance, battlefields we did not choose. Serengeti models of predation (Lotka/Volterra, etc.) bring into the discourse our ability to resolve differences, or be destroyed by them, a reflection of what our kind has already done, in rapid succession, to the majority of remaining other large >50 kg vertebrates. What is now likened to, not a sixth, but a seventh extinction spasm.

Is our near-term future simply a given? Or will we have to do something to shepherd it along day by day? Ukrainians, Haitians, Somalis, Yemeni, Congolese, all those caught up in the seismic whorls of collapsing systems. Various famines, distributed chronic malnutrition (affecting nearly one billion of our kind at present) have a single focus; what we (Jane Gray Morrison and I) have elsewhere termed the "Pain Points Index." It refers to all species — comprising trillions of individuals who are slaughtered for human consumption or destroyed by opportunism in the wild. It tells a vague story of Social Darwinian crimes against humanity, and by far greater implication, the earth, both as a mirror and catastrophic impact; of hatreds and oppressions, of massacres and disastrous entanglements we are, all of us feeling at some frequency of the ecological tuning fork. A critical mass of *H. sapiens*, discouraged, at risk, depressed and frightened by the seemingly unique turn of events that is, in sum, the Mis-Anthropocene; compounded by the looming threat yet again of what the Bulletin of the Atomic Scientists liken with their "doomsday clock" to 100 seconds to midnight. For all those dying at this instant, they are, as poet James Dickey once wrote, "dying out." This is their last second to midnight.

We know well enough to mistrust simple anodynes — to eschew white noise parading as facile solutions to the unsolvable, buttressing greed, rapacity, and the astonishing gulf between trillion-dollar empires and more than a billion people who live on less than one dollar per day. But let us turn to a simple enough equation that encompasses the underscore of the most perilous, critical time in our species' — in most species' — history:

$$L = CEP \times 1^2\,(+1)$$

Where L is equivalent to any life form, by any phylogenetic definition, in common usage or not; C refers to "compound" as a verb, but also to "community," as in a community of life forms by association, a noun; E = expressive, in whatever manner of behavior (a totality of thoughts, morals and choices); and P is equivalent to Potential; 1^2 is to be perceived as a rational number with a repeating decimal, implicative of a population with unwavering collective consumer impacts; and +1 references the all-important final narrative, an individual who survives and overcomes the current and coming ordeals, that one final measure of humanity and kindness, of sanity and tolerance, that will not be stayed.

The (+1) assumes a survivor and is added to a population whose growth — linear, non-linear, exponential, erratic, rational, irrational — nonetheless prevails, by whatever means. We cannot divine outcomes or forecast the cumulative, syncretistic tumult that is upon us. But we can irrefutably insist on the freedom, the dignity, and compassion of a theoretical individual who represents coherence within complexity. By common assent, even amongst a diminished hamlet conforming to British anthropologist Robin Dunbar's "150" numeric designation for a sustainable number of hominids living together, we can envision from today's physical anthropological record any number of viable scenarios of human life on this earth in the near future. Such peoples include the Todas of Tamil Nadu and the Bishnoi of Rajasthan — and the millions of devoted followers of PETA (People for the Ethical Treatment of Animals). Of all those in kind-hearted unions and communities throughout the world who have conceded that a softer, gentler footprint is essential, and they are going to be the ones of all ages and persuasion who implement their local and regional pathways to getting there. By the powers vested in their parities and the power of spending differentiations, choices at the polling booths, consumer habits and daily conversations with others who will be turned round before the spellbinding obvious network of solutions in every domain.

Now, consider the following thought experiment (*Gedankenexperiment*) of the aforecited (+1) more deeply; a technique for jettisoning hypothetical propositions towards some salutary, solutions-driven point of view. Einstein's notes on his General Relativity Theory in 1905 occupied all of three pages. Other such experiments, like Ashoka's Edicts (268-232 BCE) were far more extensive. But a relatively similar motive catapults the thought experiment genre as documented from at least the time of the earliest Stone Age tool work, the first fire pits in East Africa (1.5 mya) and throughout the known cultural Middle and Late Paleolithic Periods that gave us emphatic and all-embracing signatures in the name of the Maltravieso cave in Spain, approximately 64,000 years old; the nearly 44,000-year old cave paintings at Maros-Pangkep in South Sulawesi, Indonesian Borneo; and a host of other spectacular cave painting sites from Timpuseng in Sulawesi (ca. 40,000 BCE) to Chauvet in France (ca. 30,000 BCE), and of course, Lascaux and Altamira.

Most recently, I was involved in the exploration of 11 rock sites and over 5,000 newly discovered petroglyphs and rock wall paintings throughout remote, largely unexplored canyon lands in the Tamaulipas State in northern Mexico, as well as the also recently discovered (2000) cave site known as Werehpai in southern Suriname, on the northern Brazilian border area deep in the Amazon, at Kwamalasamutu, home of the indigenous Trio and Wai-Wai peoples. In these two latter cases, particularly the first, in Mexico,

I managed to sit quietly for many hours and days meditating on the rich constellation of unknown species colorfully represented, along with pantheons of early human abstract and expressive symbolism — ladders to new galaxies; interspecies co-occupational communiques; mutualistic events, interdependencies, and symbiotic venerations.

At length, I photographed thousands of points and lattices of conceptually challenging artwork, entirely indebted to my great French mentor, André-Leroi Gourhan (1911–1986), whose comprehensive insights and computational biology featuring most of the major paleolithic sites throughout Europe, would tutor all of the 20th and early 21st centuries. He formulated cornerstones of the language and methodologies for approaching these endlessly labyrinthine, elusive components of our near ancestral, artistic heritage across every Western geographic vortex of philosophical speculation. In each of the great Paleolithic sites of genius, a common thread is readily discernible: the idea that our love and veritable worship of nature is a key to our survival, *or not*, as a species.

Early on in my quest to be immersed in some shamanic qualia of these sacred penetralia so powerfully utilized by our genetical and artistic ancestors, I discovered caves teeming with remarkable, Mondrian-like imagery which I examined by torchlight in a deep gorge, solo climbing in the 1960s near the Source du Pontet, and the Verneau complex in the Doubs department in France. I never revealed the whereabouts of the caves I discovered, nor what I was astonished to discover inside each.

From these modest expeditions, through the explicit lens of ecological matrices, and the accelerated data sets deriving from the latter-day ethological schools of biophilia, physiolatry, biosemiotics, bioacoustics, and quantum biosemiotics,[37] a most potent Gedankenexperiment has arisen in my deliberations concerning the International System of Units (SI). In 1948, the *Conférence Générale des Poids et Mesures* (CGPM) Resolution 7 embraced the *newton* as the signaler of *one unit of force*, that same measurement akin to humanity adopting the *second* as a basic fraction of our subjunctive time experiential. In either case, no one can actually convey the meaning of a newton or a second in common parlance. Nor was there anything down to earth, so to speak, about Einstein's reliance upon these agreed-to standards in formulating his elegant and seemingly simplistic $E = mc^2$.

How are we, in the 21st century, to accommodate Sir Isaac Newton's Second Law of Motion, which is intrinsic to Einstein's work? To imagine a single newton accelerating a single kilogram of mass by one second per second? Other units (Imperial, etc.) are commingled to single out in mathematical parlance pound-force, weight, mass, the nature of acceleration and deceleration, pressure, gravity, and all of the pre-figurations of classical quantum mechanics that have shifted the dialogue between specialists in their attempts to express the speed of light per second per second, and how it relates (relatively speaking) to the observer.

All of this breaks down into very practical if sinister engineering tactics and political strategy, like the tragedies enshrouding Hiroshima and Nagasaki, and the madness of Mutually Assured Destruction. Aeschylus and Shakespeare anticipated all of it. That is where, subsequently, the thought experiments turn fundamentally evil. Science (and the legacy of Einstein and compatriots) cannot eschew the ethical responsibilities of these machinations that have come to define the underlying threat, for example, in the current horror show that are Putin's psychotic war crimes committed in Ukraine by the hapless complicity of those hundreds of thousands of Russian troops conscripted beyond every red line of rational human experience to commit genocide.

The thought experiment that won Einstein and many others their Nobel Prizes has backfired in ways that mirror the Mis-Anthropocene (think of

Fritz Haber and Norman Borlaug, each Green Revolution heroes whose work also quickly showed the dark side), our species' apparent insistence, despite our fundamental kindness as individuals, on perpetuating the backfire as a paradoxical mode of being. The late sociobiologist E. O. Wilson questioned whether our species was, in fact, suicidal. This is no conjecture we can shove aside because the myriad examples of ecocide are raining down upon our eight billion and counting with a ramshackle, unrelenting illogic which all of us are conspiring — whether we realize it or not — to empower. Over a quiet breakfast in San Francisco with Wilson many years ago, he told me, in so many words, that he was desperately unsure — unsure of it all!

This paradox is indeed a make-or-break debacle. It poses the most fundamental and disturbing abyss our species — in some 350,000 years of its existence — has ever experienced/inflicted. We must take note of the experiment which devolves, ultimately, to the self-recognition, mirror test of the (+1). If this planet of miraculous biomes is to function, then $L = CEP \times 1^2$ (+1) needs to be tested. That is both the only direct scientific model, as well as the only practical one. Compound expressive potential realized in its various forms of impact on populations at large, as applied by an individual, one individual at a time in the irrepressible endeavor to cherish and preserve, to conserve and venerate life.

Consider a young girl, born without eyesight or limbs, who has heard and dreamt enough to know that she must somehow climb Mount Everest. Moreover, she insists on wearing only white clothing on the expedition, where she is helped along by fellow climbers and parents and Sherpas devoted to and inspired by her passion to accomplish this feat. This little girl makes it to the summit. As others who have accompanied her are celebrating like astronauts at 29,032 feet, the little girl suddenly throws herself off the summit, disappearing forever. Her friends, family, and loved ones — and the world — are stunned by this seemingly senseless suicide. And because she had insisted on wearing all white, her body — as if an entire civilization has vanished — will never be found. Why did she do it? What did she know that we don't know?

There are no equations for that kind of behavior. Nor, for that matter, could science have predicted a Sisyphus, or a John Kennedy saying that we chose to go to the moon not because it was easy but because it was hard. The fictional thought experiment of the little girl is also a (+1) in her enigmatic message to humanity. It is the same cautionary tale of which so many historians have warned: wars, disasters, collapses, the disappearance (as Arnold Toynbee documented) of 22 civilizations through their internecine violence and ecological overshoot. Witness Edward Gibbon on the final days of the Roman Empire, and the revelations of so many genocides and holocausts in human history.

That little theoretical girl atop Everest choosing to perish is not entirely a fiction. We see her rooted to much that now — in true quantum entanglement — confuses coherence and incoherence, the prevailing doctrines of human superiority versus the psycho-social development towards maturity that thinkers like Erik Erikson, or a Rachel Carson, back in the 1950s urged their fellow citizens to contemplate.

Humanity, as Paul R. Ehrlich and Robert E. Ornstein have written, now finds itself on a "tightrope." E. O. Wilson's query — Is humanity suicidal? — and the image of that ghost atop Everest, reflect the anatomical anomaly of human embryology. Many specialists have argued that our species is born too soon, our gestation cut short, with serious consequences.[38] 800,000+ people choose to commit suicide annually. 82 million other people are born and try to survive. At that birthrate, we are destined to see 10-to-12 billion humans teeming on this planet by 2100, assuming there is a year 2100. For some reason, the success of the long obsolete one-child policy in

China has now engendered what Chinese mouthpieces are calling a "demo-graphic crisis," as they call upon couples to have many more children. This is an insanity that comports with the biophysical truth that fertility, per se, does not connote biological success, and most of us who feel the pain inflicted by our kind must both privately and publicly confront the prom-ise and peril of so many precious individuals. (+1), however, leaps from the equation I have cited with astounding resources, imagination, dreams, and favorable hopes. This individual is not some cold calculus, neither lost in the wilds of quantum entanglement, or morose to the point of leaping from a mountaintop, having become, what many might think of, as the heroism of human life. Rather, this is someone who will be just as Nikos Kazantzakis once wrote, after he had come down from a wintry pilgrim-age to Mount Athos where upon he found a secluded courtyard in which stood an almond tree, struggling against the cold weather. He stepped up to that tree and said, "Sister, speak to me of God. And the almond tree blossomed."[39]

The mythopoesis of our coming days will go dark, blank, vanishing altogether, along with the entirety of our species, if our only exemplars and paradigms comprise hero worship, ventures into space and to the sea floors, conquest by the agency of superego and the dollar. Like never before we must seek to distance ourselves from the harsh statistics and equations outlining one misery after another. How difficult is it, really, to offer some food, some love, to another — a few organic soupçons (the more the better) to a little bird?

We are all strangers in this world, tied by nebulous claims and fast dis-appearing ancestors. Our DNA will not halt the storm clouds rapidly gath-ering over the surface of the planet while we sit back and take our potshots from the galleries. That will not do. It is, admittedly, easier to criticize than to proffer realistic assistance. But that is precisely the dominant theme of 21st century pan-biological survival.

We are all that little girl, and that little bird, born miraculously, but with the baggage of a writhing, short-lived past. Our cultural motifs today are pressing us to climb that mountain. Unseen, little spoken of, are those demonic forces from within — reacting to the many psychoses of our age — pushing us off summits in despair. We know it's true. We also know what we should do.

Our obligation, the one simple, moral duty we are all compelled to observe, acknowledge, and steward, is the preciousness and vulnerability of life herself. I am acquainted with many individuals who will agree. Many others could care less about these issues. If it's not a "30 second read," they are not interested, if there is interest at all. So, I implore readers to step out and begin: adopt orphans rather than siring more who are likely to suffer in this world; embrace veganism, a total non-violent regime of minimalist consumption; and partake of restraint and non-absolutism, of authentic voice and unrepressed feelings, of a singular expedition out into the wild barefoot and with no intention other than to love, to be guided by love, and to introduce calm and poetic revery into the illogic of everyday life. Realize that if you think it's bad now, it's going to get a lot worse. To be that +1, liberated outside the parentheses of any oddball equation, to be yourself, in all its authentic trappings, with a paramount focus upon the uniqueness of life on earth, it now perilously falls upon us to shoulder the courtesies and civility, the attuned compassion, and the sincere restraint that will collectively be necessary to save all those who remain. Short of that... a silence, beyond which we would never be forgiven.

CHAPTER 28

UPSHIFTING OUR THINKING: AN OVERVIEW

DAVID LORIMER

In Lewis Mumford's brilliant and prophetic book, *The Transformations of Man,* published in 1957, the final two chapters address world culture and human prospects. At the end of the previous chapter on post-historic man — 'a wholly subservient creature of the machine' — Mumford already refers to previous utopian aspirations to 'impose upon the whole community a common military discipline.... to banish the poet and artist.' Under such repressive systems, 'every form of privacy is either diminished or denied; every form of tender feeling is repressed. The end product is a community unified, centrally directed, uniformly responsive to command: freed from anxiety, insecurity, mischance or error; and by that fact equally freed from possibility of growth and improvement.' (p. 130) The danger is that superhuman technological powers can now be used for subhuman and ultimately dystopian purposes.

Mumford continues (p. 138) that 'Man's principal task is to create a new self, adequate to command the forces that now operate so aimlessly and yet so compulsively [even more so in our own time]. This self will necessarily take as its province the entire world, known and knowable, *and will seek, not to impose a mechanical uniformity, but to bring about an organic unity* (my italics).' He continues that 'such a culture must be nourished, not only by a new vision of the whole, but a new vision of the self capable of understanding and cooperating with the whole. In short, the time for another great historic transformation has come.' Even then, Mumford realized that 'the political unification of mankind cannot be realistically conceived except as part of this effort of self-transformation.' Since his time, we have seen the development of systems views of life, autopoiesis and self-organization, chaos and complexity theory, Gaia theory, epigenetics, experimental proof of non-locality, psychoneuroimmunology, holistic and mind-body medicine, and many other avenues explained in this volume. This means, as we have seen, that upshifting the world and upshifting ourselves are two sides of the same coin, or rather outer and inner mirrors of the same process.

Mumford's basic assumption (p. 142) is that 'the destiny of mankind, after its long preparatory period of separation and differentiation, is at last to become one' after the progressive widening of the base of human community. This new unity, as already explained above, 'lies at the other end from totalitarian uniformity' which technocratic forces are currently seeking to impose on us, as has been apparent over the last few years of cancelling and censorship of views that do not correspond to the mainstream narrative largely dictated by transnational business interests that have inordinate influence through campaign contributions on ostensibly democratic political processes, and who have captured regulatory agencies. Many commentators have remarked on the prescience of Aldous Huxley and George Orwell in this respect, and one should add C.S. Lewis, whose book *The Abolition of Man* also warned of the dehumanization implied in scientism, mechanistic metaphors, and the merging of human and machine on the basis that we are already nothing more than complex, carbon-based biological machines. The aspirations of this BOOK are clearly towards organic unity rather than mechanical uniformity. For me, organic unity also highlights the importance of the principles of decentralized community, localization, cooperation, reciprocity, and mutual aid based on personal I-Thou (Martin Buber) relationships rather than impersonal and bureaucratized I-It relations.

Like our contributors Alfred de Zayas and Elena Mustakova on principles of global order and unitive justice, Mumford insisted on an open society with basic human freedoms and securities as the very anchors of any form of world governance. These included freedom of thought and belief, freedom of expression, freedom of association, and freedom of movement and the securities of life and property, security from arbitrary arrest and coercion, and security from random violence. These have all been violated by recent government biosecurity measures, including unwarranted online coercion and digitally-enabled violation of the freedoms and securities listed above. This is a dangerous precedent, and people must stand together and insist on universal recognition of such freedoms and securities that are in fact already enshrined in key UN documents. And we must also resist the reduction of us as subjects to objects, of organisms to mechanisms, and of persons to things, while affirming intrinsic values and purpose.

Mumford expresses this by saying that 'our philosophy must respect the main attributes of life, balance and growth, freedom and choice, persistence and variation, adaptation and insurgence, above all, the tendency to self-actualization and self-transcendence.' (p. 182) He calls for a philosophy of the person based on integration, 'with values and goals already embodied.' He says (p. 184) that 'in the development of the person love is actually the central element of integration.' He adds, 'Without a positive concentration upon love in all its phases [including erotic desire, delight, fellow feeling, neighborly helpfulness, parental solicitude and sacrifice], we can hardly hope to rescue the earth and all the creatures that inhabit it from the insensate forces of hate, violence, and destruction that now threaten it. And without a philosophy of the person, who dares to talk of love?' Indeed, love is the symbol and agent of this organic wholeness and underpins 'a radical transvaluation of values.' In educational and developmental terms, 'Growth and self-transformation cannot be delegated.' We are responsible for our own personal upshift process.

Mumford's vision reflects the thrust of this volume. Multiple contributors recognize that we are in the throes of a metacrisis or polycrisis rooted in a crisis of perception and an outdated story of separation and competing interests. This creates inner psychological tension and outer pressure toward not only a new story but also a fundamental shift of mindset and paradigm across multiple disciplines, as we already highlighted in the Foreword. We have reached a crucial bifurcation point with two very distinctive potential evolutionary trajectories: one of conscious evolution and an evolution of consciousness that aspires for us to become, as Albert Schweitzer put it, 'more finely and deeply human,' embodying the wisdom of the heart; and the other toward the transhuman and post-human based on a narrow view of cleverness and intelligence and the instrumental values of efficiency and control. Only machines can be efficient; humans can be effective as well as affective. As Wesley Smith pointed out in a recent article, the ultimate value of the great spiritual traditions is love [and I would add wisdom] while that of the technocrat is a disembodied intelligence. As the famous passage from Deuteronomy suggests, we should Choose Life.

It is now well-documented that mystical and near-death experiences give us access to what one might call deeper structures of reality, suggesting that we are embedded in spiritual dimensions and subject to cosmic moral laws, as is evident in the life review sometimes experienced in NDEs. The emerging picture is that of One Mind and One Life, meaning that we are intrinsically interconnected, both ontologically and ethically. If we are one another, then what we do to 'the other' we are in fact doing to ourselves. In this way, a metaphysics of unity entails an ethic of interconnectedness or, more simply, the Golden Rule. This finding has the most far-reaching implications if understood and applied. Violence is ultimately self-defeating, while love is self-fulfilling.

A worldview implies both a view of the world and a view of the human: world image is reflected in human image. The scientific, ecological, and spiritual worldviews articulated in this volume are all based on similar principles that are reflected in corresponding values and priorities. For my part, Peter Deunov's five principles of Love, Wisdom, Truth, Justice, and Goodness are absolutely fundamental. He explained that Love brings life, Wisdom brings light and knowledge, and Truth brings freedom. He insisted that 'there is nothing greater than these principles; there is no straighter or surer path. In these three principles lies the salvation of the world!' It is not a question of believing the right propositions, but rather of embodying these principles in our lives to the best of our ability. Evolved individuals realize that they are embedded in larger wholes, which they seek to serve. As Deunov put it: 'The supreme goal of human life is that people should be free and to serve Love, Wisdom and Truth.'

Values and principles are in turn reflected in organizational systems that shape individual and collective behavior. Our existing — and corrupt — systems are predominantly a reflection of individual, collective, commercial, and national interests to be pursued in a self-interested competitive fashion. The central material values are those of power and wealth, where wealth can be transformed into power and influence through philanthropy or what has now come to be known as philanthro-capitalism. Such corrupt systems are underpinned by militarism informed by intelligence services in pursuit of these same values seeking competitive advantage and dominance at the expense of the common planetary good. Their operations can be and often are completely ruthless and inhuman — the end justifies the means, especially if it is highly profitable, as is the case with the military-industrial complex. We are still immaturely and shortsightedly applying the law of an eye for an eye and a tooth for a tooth, leading inexorably to further cycles of revenge and retaliation. Jesus was already proposing the alternative way of forgiveness and nonviolence 2,000 years ago, but we have yet to take it seriously, and many of those who did so have been assassinated. It is now high time to enact peace through peaceful means and justice by just means on the basis that ends and means must be consistent. Such an approach would be in harmony with rather than contracting cosmic moral laws and principles.

Imagine if we sought to co-create new systems on the basis of an under-standing of cosmic laws grounded in love, wisdom, truth, justice, and goodness. Such systems would tend to elicit corresponding positive behav-ior patterns — as Thomas Legrand suggests in the Politics of Being — and could begin as a thought experiment. This process would align with a gen-uinely human evolutionary trajectory towards both freedom and loving order. Indeed, this volume contains an inspiring series of just such thought experiments and proposals in the fields of science, technology, philosophy, psychology, spirituality, ecology, health, education, politics, economics, and business.

I believe that we are capable of the kind of systems evolution and trans-formations described in this volume and that these will ultimately come about, though perhaps in a longer timeframe than we would like. As I argued above, there are powerful economic and political forces driving us towards a technocratic post-human future, a prospect which I regard as a dehumanized downshift. Technology must serve humans rather than humans serving technology. What we are proposing here is a humanized upshift based on the principles of an ecological and spiritual worldview.

Deunov suggested, and more recently Chris Bache has concurred (*LSD and the Cosmic Mind*), that a new culture will either come about through the awakening and inner transformation of human consciousness or by the path of suffering through catastrophic breakdown. And Jim Rohn suggested that there are only two reasons why we change: inspiration or desperation. In the absence of inspired thought and action, breakthrough is likely to come about only through breakdown and desperation. However, the contents of this volume surely provide sufficient inspiration for positive and proactive change. And the time for us to make the choice is now! Readers can begin this in their own lives and circles of influence.

To conclude: a poem to illustrate the need for, and the effects of, upshifting our thinking:

Deliverance

Every year the Earth
Gives birth to new life —
But what about us?
Can we give birth
To a new culture,
A culture of love
A culture of wisdom
A culture of truth
A culture of justice
A culture of freedom
A culture of kindness
A culture of peace

A culture of beauty?

Or will we remain
Huddled in darkness
Trapped in fear
Stifled by control
Cowed into compliance
Cancelled by censors —
Unable to breathe freely,
Sleepwalking backwards
Into digital slavery?

Deep grief wells up —
A sense of human future lost,
Of time being short,
Earth in the balance,
Breakdown and breakthrough
Coming into view.

Will this culture of hope
Be stillborn again?
Or can we finally deliver
This new world together
With courage and love?

The Earth has long awaited
This moment of deliverance
From violence and secrecy,
From deception and evil.

The world can torture

And crucify the good

But the light of love

Endures,

Comes through —

Human hearts crack open,

The birth pangs of one humanity

Awakening oh so slowly,

Agonizingly

Emerging

From the cave of suffering

To greet the rising sun.

NOTES & REFERENCES

▌CHAPTER 22

1. Guarnaccia, S. (2021). The Ecozoans: The Anticipation and Birthing of an Ecological Era. *Kosmos.* https://www.kosmosjournal.org/kj_article/the-ecozoans/

2. Laszlo, A. (2020). Practices that Ensoul the Cosmos: Expressions of Connectedness. *Medium.com.* https://medium.com/@Alex8er/practices-that-ensoul-the-cosmos-f36f4217f00b

3. Robèrt, K. H. (1997). *The Natural Step: A Framework for Achieving Sustainability in Our Organizations.* Cambridge, MA: Pegasus Innovations in Management Series.

4. Cai, D., Winslow, R. L., & Noble, D. (1994). Effects of Gap Junction Conductance on Sinoatrial Node Cells: Two-Cell and Large-Scale Network Models. *IEEE Transactions on Biomedical Engineering,* 41(3):217–231. https://doi.org/10.1109/10.284940

5. Montuori, A. (1989). *Evolutionary Competence: Creating the Future.* Amsterdam: J.C. Gieben.

6. Rowland, G. (1992). Do You Play Jazz? *Performance & Instruction,* 31(10):19–25. https://www.academia.edu/7742910/Do_you_play_jazz

7. Laszlo, A. (2018). Living the New Paradigm: Syntony and Spark in Life, Being and Becoming. *The Handbook of New Paradigm Research.* A Publication of the Laszlo Institute of New Paradigm Research. Cardiff, CA: Waterfront Press.

▌CHAPTER 23

8. Sheldrake, R. (2012). *The Science Delusion: Freeing the Spirit of Enquiry.* London, UK: Coronet Books.

9. Theobald, R. (1997). *Reworking Success: New Communities at the Millennium.* Gabriola Island, B.C.: New Society Publishers.

10. Artigiani, R., Combs, A., Csányi, V., & Laszlo, E. (1996). *Changing Vision: Human Cognitive Maps: Past, Present, and Future.* London: Adamantine Press; Westport, CT: Praeger.

11. Abraham, R. (1998). Social interventions and the world wide web. Loye, D. (Ed.). *The Evolutionary Outrider: The Impact of the Human Agent on Evolution, Essays Honouring Ervin Laszlo,* Westport, CT: Praeger.; and Anderson, P. B. (1998). WWW as self-organizing system. *Cybernetics & Human Knowing: A Journal of Second Order Cybernetics, Autopoiesis, and Cybersemiotics.* 5(2), 5–41.

▌CHAPTER 25

12. Invocation of Genesis 1:1: "In the beginning God created the heavens and the earth."

13. Invocation of Genesis 1:3: "Let there be light."

14. https://dml.eecs.ucf.edu

15. https://www.azquotes.com/author/14543-Nikola_Tesla

16. https://www.goodreads.com/quotes/161207-concerning-matter-we-have-been-all-wrong-what-we-have

17. https://www.azquotes.com/author/4399-Albert_Einstein/tag/energy

18. https://www.goodreads.com/quotes/872306-i-was-originally-supposed-to-become-an-engineer-but-the

19. It's~A~Resonating~World: www.ItsAResonatingWorld.com

20. Resonating~Person: https://www.itsaresonatingworld.com/resonating-person

21. Resonating~Couple: https://www.itsaresonatingworld.com/resonating-couple

22. Energies~Community: https://www.itsaresonatingworld.com/energies community

23. https://en.wikipedia.org/wiki/Natural_frequency

24. https://www.toppr.com/ask/content/concept/forced-vibrations-254844/

25. Quote of Dr. Rollin McCraty during the Energy Medicine Summit, 14 Nov 2022: https://energymedicinesummit.com/program/51362

26. The Upshift Movement: https://www.UpshiftMovement.com/

27. Upshift for Business: https://www.UpshiftForBusiness.com/

28. Laszlo, E. (2022). *The Upshift: The Path to Healing and Evolution on Planet Earth*. Cardiff, CA: Waterside Productions. Available at https://ervinlaszlo-books.com/product/the-upshift.

29. Resonating~Business: www.resonatingbusiness.com

30. https://quoteinvestigator.com/2017/10/23/be-change/

31. Invocation of Genesis 12:1: "Leave your country, your people and your father's household and go to the land I will show you."

32. Quote from Mario Puzo's novel, *The Godfather*. https://www.goodreads.com/quotes/89874-tom-don-t-let-anybody-kid-you-it-s-all-personal-every

33. https://en.wikipedia.org/wiki/Business_purpose

▌CHAPTER 26

34. For Chaps Ltd. (2023). The Evolution of Stress: How Our Hunter-Gatherer Ancestors' Stress Response Still Affects Our Health Today. *www.forchaps.com*. https://www.forchaps.com/blogs/learn/how-the-stress-response-of-your-hunter-gatherer-ancestors-helped-them-survive-and-why-it-may-now-be-damaging-your-health

35. Lovelock, J. (2019). *Novacene: The Coming Age of Hyperintelligence*. The MIT Press. Cambridge, MA.

36. Kasparov, G. (2017). Don't fear intelligent machines. Work with them. *TED Talk* [Video]. https://www.ted.com/talks/garry_kasparov_don_t_fear_intelligent_machines_work_with_them

▌CHAPTER 27

37. Some data from the recent book, *The Quantum Biosemiosphere*, by M.C. Tobias and J.G. Morrison (New York, NY: Nova Science Publishers, 2021), and earlier research from an unpublished manuscript by Nobel Physicist (2006) George Smoot III and M.C. Tobias and J.G. Morrison (2021) entitled *Quantum Eco-Dynamics*.

38. See, for example, Bluestone, C. D. (2005). Humans are born too soon: impact on pediatric otolaryngology. *International Journal of Pediatric Otorhinolaryngology*, 69(1):1–8. https://doi.org/10.1016/j.ijporl.2004.07.021

39. Kazantzakis, N. (1965). *Report To Greco*. Translated from the Greek by P.A. Bien. New York, NY: Simon and Schuster Publishers (p. 234).

ROADMAP CLUSTER V

UPSHIFTING OUR INTUITION

- *Keynote*: Intuition and the Great Evolutionary Upshift
- We Have a Bright and Beautiful Future
- Love — The Force of All Creation
- A Heart-Mind Path Toward Unitive Justice and Human Security
- Upshifted Relationship to Beauty
- The Ensoulment of Reality: The Soul, Art and Technology of Life-Centric Realities

CHAPTER 29

KEYNOTE

INTUITION AND THE GREAT EVOLUTIONARY UPSHIFT

ANNA BACCHIA

This contribution is a synthesis of my intimate intuitive interrelation with Life, and of my Teaching and my Essays.

▌THE GREATEST EVOLUTIONARY UPSHIFT OF ALL TIME HAS BEGUN

The human being has passed from the Pre-verbal Age to the Age of Word and then the Age of Logic in which man is informed by pre-existing thought and patterns. Today, we are living the passage to the Age of *Analogic Intuitive Wisdom* where man is informed by Life, through an *unexplored* intuitive information, to which he gives shape of works coherent with Life — Life from which he is not 'other.' Thus, he becomes an aware *instrument of the constant process of creation-evolution.*

There is a quality within us,
in which breathes the Life we are, the flowing, the being.
Where we receive all the mutable orientation
toward the blossoming of the plant which we are,
toward the expansion of evolutionary consciousness.

What if Life, the Life we are, were not as we define it while we observe it?

What if the vital solutions needed for today's Great Upshift,
were innate in us since always, we just aren't aware of them?

▌PRELUDE TO INTUITION

What if we sparked the Upshift
through Art: the Art of the Life which we are,
through intuitive actions that do not ask us for energy, but offer us energy?

In these perspectives, the Intuition we are about to explore is ignited by activating in us an innate quality, an extension of our sentience: our attitude to contemplate, which like a prelude, promises and suggests the symphony of Life to which it introduces us.

Contemplation makes us aware threads of the very fabric of Life.
Contemplation is not reachable; it is already here.
It does not know any measure or definition. It is unrepeatable.
It does not involve will or time.
We can contemplate even the flash of a lightning in the night,
an avalanche of ice, an invisible rumble.
Contemplation is not created by us. It creates us.

Contemplate that here on such a small planet in the universe, we human beings are travelling at 1,600 kilometres per hour while the earth rotates on its axis, and at 100,000 kilometres per hour around the sun, while the intelligence of Life constantly transforms every thought of ours into matter, into neurotransmitters. So, instantly, the 50 thousand billion cells which we are are informed and implement vital responses to our every fear or enthusiasm — and we are no longer who we were yesterday.

Contemplate the nature of existence where the silent emptiness reveals itself while generating Life and manifesting itself as vital intelligence which conducts the whole symphony of existence — that ocean of frequencies in which we are immersed and of which we are made, that intelligence that ancient Indian texts recognize as ubiquitous and which state that those who never find it would be like fish that never find the ocean.

Contemplate that we are 8 billion faces, 8 billion different voices with many native languages but one *human* language: the language of Life in which breathes memories and archetypes and the greatest database of human wisdom existing — the collective unconscious, which opens us to the greatest poetry and understanding and to discover in us the human being of all time on Earth.

ÌNIN

I have named ÌNIN[1] the ordinarily *unexplored* INsight and INtuitive INtelligence in which Intuition, intuitive person, and intuiting are *one* process. ÌNIN expands our awareness from logic thinking toward an analogic (beyond dual, causal logic) intuitive wisdom in which we can grasp that even our usual distinguishing 'or.. or.' (e.g., 'here or there') can become a unified 'and.. and.' where diversities are waves of a unique ocean.

In the ĪNIN experience, we do not pre-define a target, but the target emerges as a consequence of our being aware and opened to the constant processes of resonance which create Life and where target and archer are not two anymore.

Particularly, the ĪNIN vision grasps both the constant eloquence emerging from every daily relationship and the perfection of such eloquence, which, as we shall see, orients every gesture of our life. It is a vision where, in front of words, gestures, and events, the intuitive eye *grasps and hears* their implicit symphony, their *invisible* meaning, which leads us to recognize that conscious, unconscious, collective unconscious, and contextual relationships are interwoven while we naturally can grasp that local and nonlocal extensions are blended.

Such experience opens us to an expanded intuitive mode of knowing, thinking, and conceiving ordinarily unexplored in western culture, a wisdom that is generated from *being* and which, from *direct experience*, grasps in an illuminating flash that we are 100% diversity and 100% oneness: where $1 + 1 = 1$.

In the ĪNIN mode, knowing becomes recognizing — here, in spacetime — what we have known and been since always, and it opens us to the conscious experience that what *emerges* reveals what we conceive as *possible*.

Furthermore, the unique eloquence emerging from all of our daily interrelations pours out waves of intuitive information, which orients every motion (micro and macro, conscious and unconscious) of the life of every living being, toward the blossoming of the unique 'plant' that every creature is. Such eloquence is the source of an extraordinary creative energy, an energy of evolutionary transformation inspiring innate human responsibility and natural effortless operating, which we can concretize with new projects and innovative works that infuse breath, life, and accomplishment.

▌INTUITIVE CERTAINTY

ÌNIN processes are an 'Art' emerging from ineffable extensions of Life, which the 'here-now' does not contain. They are an Art inspired by the poetry of life, by the harmony of the resonances which creates our life, a poetry revealed by the intimate force and naturality by which we bring an Intuition to light, a spontaneity from which the intuitive work emerges from our innate *art*isan attitude to give form to the Intuition which is involving us and which we are following and which is able to orient us like a compass.

Picasso: *"I don't search. I find."*

There is no protocol to apply. We cannot choose Intuition. We can only be invited by it: touched, transformed, re-created.

There is an Eloquence emerging from events, from relationships, constantly flowing. Ubiquitous.

And eternally intuitive information vibrates, springing up from the fields of Life.

So, what Intuition calls us to follow and to do next, unveils (the grand workshop of) the bigger whole.

The ÌNIN vision is engendered by and engenders a natural *relational syntony*. It is nourished by our *innate sentience*, which, by its nature, responds with appropriate spontaneous coherence. It is similar to the sensitive perception of an eye to a ray of light, which manifests a perfect response in coherent resonance with the qualities of the light received.

In such awareness, the ÌNIN intuitive perception opens us to the vital natural coherence innate in man. The ÌNIN experience makes us aware that our sensitive and vibrant existence on Earth is not distinct from our

Self: Our Being is at once Unique and One. In such experience, our actions do not spring from intellectual learning, but arise from *self-insight*. Thus, the full clarity of mind-body unity emerges, of how conscious mind and unconscious biological perception influence body, health, and well-being.

Even the meaning of our Life lets itself be seen through the ineffable perfection of each emerging event. Intuition focuses this instantly whereas ordinarily we rarely see immediately the perfect vital sense of any event which involves us. Usually only in time do we acknowledge: *'If that day I had not seen... met... I would never have...'*

Yet, within an acquired intuitive insight, we begin to look forward like we look backward: where we recognize the perfection of Life. In such perspective, even the human *sense of hope* gives way to *intuitive certainty*. In Marco Bersanelli's book, *From Galileo to Gell-man,* the words of the greatest scientists and artists of every age emphasize that *"Intuitive Certainty constitutes the most fundamental form of knowledge on the basis of which all subsequent rational investigation proceeds."*[2]

▌THE ART OF CHANGE

> *Just as the flow of movement arises from emptiness, at the center of the hub,*
> *evolutionary transformation arises from silent insight.*

The ÌNIN training orients us toward goals and solutions that come to light as an *'a posteriori'* effect, when we follow our innate INtuitive INtelligence, which inexorably draws the Self to the center.

Since always, Intuition has sparked enlightening, decisive, resolutive views and gestures, and it has led man to give form to unique works of art and discoveries which have influenced and marked history (such as the wheel, the electric current, or the microprocessor).

But today, in the evident complexity, and in the human affinity to complexity, ÌNIN empowers us more and more properly to an enlightened, expanded understanding, ready to give form to urgent answers, coherent with the evidences emerging from daily personal and social relationships, and ready to *answer questions that have not yet found words to be expressed*.

We are dealing with an Art of Change in which man is naturally called and inspired to transform, renew, and evolve, starting from an intuitive self-insight of holographic nature. Where *we are not explorers of Life*, as already ancient Indian sages pointed out, *we are Life itself*, and as Instruments of its marvellous creative evolutionary processes, we are today called more and more urgently to concretize our natural responsibility of co-creating vital evolution.

ÌNIN – ESSENTIAL ELEMENTS

The ÌNIN training involves the awareness and experience of some essential elements:

- The necessity to rediscover the human natural *sensitive perception*, capable of grasping reality in broad extensions, beyond predefined models: A striking example is offered by the cultural transformation of the 19th century, which, from academic painting, saw the rise of the impressionist painting revolution. Freed from all previous academic rules, impressionism was implemented from a new relationship with the world unmediated by pre-established academic rules and models. But proceeding from the sensitive perception of reality, impressionism captured life's eloquent evidences and created the masterpieces that decisively influenced the following thought and culture (of the time).

- The awareness that existence is not our *description* of existence: The nature of experience is *nonlocal.* Only its verbal definition is *local*, as a representation dropped in space-time.

- The need for a *new analogic grammar* (beyond partitioning, causal, logic): It arises today from the awareness that the nature of reality does not consist of isolated parts, but of relations, and — as Paolo Renati points out[3] — evolves in a process of circular, self-regenerating, self-conscious autopoiesis. Such a new analogic grammar takes voice from an intuitive local-nonlocal 'space' silent within us, the intimate center of the hub of our evolutionary wheel, empty as the spaces that generate words or musical notes and as clear as the original spontaneity, a space that — as we shall see — generates effortless movement.

▌AN IMMENSE LATENT EVOLUTIONARY POTENTIAL

In western culture, the innate human intuitive ability is ordinarily unexplored and undeveloped by our education founded on logic thinking, dual and causal. In the ÌNIN training, we recognize that the INtuitive INformation emerges from the field of existence, and it constitutes an infinite source of an unexplored creative energy.

Man, who receives such information, is in*form*ed by it and is naturally inspired to bring it to light and give it an explicit *form*: the form of words, answers, projects, works, solutions, and inventions. In this way, man becomes a conscious instrument of the evolutionary creative process, an instrument of the symphony of life.

At the same time, we can experience how Intuitive Information has the admirable precise function of orienting our INtuitive INtelligence toward movements, choices, and options, addressed and in tune with the fulfillment of our Life. We can all recognize that unpredictable encounters, readings, and events, not created by our will, have often been harbingers of new openings, perspectives, transformations, and needs of change. How many times has an encounter changed our Life?

But what we may miss is that the emergence of information capable of orienting us is a *constant* process of our Life, occurring in every moment. If we are not accustomed to recognizing it, *an immense potential of centeredness and evolutionary coherence risks being lost.*

In this sense, such evolutionary coherence risks to remain out of our reach because of our acquired habits, models or choices related to our cultural prejudices. The acquired logical mind frame preponderantly imprints our causal way of proceeding and constitutes the first obstacle to our natural following Intuition. Thus, we risk that Intuition escapes our awareness, and that we are distanced from the processes of syntony and vital resonances capable of polarizing us, inspiring us, and orienting every step of our evolving.

In the ÎNIN educational training, our intuitive experience unfolds in the *TTF formula*: we are Touched, Transformed, and we Follow.

▌THE MAGNET OF INTUITION

Life flows through me, rather than me run my Life. It does not feel like me doing something, but rather it being done through me.
— Peter Merry, Chief Innovation Officer, Ubiquity University[4]

By its nature, intuitive information appears unpredictable to us. It certainly does not depend on our will. In a reality which is *one*, of which we are not 'part,' but which we are, with the İNIN experience, we glimpse how the impulse that brings the intuitive information to reach us is *within us*.

The magnet of Intuition is inherent in the relationship of man of all times with reality, a relationship that, since childhood, is woven with surprise and awe and permeated with the innate eternal *wonder* invisibly inherent also in our yearnings, in dreams, and in the human aspiring for the realization of his life, a wonder interwoven with an intimate silent wordless question, which is ineffable while we face the eloquence of the emerging phenomena (from Greek: to appear, to make visible) of new discoveries, surprises, and the unexpected. The wonder within man's relationship with reality is very evident in children while in the adult it tends to be stifled by the objectivity of logical quantifying, explaining, and defining.

Our vibrant attitude of wonder, nourished by our sensitive perception, flows into the great ocean of vital autopoiesis, while radiating a wave. This wave evokes a resonance from the field of existence, a kind of response wave, and such response manifests the Intuition we receive. This process involves every human being, at any age, when we remain sensitive and amazed like a child. In this regard, in the words of eminent scientists and artists of all times,[5] we find the binomial "Wonder and Knowledge," where to the human *wonder* corresponds an intuitive *knowledge*.

VEILED UNVEILED REVEALED

VEILED: In the field of infinite Vital Possibilities, some of them will come to light in the dimensions of space-time as future discoveries, works of art, or new solutions. They constitute a latent potential, a potentiality that is

invisible or metaphorically *veiled* to the local vision. In the wake of eloquent inputs emerging from readings, or touching and interesting events,
sensitive waves of human wonder evoke unexpected insights. Such insights
can develop inspiration and creative inputs in the inner vision both of artists and scientists as Michelangelo, Wagner, or Einstein, as well as of any
man. At any time, anyone can be touched by the Intuitive Inspiration to
write a book, to create new answers, projects, or solutions, or to bring to
light creative forms that do not yet exist. *"Something is saying to me... has
brought me... has suggested to me..."*

UNVEILED: In such process, a *veiled*, nonlocal, invisible potentiality (as
was the image of the wheel, before it was discovered) is distilled in spa-
tiotemporal dimensions and becomes an intuitive image that is *un-veiled*,
devoid of its *veil*, and exclusively in the vision of the discoverer. No one
other than the discoverer 'sees' the book or sculpture that is intuited before
the discoverer gives it form. Such *ineffable* process is recognized by ancient
Indian Brahma Sutras as *Shruti*. Says Michelangelo, *"The Pietà was already
in the stone. It was only a matter of extracting it."*

REVEALED: When the discoverer brings to light and concretizes the
received creative Intuition, he *re-veils* it: the invisible intuitive image that
has been received and grasped by the discoverer now becomes visible for
all, having received 'a veil', i.e., the *form* (verbal, sculptural, musical) that
makes it accessible, available, and concrete in the dimensions of space-time.
It is not created by voluntary choices, but we see it arising as an emergent
reality from our *art*isan hands, which proceeds following Intuition with an
original unawareness, like the hands of a composer moving by themselves
on the pentagram paper as they write the Music which is being heard and
of which the composer will be called 'Author.'

▌SURFERS IN THE GREAT UPSHIFT

In the process in which the human is in-*form*-ed by an intuitive information emerging from Life, and is called and inspired to give it a *form*, it
is fundamental for the Great Upshift that our intuitive analogic wisdom
takes *form* — Consciously — and brings forth concrete, coherent works
and solutions in symphony with the analogic nature of Life.

In such awareness, the ÌNIN experience trains us to catch the intuitive flash which enlightens the surfer as he follows, quick as lightning,
the unpredictable change of the winds (i.e., change of events or emerging
unpredictabilities), the intuitive flash where the goal emerges *a posteriori*
and follows a flowing in which man becomes target, arrow, and archer
together.

Thus, as surfers, we train ourselves to proceed *without knowing* a
moment *before* how to change and orient the sail of our daily windsurf-
ing while we follow the unpredictable wind of the emerging events and
stay elegantly on the constant wave of Intuition which is speaking to us. It
inspires us and calls us, as instruments of vital creation, unto a coherent
Great Evolutionary Upshift.

Acknowledgements

*My most heartfelt gratitude goes to the Architect Roman Calzaferri who has
greatly supported the steps of compilation, translation, and editing of this
essay.*

CHAPTER 30

WE HAVE A BRIGHT AND BEAUTIFUL FUTURE

TED MAHR

We are on the verge of creating a bright, beautiful new world, based upon love, compassion and understanding. As Ervin Laszlo writes in Chapter 1 of *The Survival Imperative*, "We face a survival challenge: evolve or perish … to live in harmony with each other and with life on Earth," and as he rightly points out, "Where there is no vision, the people perish (*Proverbs* 29:18)."

Because of my upbringing in a psychic family, I learned how to talk to Angels and guides on the other side. My foster mother (Teri) even worked very effectively with police departments finding lost and missing children. She taught me how to talk to spirits on the other side. Now, with over 30 years of experience, I have no doubts that there is a nonlocal universal consciousness that connects to other worlds and other dimensions, well beyond the constraints of this Third Dimensional reality. This universal consciousness connects to God or the Supreme Being, the being who created all that there is, and that spark of creation is within each and every one of us on this planet. (This is further detailed in my newest book, *Journey to the Other Side: Talking to Angels and Other Benevolent Beings*.)

As with many of us on Earth, my soul journey actually started in Atlantis 12,500 years ago. At that time, I was one of the priests in Atlantis trying to stop a military and political elite from destroying the planet. We failed to stop the destruction. Here we are today facing the same issues. This spiritual pattern of repetition is required until the lesson is learned. Today, many have evolved past the lower levels of negativity and are now waking up humanity to create a better world. I know that this time humanity will identify the power of love to create a beautiful new world, and we will ascend into the higher dimensions. Each of us has a duty to prepare now, so we can continue to co-create this bright, beautiful future for all of us.

We experience reality on this planet in the Third Dimension, but it is important to realize that there are many other dimensions beyond this Third Dimension. For example, there is the Fourth Dimension of time, the Fifth Dimension of what some people call "heaven," and then seven other dimensions leading all the way up to the Twelfth Dimension where God or the Supreme Being exists. When someone can access the higher dimensions in the Fourth and Fifth Dimensions and beyond, all of the information they access is Truth, and my Angels tell me that the destiny of this Earth is to become a loving, harmonious, and beautiful planet.

The Earth is slated to ascend into these higher dimensions. The process started in September of 2016 when the planet shifted into higher positive energy for the first time in at least 26,000 years. For example, for thousands of years, the Schumann resonance or the vibration of the planet was at 7.8 hertz. Then, on January 31, 2017, for the first time in recorded history, the Schumann resonance reached frequencies of 36+ hertz. Since then, it has gone even higher to many thousands of hertz, surpassing the frequency of love, which is 528 hertz. As we shift into the Fourth and then Fifth Dimensions, the frequency of this planet should shift even higher.

This ascension process would have happened over 50 years ago if U.S. President John F. Kennedy's life had not been cut short on November 22, 1963. If JFK had lived, the U.S. (and other countries) would have upshifted into the Fifth Dimension, and we would now be exchanging ambassadors with other benevolent human and extraterrestrial civilizations. Our longevity would have easily increased five times to over 300 years. Money would be de-emphasized as a medium of exchange because there would be free energy, and diseases would have been eliminated. There would be no rich and no poor because everyone would live in abundance. The entire planet would now live in peace and harmony — we would be far more materially and spiritually richer than we are today, as war and conflict would have become a thing of the past.

Many Angels and many advanced civilizations beyond this planet are also helping us. As one example, Kennedy is still the U.S. President in the spiritual world; he has never stopped being our President and is still constantly working for peace on the other side. For example, he tells me that he was responsible for helping the United States and North Korea achieve a peace agreement in 2018. He is also working on achieving peace throughout the world now.

The changes that Kennedy tried to implement were from the top down. Today, the changes are coming from the bottom up — from the majority of people around the world who want to create a peaceful and beautiful planet, free of conflict and war. He has repeatedly told me that if we all recognize that we all have God within us, we would realize we are all one, and we would stop fighting. If we are all one and fight among ourselves, we are just hurting ourselves.

This is a pivotal time in human history, I am prayerfully confident that humanity will make the right choices to live in harmony and peace. In the future, Nostradamus has told me that the kind of heavy government regulations which we have in place now will not be needed. People will tie into God and know how to treat each other with honesty and respect. Nostradamus has told me we will still have governments, but governments in general around the world will be much smaller because they will only deal with Extraterrestrials beyond this planet. Any military needs will be taken care of by our alliance with a group of benevolent ETs called the Galactic Alliance (which is a benevolent alliance of 450 million planets and 7 trillion mostly human souls).

As part of this transformation, people will upshift from this Third Dimension into the Fourth and then Fifth Dimension. As they shift into the Fifth Dimension, language itself will become secondary, and most people will communicate telepathically. So many conflicts today are the result of misunderstandings and miscommunications. However, as people learn to communicate telepathically, they will learn to be totally honest with each other because they will instantly know if someone is lying to them or not telling the truth.

For corrupt politicians and others, they will be replaced by persons of high integrity and honest motives. Criminals will not be able to lie to the people they are supposed to represent because people will be able to read their minds and readily see the truth. The good news is that criminals will not be able to commit crimes. This is because everyone will be telepathic and able to read each other's minds.

Many indigenous peoples know the true history of this planet and have seen into our future. They realize like Ervin Laszlo that this is a crucial time in humanity's history because we have to make the right choices for us to create a much better and happier planet.

The Hopi Indians in Arizona have what they call "Prophecy Rock" that dates from 4,000 years ago. The rock itself has two lines. One line goes around the bottom of the rock in a straight line. It represents humanity living in peace and harmony forever if we all learn to live in peace and harmony with each other, Mother Earth, and the environment. The other line is above the first line. It goes straight through five different boxes, and then, just before the fifth box, zip zags up at a 45-degree angle and stops. This line represents what will happen if we do not take care of Mother Earth and the environment and do not live in peace and harmony with each other. Each box on the rock represents a different dimension, with the fifth box representing the Fifth Dimension. If we do not live in peace and harmony with each other, we will destroy ourselves, and our civilization will end like it ended in Atlantis 12,500 years ago.

However, all the Angels and great spirits say that our future is very, very bright! There are many points of light coming into the planet now from God and the Central Sun of this Universe. As time goes on, these points of light will become even more prevalent. According to Kennedy, eventually, the entire Earth will become like one huge ball of light as it ascends into the Fourth and then Fifth Dimensions. People will wake up to a brighter and happier future for themselves, their children, and all future generations. When this happens, there will be no more war, no more poverty, and no more hunger; people will truly live in peace, harmony, and prosperity.

People will demand that these changes be implemented democratically from the bottom up (and not from the top down). As the Canadian truckers showed the world in the spring of 2022, people around the world are tired of being forced into tyrannical societies where they are told what to do, without any meaningful say. People do not want to be controlled. They do not want some big government trying to control and harm them, and the old economic and political systems based upon greed, selfishness, and service to self will not be a part of this New Earth. Instead, the New Earth will be based upon love, peace, harmony, and service to others.

As noted by former Canadian Defense Minister Paul Hellyer in the Foreword to my book, *Messages from the Masters*, "The most re-assuring words came from Nostradamus and Leonardo da Vinci who indicate that the woeful predictions of an apocalyptic Armageddon no longer apply … the future of humanity is very bright if we strive for ascension to a higher dimension, and accept the fact that the universe is a unity, and the glue that holds it together is love. All we have to do is seek to love and serve the God who created a universe of love and light."

The 2020s will be pivotal decades in the spiritual evolution of humanity; we are at a crossroads! We can either take the high road and continue our spiritual progress, or we can go down the negative path of conflict and war. However, I know we will make the right choices to transform the Earth into a beautiful and wonderful place where people will live in peace and harmony. I know there is a bright, beautiful future ahead of all of us!

As Albert Einstein said, "The unleashed power of the atom has changed everything except our thinking. Thus, we are drifting toward catastrophe beyond conception. We shall require a substantially new manner of thinking if mankind is to survive." As part of this, we will need a new paradigm based upon service to others rather than service to self, and of love, compassion, peace, and harmony, rather than war and conflict.

As Lao Tze has said, *"The journey of a thousand miles begins with one step."* In other words, no journey is too long or too difficult when we break it down into small, manageable steps. It's a powerful reminder that even the most daunting of tasks can be accomplished when we take that first step and begin our journey.

So, I hope you all will join Ervin Laszlo, David Lorimer, myself, and all the others in this beautiful, inspiring book to co-create a beautiful, harmonious, and loving New Earth where war and conflict are just distant memories and, in the words of John Lennon, "all the world will live as one!"

CHAPTER 31

LOVE – THE FORCE OF ALL CREATION

RAYMOND BRADLEY

Someday, after we have mastered the winds, the waves, the tides and gravity, we shall harness for God the energies of love. Then for the second time in the history of the world, man will have discovered fire. — Pierre Teilhard de Chardin, *On Love* (1967), Pp. 33–34.

OVERVIEW

The world teeters on the cusp of planetary catastrophe. An urgent imperative is societal transformation: a shift from greed, inequality, and environmental degradation to an order of *harmony* both among humanity and with nature. This requires empowerment using *all* human faculties to achieve sustainability. Research in neurobiology and psychosocial science documents love's key role in psychobiological development, social relationships, and collective organization. Moreover, groundbreaking studies in psi research reveal love's subtle but crucial role in psychic proficiencies, such as intuition, prescience, and telekinesis — the basis of creativity, foresight, and the power of mind and spirit to shape reality. These findings suggest principles to guide the *upshift* to societal transformation. They also point to a *general equation* expressing the fundamental creation relations among Love, Consciousness, Energy and Matter.

I. LOVE AND PSYCHOSOCIAL ORGANIZATION

We begin by showing how love is organized as a tacit field of socioaffective connection that mediates development of effective psychosocial organization throughout the human life span and across levels of neuropsychosocial order. The field is organized along two relational dimensions: one involves love — the arousal of bio-emotional energy; the second involves social regulation of the aroused energy. The conjunction of values on the two dimensions mediates the generative processes that *in*-form (literally, *give shape to*)[6] the emergence of psychosocial order.

Neuropsychosocial Development

In his seminal work, *Affect Regulation and the Origin of the Self*,[7] Allan Schore documents how the interaction between a mother and her infant directs the development of the child's brain with enduring psychosocial consequences:

> The child's first relationship, the one with the mother, acts as a template for the imprinting of circuits in the child's emotion-processing right brain, thereby permanently shaping the individual's adaptive or maladaptive capacities to enter into all later emotional relationships.[8]

Signaled primarily by mutual eye contact, body gestures, and movements, and especially facial emotional expression, data on their psychobiological states and the socioemotional structure of their interactions are communicated in split-second sequences of highly coordinated states of *socioemotional attunement*. Structured along two dimensions — love/affect and regulation/modulation, the interactions involve the mother stimulating her baby's positive emotional states and then regulating the infant's aroused affective energy.

During a critical period — the first eighteen months of life — brain development is optimized when the interactions are charged, primarily, with positive emotions and modulated appropriately. These socioaffective exchanges stimulate the neurochemistry and production of neurohormones that orchestrate development of neural structures and circuitry, and, as patterns of interaction, are imprinted in the infant's developing brain, thereby encoding the neurological templates that govern psychosocial function. By the onset of speech, the basis for psychosocial autonomy, self-consciousness, and agency are all in place.[9]

Schore's primary conclusion can be expressed as a principle to guide parental behavior:

> *Principle 1.* Appropriately modulated love generates optimal neuropsychosocial development, creating the requisite foundation for psycho-social autonomy and self-conscious agency for life.

Intimate Relationships

Grounded in research, Sternberg has proposed a triarchical dimensionality to account for the development of stability in love relationships.[10] The first is *passion*, the drives of motivation and affective arousal that generate romantic and physical attraction, and sexual relations. The second is *decision/commitment,* a cognitive component involving two temporal considerations: a short-term decision that one loves someone else, and a long-term commitment to maintain that love. The third dimension is *intimacy,* the feelings of closeness, connectedness, and bondedness that produce emotional warmth and attachment in a loving relationship. Sternberg observes that while passion, relationally, is "relatively unstable," commitment and intimacy are "relatively stable."[11]

Of the eight kinds of love generated by the different logical combinations of the presence or absence of these three elements in a relationship, only "Consummate Love" encompasses the requisite intimacy and maturity for stability.[12] In our terms, optimizing the coupling of passion with decision/commitment to create a co-evolving order of socioaffective dialogue improves the likelihood that intimacy, and hence durability, will develop. Thus, codified as a principle for creating durable intimate relationships:

> *Principle 2.* Coupling passion with decision/commitment creates an adaptive, co-evolving bond of mutual love which increases the likelihood of developing intimacy and durability in relationship.

Collective Organization

In an earlier study, *Charisma and Social Structure,* I found that two patterns of relations characterized the social structure of durable collaborative groups.[13] One was a dense network of 'loving' relations interconnecting virtually all members. The second pattern was a densely interlocking hierarchy of 'power' relations, extending down many levels of strata.[14] A balanced coupling was found between these two orders which, in turn, was associated with group stability. These findings were *invariant*: they held for groups with different ideologies, leadership type, group size, and history and were not explained by member characteristics. There was also compelling evidence that a tacit *holographic* process communicates information on group structure throughout the socioaffective field to all members. In a follow-up investigation, using multivariate techniques, Karl Pribram and I found that structural measures of collective love and collective control *predicted group survival some 24 months into the future.*[15]

Taken altogether, these results and others (Table 1) suggest that a general order of endogenous dynamics, involving the arousal and regulation of affective energy — *love* — is operative in *all* collaborative groups and mediates collective organization and function. Additional analysis across levels of scale reveals these same dimensions and dynamics involving love appear involved in generating stable forms of psychosocial organization (Figure 1). This suggests a basic principle for collaborative organization:

Triarchical Models of Development Across the Human Life Span*

	Development Stage				
	----------Child----------		------------------------Adult------------------------		
Dimension:	Infant (Schore)	Pre-Schooler (Hinde)	Personal (Csikszentmihalyi)	Interpersonal (Sternberg)	Organizational (Bradley)
Affective Energy	Emotional arousal	Maternal warmth	Action opportunities (challenges)	Passion	Network of positive affect
Social Control	Modulation/ regulation	Maternal control	Action capabilities (skills)	Decision/ commitment	Hierarchy of social control
Emergent Psychosocial Form	Optimal brain/mind development	Cooperative peer relations	Flow state/ peak experience	Intimate relationship	Collective agency

*Adapted from Bradley (2003).

Table 1. Modulated Love and the Emergence of Psychosocial Order

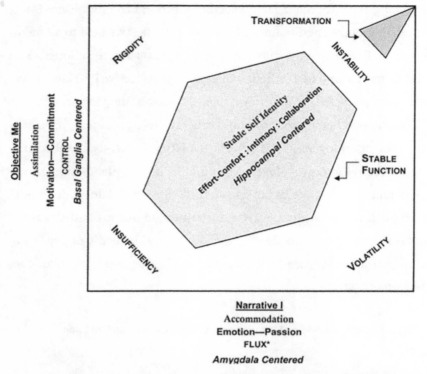

Figure 1. Postulated Relations Between Triarchical Structures at Various Scales of Order (Neurological to Psychosocial) and the Resultant Effects on Stability. (Adapted from Pribram & Bradley (1998), Figure 10.4).

Principle 3. A balanced, dynamically adaptive coupling of bonds of affective attachment with regulating relations of social control creates an optimal order for collaborative organization.

Overall, a general proposition can be formulated:

When bonds of love and social regulation are coupled in a dynamically adaptive, co-evolving system of reciprocal interaction, neuropsychosocial development is optimized and effective forms of intimacy and collaborative organization emerge.

Moreover, this proposition can be expressed as an equation, denoting the logic of the process:

Equation 1.

▍II. LOVE AND PSYCHIC INTERACTION

In their acclaimed work, *Margins of Reality*, Jahn and Dunne reflect on what accounted for the nonrandom departures in their mind-machine telekinesis experiments:

> Careful application of scientific knowledge and rigor of method, *within a permeating atmosphere of "love"* … appears particularly pertinent … for the realization of the phenomena themselves, for it is precisely through the *bonds of consciousness* established between human operators, or with their technical devices and processes, that the anomalous [nonrandom] data seem to emerge. Thus, the spiritual component participates in a very pragmatic sense: *selfless investment of self can affect physical reality.*[16]

They condense their conclusions into a basic equation expressing the role of consciousness (Love) as a fundamental organizing principle in nature:

> Whatever may be assigned to this chaos-reducing capability of consciousness, if *L* [Love] is its symbol, the process it defines is clearly of the form:

Equation 2.

$$L = -\Delta s$$

where $-\Delta s$ denotes the decrease in entropy of the relevant system, the increase in its information, the establishment of its reality.[17]

Forty years later, in a truly ground-breaking study, reporting on a 30-year series of experiments documenting the effect of "lovingly held" intention on various remote targets,[18] William Tiller and his associates conclude, "*Every one of us can influence all biological life forms around us via our biofield emissions and the information that they carry whether we consciously intend to or not.*"[19] And:

> ... aspiring humans, through their *conscious intent* acting on and through their acupuncture/chakra systems into the U(1) level world [our space-time reality], *can slow down and perhaps even reverse the degradations of that world via lifting themselves and their surroundings* to ever higher EM gauge symmetry [higher dimensional] states![20]

Moreover, their groundbreaking discovery of change in the hydrogen ion ($\Delta\psi$ H+) as a marker of the shift to a higher dimension of reality, wherein a special kind of "*information entanglement*" operates, may well be the long sought-after *physical* instantiation of an *emotional field — beyond space and time* — mediating psychic communication:

> A postulated substance, called *deltrons* from the domain of *emotion* (outside of physical reality), exists and has the quality of being able to travel at velocities both above and below c [the speed of light] and to interact with substances from both levels of physical reality [viz, that below or equal to, and that above the speed of light].[21]

In short, *emotion* (love) plays a key role in the psychophysics of *how* such psychic/anomalous consciousness phenomena occur. The heart is equipped with its own set of neurons and operates as the 'grand conductor' in the processing of emotions by the body.[22] As Tiller explains:

> When focusing on the heart with *loving intent*, the human EKG becomes *harmonic* at the baroreflex frequency, 0.014 hertz, where the heart entrains the brain and simultaneously all the other major electrophysiological systems of the body.

He then goes onto to make the all-important point:

> In this heart entrainment mode of functioning [*heart coherence*], body chemical production becomes healthier and *focused intent can psychokinetically influence molecular structures both inside and outside of the body.*[23]

Overall, we can deduce three principles that guide access to and use of psychic faculties:

Principle 4. Our bio-emotional emissions interconnect us to everything around us, whether it is a physical, biological, or a social system, or it is proximate or distant.

Principle 5. This ever-present bio-emotional connection means that we influence all systems whether, consciously, we intend to or not.

Principle 6. Using a loving focus we can communicate intention, via heart coherence, and exert an influence on a target object, even when it is remote.

III. LOVE: THE FUNDAMENTAL CREATIVE FORCE

Tiller's group goes on to construct a general "reaction equation":

Equation 3.[24]

They explain the equation's significance in these terms:

> Einstein provided us with the quantitative relationship connecting
> the first two terms on the left $[E = MC^2]$ .... The last term on the
> right [Love] *is the force of all creation* .... [and] centering one's con-
> sciousness within a framework of *unconditional love,* nurturing,
> caring, etc., *can allow the healing process to unfold* from right to left
> in the above equation ....[25]

Although they depict a reciprocal relationship between each pair of factors in a specific order, wherein Love does *not* have a *direct* effect on Energy
or Mass/Matter, many studies find direct evidence of an *emotional* component.[26] For instance, studies of the Global Consciousness Project's (GCP)
database mark 'emotion' as the nonlocal mediator of mass consciousness
effects on the behavior of the GCP's worldwide network of random number
generators.[27]

Love and Consciousness: A Quantum Holographic Account

It is the field of emotional connection — our intrinsic bond of *love* to
everyone and everything in the universe — that is the channel for psychic information, both in relaying precognition and in communicating
intention nonlocally. Based on Tiller's discoveries, this field of emotion is
mediated by deltrons and operates through a special kind of "information

entanglement" akin to a holographic field. In the thumbnail sketch that follows, the entire process can be described in *quantum holographic* terms, which is fully elaborated elsewhere.[28]

Briefly, *passionate attentional focus* attunes the bio-emotional energy of a percipient's psychophysiological systems, via Phase Conjugate Adaptive Resonance (PCAR), to the resonant frequency of the object of interest, thereby establishing a phase-locked, co-adaptive, two-way communication channel.[29] The incoming wave field of energy to the person contains quantum holographically encoded information on the object's future potential, which is perceived as precognition — *intuition*. During sustained *passionate intentional focus*, the outgoing wave field from the percipient encodes the intention as a hologram — an *unchanging* image, which is communicated, via a quantum holographic process, and can influence the object's organization and behavior (see Figure 2). Although the psychokinetic effect can be small, Prigogine's discovery of 'sensitivity to initial conditions' in far-from-equilibrium systems, means that targeting at the bi-furcation moment (tipping point) can produce a *radical transformation* in a complex dynamical system: essentially *all* living systems in nature.[30]

Finally, the logic of the processes involved can be denoted in a reformulation of Tiller's equation in which we surmise, for each pair of factors, the likely psychophysical mechanism and mathematics (in parentheses) implicated:

Equation 4:[31]

Conscious Intent*	→	Love	→	Energy	→	*In*-formation	→	ΔMaterial/ Living Systems
	activates		attunes		encodes		gives shape to	
(Δ to Heart Coherence)		(PCAR)		(Gabor EF)		(see below**)		

Notation
* Encoded as a hologram
Δ = Change
PCAR: Phase Conjugate Adaptive Resonance
Gabor EF: Gabor Elementary Function
** Target disposition feedback: Quantum Holography
   Nonlinear Δ: Complex dynamical systems theory

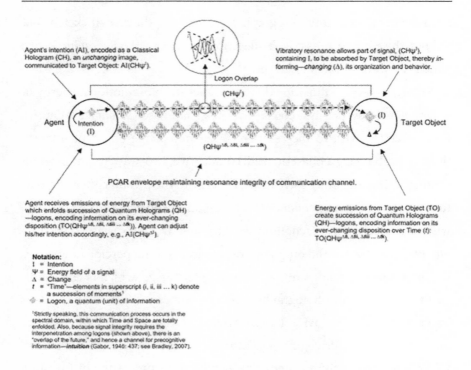

Agent's intention (AI), encoded as a Classical Hologram (CH), an *unchanging* image, communicated to Target Object: AI(CHψ²).

Vibratory resonance allows part of signal, (CHψ³), containing I, to be absorbed by Target Object, thereby *informing—changing* (Δ), its organization and behavior.

Logon Overlap

Agent receives emissions of energy from Target Object which enfolds succession of Quantum Holograms (QH) —logons, encoding information on its ever-changing disposition (TO(QHψ$^{1,δ, Δδi, Δδii ... δk}$)). Agent can adjust his/her intention accordingly, e.g., AI(CHψ^{5}).

Energy emissions from Target Object (TO) create succession of Quantum Holograms (QH)—logons, encoding information on its ever-changing disposition over Time (*t*): TO(QHψ$^{1,δ, Δδi, Δδii ... δk}$).

PCAR envelope maintaining resonance integrity of communication channel.

Notation:
I = Intention
Ψ = Energy field of a signal
Δ = Change
t = "Time"—elements in superscript (i, ii, iii ... k) denote a succession of moments[1]
⟠ = Logon, a quantum (unit) of information

[1]Strictly speaking, this communication process occurs in the spectral domain, within which Time and Space are totally enfolded. Also, because signal integrity requires the interpenetration among logons (shown above), there is an "overlap of the future," and hence a channel for precognitive information—*intuition* (Gabor, 1946: 437; see Bradley, 2007).

Figure 2. Quantum Holographic Model of Nonlocal Agency (adapted from Bradley, 2023)

CONCLUSIONS

The conclusions, principles, and equations presented here illuminate love's fundamental role both in generating psychosocial organization and in facilitating access to psychic proficiencies. By harnessing the energies of love, thus, humanity can empower itself with the requisite knowledge and practices to create a harmonious sustainable world.

In closing, we may finally be approaching the monumental turning point Teilhard de Chardin had in mind: the moment when humankind "discovers fire" for a second time, by harnessing "for God [and the Planet] the energies of love." Given the dire warnings of looming, irreversible, catastrophic climate change, Teilhard de Chardin's moment of transformation cannot come quickly enough![32]

Acknowledgements

I am grateful to Ervin Laszlo for the invitation to contribute to this book, and for his patience with my revisions. I thank Rob Nixon, Dr. Robert Rees, Prof. Dragan Milovanovic, and my wife, Chaarenne Torris, for their helpful comments.

CHAPTER 32

A HEART-MIND PATH TOWARD UNITIVE JUSTICE AND HUMAN SECURITY

ELENA MUSTAKOVA

Walking the mystical path with practical feet... — 'Abdu'l-Bahá[33]

I had no sense at the time of what conflict reporting actually entailed. I didn't understand that straddling different worlds would require taking a wrecking ball to much of what I thought I knew about life, politically and personally. That gradually, but unmistakably, there would be a smashing. A smashing of my preconceived notions, a smashing of what I thought I knew about history, about myself. I didn't realize that I would have my heart broken in a hundred different ways, that I would lose friends and watch children die and grow to feel like an alien in my own skin. I didn't understand that the privilege of witnessing history came at a price. But in that moment, only one thing mattered to me: I had a calling. — Clarissa Ward, *On All Fronts*

For the length of human history, we have lived in and reproduced contexts of structural violence — social systems that have relied on large masses of people being treated as unworthy based on gender, race, and social class, controlled and ruthlessly exploited. Now we celebrate the courageous people who uncover these systems but omit to acknowledge that all their individual courage and sacrifice will not go far enough in uprooting these systems which are still upheld by the dominant global power paradigm.

Violence toward fellow humans runs through the whole history of humanity. Even as civilization has advanced immensely in its social forms of organization, its grasp of nature, and its ability to create sophisticated technologies for an ever-broadening range of purposes, the plague of violence continues to degrade human character, inflict enormous suffering, compromise civilization, and destroy the possibility for human security. It is safe to say that *we do not have true civilization* on this small planet, regardless of our technological savvy, while violence continues unchecked.

Systems of justice have developed over the centuries to protect the inherent balance of life and to restore relative social harmony. However, these punitive systems themselves have often relied on violence, and have been shown to be systemically skewed to enforce structural oppression. While social systems of justice have evolved with the evolution of consciousness and society, it is only at *this* stage of human evolution that we are collectively poised to create a system which is *genuinely and comprehensively just* for all life in its interdependent oneness and ensures the harmony of the planetary community.

ONTOLOGICAL AND EPISTEMOLOGICAL PARADIGM SHIFT

The dominant mechanistic paradigm of separateness through which we understand reality and organize social life has outworn its usefulness. A holistic and comprehensive approach is now needed to reflect the emergent scientific understanding of oneness as our fundamental reality and to move us beyond repression and control toward regenerative solutions to planetary human and other crises.

Human ontological beliefs have evolved over the past 30 centuries or so, from magical thinking about the world, to literal understanding of natural phenomena, and social and spiritual rules, to a gradual analytical grasp of abstract processes that allowed science to flourish in the last two centuries. Instrumental reason reliant on logical operations has developed the capacity for sophisticated organ transplants, has freed people from many of the prejudices of the past, and has allowed us to land on the moon and to explore interplanetary travel. Yet, as the scientific approach increasingly mutated into narrow rationalism, scientism, and physicalism — the belief that other approaches to knowledge cannot be as valid, and that materialist science alone can provide the most reliable worldview — this led to a moral and spiritual void that has pushed the planet well beyond its carrying capacity and continues to perpetuate unimaginable structural violence on millions of people. Religious forms of knowledge manifest similar physicalism, and although the majority of people on the planet claim some form of religion, the sanctity of life is by far not a central and lived value. Clearly, our current ways of thinking about reality, and coming to know what needs to change, are profoundly skewed.

At the deepest level, our ontological understanding and epistemological methods prioritize the visible — physical strength, separateness, and the power to control the environment — the masculine principle. This approach has created exclusionary hierarchies of power, held into existence by structural violence and a deepening gap between wealth and poverty. The feminine principle of connectivity and grasping the invisible through the powers of the heart and soul and aligning oneself to it through the spirit of love and service, remains neglected, radically undervalued, exploited, and violently repressed. The war on women and the feminine actively continues in the 21st century, as the account of investigative reporter Sue Lloyd-Roberts shows.[34]

Collective understanding is rapidly evolving toward a holistic view of life. Advanced science increasingly suggests a radical shift in worldview: reality as a universal field of consciousness, a subtle interdependently co-arising energy system. Such ontological understanding calls for a heart-mind epistemological approach to life and society.[35] A heart-mind way of knowing and decision-making draws consciously and intentionally on the cultivation of heart-centered expanded perceptions of spiritual reality, through depth states of gratitude, care, and compassion, as it also draws on the rational powers of the mind to develop practical solutions that protect the inherent unity and sanctity of life. It involves deep listening to all the traumatizing social and historical polarities of human experience, which allows for a healing, holistic, and forward-looking unitive perspective to emerge.

This emergent heart-mind epistemology encompasses all human potentialities and aspects of human consciousness and reflects a coherence of mind, feelings, and will.[36] It is based on the convergence between universal laws across spiritual systems and the findings of advanced science about the unitive nature of reality.[37] Convergent understanding recognizes that *it is only in our movement toward greater unity that we find greater justice.*

EDUCATIONAL EFFORTS IN THE MOVEMENT TOWARD UNITY: CHANGING CULTURE

A massive and rapidly growing global effort, led by thousands of non-profit organizations and global initiatives, is striving to help communities and cultures appreciate the impossibility of continuing to exist separately and in a disconnect between mental beliefs and the wisdom of the human heart. The United Nations, by its very existence over the past 75 years, has been a beacon of the value of unity. The UN community has persevered in developing goals for a global society, but it has no power to move beyond recommendations. Many other groups seek to promote holistic unitive values and approaches to change, yet efforts often remain partial — either limited to a particular intellectual group or focused more broadly on social issues but not touching the ontological and epistemological roots of the system of patriarchy and structural planetary violence.

Educational efforts on every level of societies need to become systematic in illuminating the roots of structural violence and illustrating the practical reality of interdependence through examining concrete interactions between different cultural groups. These efforts need to be informed by the two wings of human understanding — spiritual and scientific. Scriptural scholarship and advanced science, rather than divisive media influences, can help communities to gradually appreciate how far accepted cultural ways have strayed from the spirit of their claimed spiritual traditions. From a heart-mind epistemological perspective, many culturally accepted practices have forced people of all classes, genders, and races to close their hearts, repress their emotions, and go along with hierarchies of power to perpetuate systemic violence.

Now, we must ground ourselves in holistic heart-mind approaches to pressing issues and must overcome the fear of speaking from the universal ethical principles that underly unitive reality and cut across wisdom traditions and the science of reality. We must find the courage and consistency to educate for values that can regenerate oppressive and unjust structures and systems.

As an example, mothers from poor rural communities can be supported to no longer view their baby girls as a lot less valuable and less worth feeding than the boys who have more physical stamina to work in the field. Uninformed mullahs need to learn from Islamic scholars that Islam views marriage as an important social contract which is void without the consent of both partners and does not endorse forced marriages, considering sexual relationship within a forced marriage as rape. Masses of men, whose cultural beliefs support the claim that rape is always the girl's fault, and that killing a sister, a daughter or a wife will restore honor to a man, need to be encouraged to engage in deep spiritual study of their respective religious traditions until they develop spiritual understanding of where individual responsibility lies and what is the source of honor.

The most systematically envisioned effort I know at global society restructuring through educating unity consciousness and heart-mind ways of working together, is the Bahá'í-inspired Institute approach to community development, which currently spreads to over 180 countries and advances, over decades, to new frontiers of learning and being. [38]

What is unique about this effort is that it extends to all classes in societies and does not require a particular religious identification, nor does it seek to create an exclusive religious community. Rather, it takes an open-ended and encouraging view of community life as an ongoing and multifaceted developmental process which seeks to open a path for everyone. The emphasis of the Institute process is on spiritual empowerment and community building as it engages people in developing a spiritual understanding of life and a long-term vision of social evolution. It works through uplifting the soul, setting a clear standard of spiritual maturity, and adopting a service orientation and a systematic and constructive long-term educational approach to developing cohesion.

Its results vary from community to community, but an impressive example is the impact men in some remote rural areas share — the spiritual shift in their thinking about the status and role of women in society. Another impact on both men and women has been rethinking the validity of the practice of child marriages and the caste system in Indian society. Across cultures and communities, people report a profound culture change toward unitive values as they learn to harmonize the human powers of will, reason, and love.

While this pedagogy is at a relatively early phase of development and is yet to be studied as a potential model and enriched by the input of social scientists, it is successful because it draws on the only spiritual system that I am aware of which *expressly* abolishes any form of oppression of and violence against women and people of different racial and social backgrounds and upholds a standard of equality and unity. This spiritual system recognizes and emphasizes its roots in all the earlier spiritual systems in human history and, thus, upholds unity and continuity in the evolution of collective consciousness. It emphasizes the dialectic interdependence between unity and true justice for all of humanity.

▎PROCESSES OF UNITIVE JUSTICE

Unitive justice was first practiced by Indigenous communities where men and women came together in balance and inclusion, to acknowledge a living web of interconnectedness of all life and to offer meaningful support to all involved in instances of injustice by simultaneously restoring and maintaining community harmony.[39] In recent decades, Virginia civil trial attorney Sylvia Clute, founder of *Alliance for Unitive Justice*,[40] developed a theory of unitive justice which compares 14 structures found in punitive systems to 14 structures found in unitive systems, providing a roadmap for the transition to a unitive system.[41] A methodology for unitive justice circles gradually emerged. There is now a growing recognition that for planetary issues to be genuinely and systematically addressed, processes are needed that bridge deepening divides, draw on holistic heart-mind ways of being, and bring together the *two central organizing planetary principles* of *unity* and *justice.*

Processes of unitive justice arise, at this time, in communities, like the ones described in the section above, which seek to create *spiritual and social coherence through harmonizing the ways people use their powers of will, reason, and love.*

Now, *unitive justice as the next level of planetary social integration needs to become the foundation for global ethical, educational, and legal structures,* which both leave room for the richness of diverse cultural traditions and purge them from elements of structural oppression and violence.

Processes of unitive justice have two critical aspects. One is the conscious use of an evolutionary spiritual language, which bridges divides, heals dichotomies, and transforms invisible and entrenched patriarchal worldviews and mindsets into new horizons of heart-mind ways of being and working together for a more just world.[42] The other critical aspect is the creation of legal global governance structures that support and protect unitive justice.

▌GOVERNMENTAL AND LEGAL MOVEMENT TOWARD UNITIVE JUSTICE

How can we seriously speak of civilization when we have no global entities able to effectively protect humanity against unspeakably inhumane practices such as the use of chemical weapons on civilians, torture, rape as a method of control and systematic sexual assault as a method of war, mass murder, human trafficking, female genital mutilation, honor killings, slave labor, pillaging of natural resources, and millions facing starvation? We have United Nations conventions on many of the above, but no structures that enforce them and protect human security. This manifest political hypocrisy at the highest levels of governance creates a collective culture of broken trust, a vast chasm between spoken and actual values, and ultimately, systemic injustice. It breeds desperation, jadedness, corruption, and social disintegration. The planet can no longer sustain the resulting chaos of human planetary life, while we continue to celebrate the courage of those individuals — investigative journalists and pathbreaking environmentalists — who risk their lives to reveal up close the self-destructive nature of our current cultures. It is time to do genuine justice to individual courage and translate its findings into legal structures. It is time to move beyond the cult of unexamined traditional ethnic ways. Every aspect of our lives must answer the question: *Does it support the sanctity of life or not?*

As an example, explorations of unitive justice across the presumably developed Western and predominantly Christian world can reveal the incompatibility between the spirit of Christ and ingrained racism, sexism, and classism. Even in Bahá'í communities, which hold express values about gender equality and human oneness, people need processes of unitive justice to learn to differentiate their cultural biases from spiritual teachings and to foster genuine healing and coming together.

As people around the world realize their interdependence with other communities and cultures, and the reality that lasting justice for all is also one that unites, rather than further divides people, *each culture and context will develop its own variation of unitive justice processes that foster healing from our current disconnected, fragmented ways of being.* What will remain common across cultures is the fundamental distinction between the structures of a punitive system and the structures of a unitive system of justice.

Such a massive global effort at unitive justice must be protected at the level of global law enforcement. The use of force, clearly defined, both ethically and legally, for the purpose of stopping the rise of aggressors, may be needed for yet a long time to come, until humanity reaches such evolution of collective consciousness that it can completely dispense with the use of force. The limits and parameters of global institutions that reflect more justly, and protect, the whole of humanity have been explored in an abundance of proposals.[43] Now we need the momentum to act.

Can we imagine unitive justice spaces operating at the level of the United Nations, and calling into question existing UN structures such as the Security Council, which still maintain the old-world model of exclusionary hierarchies of power? Just as communities in the example above were able to move beyond the centuries-old caste system through spiritual empowerment and a sense of unity, so too unitive justice processes at every level, from citizen assemblies to the UN General Assembly, can create momentum for a new system of global governance that represents justly the whole of humanity and is empowered to protect human security in action.

Humanity has always longed for a relationship to the sacred. Giving up that longing in a modern age fraught with misconceptions about reality as only that which can be observed, has unleashed the greatest pandemic of addictions, corruption, soaring mental illness, and violence. Planetary crises are facing us with a moment of choice,[44] in which we can no longer depend on leaders, or groups, or industry. Our only opportunity lies in the grassroot movement of citizen assemblies which seek to restore the sacred in our collective lives through unitive justice that honors and protects the sacredness of all life.

CHAPTER 33

UPSHIFTED RELATIONSHIP TO BEAUTY

ARABELLA THAÏS

The World will be saved by Beauty. — Dostoevsky

Beauty, like time, is a strange and wondrous thing. It is fundamental to the human experience and yet so hard to pin down in words. We know when we are in the presence of Beauty because it absorbs us; it even has the power to transform us. In the words of the great poet Dante, "Beauty awakens the soul to act."[45] The question remains: Why? What *is* beauty, and what is its meaning? I propose that a renewed investigation into aesthetic principles and the implementation of said principles offer the potential to transform human consciousness and, thus, to transform our world. Because Beauty, I suggest, has the power to redeem us all.

The question of Beauty has been contemplated since the dawn of Western philosophy and once bore great influence on the cultural psyche. Unfortunately, the situation today is radically different. Post-Industrial societies are fragmented, divorced from meaning, nature, holistic thinking, and philosophical discourse, and now humanity faces a meta-crisis of catastrophic proportions. But our problems are not isolated. Sex trafficking, bigotry, the climactic catastrophe, poverty, genocide, and warfare are but symptoms of a single cause: a sickness of Mind. The only solution is to heal and evolve, to upshift consciousness. The crucial question is how?

Aldous Huxley held the belief that the mystical enlightenment of the individual would change the world, and I agree. To become mystically enlightened is the equivalent of exiting Plato's proverbial cave and beholding a whole new world outside, a world that is intelligent, creative, purposeful, and multi-dimensional, as well as intrinsically meaningful. This is the essence of what it means "to awaken." At the heart of this illumined perspective is a deepened understanding of the nature of consciousness and, therefore, cosmology, for this is not a material universe but a mental one. This is the new paradigm that Ervin Laszlo has so elegantly and meticulously articulated throughout his work.

Despite the incredible body of evidence pointing toward an intelligent, self-realizing cosmos, mainstream scientists still resist it. But scientific materialism will never be able to explain why we have consciousness as complex and self-reflexive as our own, why we dance, make art, or experience poetry in the changing of the seasons and the movement of the moon. These are not just essential facets of our conscious experience; they also make life worth living. To evolve beyond our current worldview, we must come to understand the nature of mind itself, and this requires a radical expansion of consciousness that is inherently mystical, emancipatory, and aesthetic in nature. We must go from being 'lumbering robots' (to use Richard Dawkins' colorful phrase) in a meaningless universe, to active participants in a self-discovering, purposeful cosmos.[46] This revelation unveils a tapestry of reality that is both ineffably beautiful and exquisitely profound. In the words of 18th century poet Novalis: "We dream of voyaging across the universe. Isn't the universe, then, in us? We do not know the depths of our mind. Toward the interior goes the mysterious road. Eternity with its worlds, past and future, is in us."[47]

The potential of Beauty is multivalent, but first, we must redefine our understanding of it. Unfortunately, these days, beauty is more commonly associated with "the beauty industry" — a $532 billion market that deals with our skin-deep appearance — rather than the ideal put forth by Plato who wrote in *The Symposium* that "only in the contemplation of beauty is life worth living."[48] According to Plato's theory, Beauty is a perfect Idea from the transcendental realm of Forms and is also the highest Good. While Plato's metaphysics are not the final word on the nature of reality, his ideas are coherent with cosmic consciousness and indicate new possibilities for us to relate and respond to beauty — specifically, that beauty confers cosmic truth and is to be revered as such.

BEAUTY AS DIVINE EXPRESSION

Beauty, in its highest expression, appears to point toward the intrinsic nature of reality. As the poet John Keats famously wrote, "Truth is beauty, beauty truth – that is all ye know on Earth, and all ye need to know."[49] This truth, which is ultimately beyond words, is expressed *through* Beauty and *in* beauty and, yet, is also beyond it, just out of reach. It is as though the exalted aesthetic experience allows us to catch a glimpse of "the whole" — the immanent cosmic intelligence that orchestrates our reality, that transcends the laws of time and space, and which sages and mystics across the ages have known as the Divine. This noetic quality does not extend to all "beautiful" phenomena, however, because not everyone has the same opinion of what constitutes beauty. Is beauty merely in the eye of the beholder? Or is there a fundamental and objective truth that transcends the lens of subjective opinion? I argue for the latter statement, that there are pinnacle expressions of beauty wherein its presence is undeniable — the starry night-sky, a rose in bloom, or a Rembrandt painting, for example — after which it iterates itself across a spectrum that becomes increasingly diluted and, therefore, more prone to subjective opinion.

That beauty is an intrinsic property of the cosmos (rather than a human projection) is indicated by the fact it exists at all. There is simply no conventional explanation for it. Conservative trends in evolutionary biology argue that all human behavior emerges from "selfish-gene" survival mechanisms, and this cannot account for the presence of awe and beauty. Beauty is, however, fully coherent with the paradigm of an intelligent, self-realizing cosmos, its presence crystallized in the intersection of creativity, consciousness, and cosmic causality. Firstly, everything has a cause — there is a reason why everything comes to pass, and this is self-evident — but this does not mean that we have to understand all the reasons and causes (for example, the question of why anything exists at all, which will always be beyond us). Secondly, the universe is undeniably creative — it is a matrix from which stars, galaxies, flowers, forests, and intelligent life have emerged — and, as Laszlo has explicated, this creative impulse is moving towards an increasing state of complexity and ultimate "super-coherence," i.e., the unification of the whole. This indicates a telos (purpose or goal) to this universe, and I propose that the telos is Beauty, that beauty is the truth and the reason, and it is pulling us forward like a magnet towards a perfect and complete aesthetic masterpiece. Our need to create art, seen thus, is simply a fractal, micro-cosmic reflection of this.

If beauty is the cause of cosmic creativity rather than just the effect, and the universe creates in order to realize the potential of Beauty, then it makes sense that Beauty is the cause of consciousness, because a self-actualizing cosmos requires self-reflective consciousness in order to experience the magnificence of its own creativity, and realize itself on every dimension.[50] Thus, the more consciousness evolves and expands, the greater its capacity to perceive beauty and, crucially, to express it. Hence, the human impulse to paint upon the walls of caves signified an evolution in consciousness beyond survival-based instincts: it was a response to the new-found perception of something greater than ourselves — something beautiful, mystical, meaningful, and inherent. Unlike Plato, who argued that art was mere imitation (and therefore a "form of the form"), I agree with German philosopher Friedrich Schelling that art reveals, "a higher truth."

However, beauty is not only visual and sensual; it also pertains to intrinsic ethical ideals: the Platonic notion of Beauty as the ultimate Form of the Good, Truth, Justice, and so on. The more beautiful something is, the closer it is to the Source, and, thus, the more coherent, harmonious, and unified it is. The more evolved a society becomes, then, the more beautiful it becomes, and this is the pathway to Utopia. The catch is that in order to attain these ideals embedded in Beauty, evolved consciousness is required, the sort of consciousness that has typically been associated with higher realms (for instance, "Christ Consciousness"). This allows us to move past the dazzling light of physical beauty and understand the deeper truth it points toward. Because Beauty, like the ring of power in J.R.R. Tolkien's *Lord of the Rings*, has the capacity to destroy those who lack strength and integrity. Without the moral fortitude to "handle" the power of beauty, expressions of it can rot at the core: exquisite refinement becomes rancid excess, the sensual becomes sordid, and the sublime becomes decadent. The character of Dorian Gray in Oscar Wilde's eponymous novel is the perfect example of this, but we see it all around us in our consumer-based culture, which thrives on people wanting 'nice things' in order to fuel sustained and rampant production.

The issue with Western culture is that we have become overly focused on visual beauty, especially as it manifests in the human form. But without moral beauty, physical beauty is a hollow mirage. We are watching shadows on the wall of the cave and thinking they are real. However, if we come to understand Beauty as an expression of the Divine, there lies redemptive power within it that may help mystically enlighten people. The scientific paradigm must shift concurrently, but understanding beauty's true nature is coeval with this. Indeed, it is *through* beauty that we can best disseminate the message of a new scientific paradigm — because mathematics is a language spoken by few, and neither philosophical nor scientific discourse delivers the truth they reach towards. They merely circle around it. But, as communication theorist Marshall McLuhan observed, "The medium is the message."[51] Truth must be enacted in order to be expressed. Art is the best way to do this, since not only can Art supply Supreme Beauty, it also can communicate this knowledge and meaning to any single human being. In the words of Terence McKenna: "The artist's task is to save the soul of mankind; and anything less is a dithering while Rome burns. Because of the artists, who are [able] to journey into the Other, if the artists cannot find the way, then the way cannot be found."

▌BEAUTY AS A WAY OF KNOWING

If Beauty is a compass to higher intelligence, then aesthetic experience is an epistemological pathway that ought to be taken seriously. Unlike scientific materialism — which is devoid of emotion and relies solely on physical instruments and data collection — the epistemology of beauty is inherently somatic, emotional, and intuitive, hence, the term 'aesthetics' corresponds with "aesthesis," which means "to sense, to feel." This is significant because our society, desensitized and disenchanted as it is, quite literally needs to "come to its senses" and re-establish its connection to the ensouled flesh of the sensible world. This includes the wisdom of the body and the sensuality of our felt experience, which is, after all, the primary means through which we come to know reality. The profound intelligence of our senses is being precluded because materialism is manacled to what integral thinker Jean Gebser called the "mental structure of consciousness." This is precisely why the aesthetic experience could help restore us to other ways of knowing, because it is not analytic in nature — it is *felt* — even if profound contemplation is entangled in it.

While the aesthetic experience does not preclude the intellect, it is the sensual response that indicates Beauty's presence. Hence, the greatness of an artwork is sensed before the mind can critique it, and it is why Oscar Wilde stated that "beauty needs no explanation." Similarly, to weep in rapture at the beauty of a Beethoven quartet or a gleaming crescent moon is hardly a "rational" response. It is emotional, intuitive, and somatic. But if Beauty is the reason for our existence, then, actually, it is very reasonable to respond like this! This is simply an upshifted conception of Reason. As the philosopher Maurice Merleau-Ponty said, "Knowledge is felt," and often this knowledge is beyond what our intellect is capable of comprehending because, to quote esteemed scientist J. B. S. Haldane, "not only is the universe queerer than we understand, it is queerer than we *can* understand."[52,53] Beauty is an epistemological pathway to the meaning that lies beyond words. Similarly, if certain artworks confer divine revelation, then art accrues religious, mystical power that transcends the dogma of all religions, as well as materialist science.

However, in order to use Beauty to upshift consciousness, encourage scientific advances, and awaken humanity, we must not privilege one means of knowing over another. The new paradigm requires holistic thinking, and beauty is an invitation for us to synthesize different pathways. The aesthetic experience is not enough, nor is philosophical speculation. The optimal coalescence is between aesthesis (sensing/feeling/intuiting) and the intellect (reason, understanding), with subsequent supporting, empirical evidence. Otherwise, theories remain just that: theoretical.

The synergy between reason and sensual delight is demonstrated when mathematicians behold a particularly elegant theorem and experience beauty; they "sense" the meaning through a kind of visual intuition. Euler's identity ($ei\pi + 1 = 0$), for example, is considered to be the "most beautiful" mathematical formula. Professor of Mathematics at Stanford, Keith Devlin, has described it in rapturous terms: "Like a Shakespearean sonnet that captures the very essence of love, or a painting that brings out the beauty of the human form that is far more than just skin deep, Euler's equation reaches down into the very depths of existence."[54] But why? What constitutes its grace? Like all art and natural beauty, the equation's aesthetic splendor arises from the relationship between its constituent parts, and what these parts point towards. In this instance, those parts include the mathematical constants *i*, *e*, and *pi* — imaginary and irrational numbers. These numbers are true, but they are *beyond* the "real plane," i.e., physical reality. These symbols point toward deeper orders of existence that confound the reason/rationale of someone with a materialist mindset. However, for those who have an aesthetic sensibility and are poetically attuned to the cosmic mind, such concepts make complete sense.

It is for this same reason that aesthetics may assist us in pioneering scientific discoveries.

We seem to have forgotten that ground-breaking forward leaps have long been entwined with intuition, imagination, and an aesthetic sensibility. This was integral to the Copernican revolution when we made the shift to a heliocentric paradigm. According to cultural historian Richard Tarnas,

"The early scientific revolutionaries perceived their breakthroughs as divine illuminations, spiritual awakenings to the true structural grandeur and intellectual beauty of the cosmic order."[55] An upshifted conception of Beauty is a call to return to our intuition, and to let that be our guide. How else did so many minds — from Plato to Parmenides, and the Hermetics to the German Idealists — intuit the same idea that was corroborated millennia later by quantum mechanics: that this is not so much a material universe, but a mental one encapsulated by physicist Max Planck's statement: "All matter originates and exists only by virtue of a force which brings the particle of an atom to vibration and holds … the atom together. We must assume behind this force the existence of a conscious and intelligent mind. This mind is the matrix of all matter."[56]

AESTHETIC PRINCIPLES AS GUIDING TENETS FOR EVOLUTION

In the upshift of human consciousness, may beauty be our guide. This is not a mechanical universe; it is musical and poetic, and we are here to create a masterpiece. Much like the way a sculptor hones a piece of marble, Humanity's task is to evolve consciousness into its most refined and exquisite expression. Our task, then, is the artist's task, and we shall not finish it in our lifetime, but we are here to play our part. In the words of Pythagoras, "There is geometry in the humming of the strings. There is music of the spacing of the spheres."[57] This universe is a cosmic symphony unfolding before our eyes, and we are part of it. The question is, then, what does our melody sound like? What chords do we need to play in order to come into resonance with the higher octaves? Consciousness — like sound, and everything else — is a waveform, and every word that we utter, every thought that we think, and every deed that we do is like playing a musical note, and as doctor and philosopher Sir David Hawkins' work on consciousness has demonstrated, human suffering does not emit coherent frequencies.[58] As it stands, our species is making a terrible noise.

But in spite of humanity's failings, I do not believe we are a lost cause, or that utopia is a childish delusion. I understand us to be a work in progress, and that is all. However, first we must believe the impossible dream: that we can and will realize utopia. The next thing is to imagine what that looks like. We have spent so much time imagining dystopian nightmares that we have forgotten to attend to our Elysian dreams. What, then, does a more beautiful and evolved society look like? What does it *feel* like? What beautiful things could we create? We need only look to the harmonic series — a nested hierarchy of coherent wavelengths that perfectly relate to each other — to see that Beauty is borne of deep, structural unity in which constituent parts amplify and enhance the others, so that the whole is greater than the sum of the parts. A more evolved society, then, would emulate this and involve the harmonious inter-relationship between all existents — people, places, animals, and things — where all systems would work cohesively and enhance each other in the service of greater joy, creativity, freedom, love, and splendor. More beauty equates to more coherence, and this means coherence of consciousness.

What we need is beautiful people to lead the world — not necessarily in their physical form — but in their character. We need aesthetic visionaries in service of divine evolution, not self-oriented politicians and CEOs. We shall know that consciousness is evolving because of how it *feels*. Aesthesis, rather than financial growth, could be our metric. The ethos of Beauty could inform the design of houses, schools, cities, educative models, clothes, healthcare, and food. The unifying aesthetic principles would not halt the freedom of creative expression but encourage it — so long as it supported the frequency of higher-consciousness. Imagine if this were our reality. Could you, just for a moment? Because coming to know Beauty is the greatest love story of all time. It is a journey of ecstatic communion, remembering, and realizing, for we are the universe experiencing itself.

CHAPTER 34

THE ENSOULMENT OF REALITY: THE SOUL, ART AND TECHNOLOGY OF LIFE-CENTRIC REALITIES

NATALIE ZEITUNY

▌OPENING – THE ENSOULMENT OF REALITY

Is humanity ready to cultivate realities that are sourced in universal principles? Could our civilization usher a global thriving on all levels: personally, culturally, naturally, and technologically? How could ensouled realities unleash boundless love, wisdom, and power that allow us all to thrive deep into the future? What is a soul, and what does humanity's soul feel like?

What I share in this paper is informed and guided by more than twenty-five years of Ensoulment research, personally and with thousands of individual clients and organizations. When we source realities in the "soul of things," we naturally and effortlessly give rise to the good, the true, and the beautiful, in all directions.

This paper discusses three primary questions: (1) What is Ensoulment? (2) What is Reality? and (3) How can humanity create life-centric realities?

▌ENSOULMENT

Ensoulment is the ongoing process of connecting, embodying, and expressing one's soul, the actualization of one's innermost essence, the realization of its higher, deeper, and wider original essence.

Your soul is your unique, essential field. It is made of your particular evolutionary experiences imprinted in your primordial, essential fabric. These experiences are recorded in your information field, made out of conscious, vibrational, energetic particles of experiences.

Your soul is connected to the universal primordial realm and to the soul of the world, and therein lies its boundless love, beauty, power, and wisdom. Your soul field is continuously updating and recalibrating based on your moment-by-moment experiences.

Everything you notice inside and around you has a soul, an inherent primordial essence. Your family, your country, humanity, and the planet all have a soul. Souls articulate through unique arrangements of form we call vessels. Your thoughts, feelings, and dreams are all vessels, containers of experiences. The cells in your body and your relationships are all examples of forms, of bodies, of vessels that carry the momentary ripples of your soul's experiences.

In the same way the pupils in your eyes record and respond to the slightest changes of light, soul fields respond to the slightest changes in your experience. This happens at all scales, in all dimensions, all the time — everything has an alive, generative, and responsive soul.

Ensoulment models describe how our personal soul is connected to our collective soul and the soul of the world through "soul particles of experience." Every person, every plant, and every animal has a soul. Every nation, every landscape, and even ideas have souls. The soul is the foundation of all existence. Each soul has its unique cosmology and reality creation process.

Your reality creation process is as unique as your fingerprints and is influenced by individual, collective, and universal realities. The reality creation process itself evolves, in the same way individuals, collectives, and cosmic souls evolve.

Reality is made out of three primary building blocks: vessels, soul particles of experience ("Sxp"), and the Soul of the World ("SOW").

1. *Vessels* are unique soul formations. They are stable carriers of the soul's experiences.
2. *Sxp* are the fundamental unit of existence, elementary particles, that each vessel generates, while having momentary experiences.
3. *SOW* is the totality of all manifested happenings (actual occasions), such as essences, souls, vessels, Sxp, and realities.

These three elements are continuously interacting and expanding the Soul of the World. Vessels have experiences and emit Sxp. Sxp articulate, weave, and actualize realities and literally bring to life the Soul of the World. The whole cosmos moves as one embodied soul, living and breathing through us. The entire world is a vibrational, energetic, conscious organism communicating through us, partly through our conscious and unconscious, personal and collective, physical, mental, emotional, and spiritual experiences.

The realities that souls create are critical to humanity's long-term global thriving. Because the soul is sourced in primordial universal principles, it embodies the highest and deepest evolutionary intelligence. Because the soul has existed since the inception of the universe, the realities that the soul generates have an inherent long-term ecological orientation as part of the Soul of the World.

Without this orientation, all other realities sourced elsewhere would be suboptimal, wasteful, and inefficient on our journey toward thriving realities. Wasting life-force energy, causing pain, suffering, and death of so many life forms, diverts our entire evolutionary trajectory toward extinction.

Now that we understand the soul, let's explore the second essential element: reality.

▎REALITY

Reality is the vessel's experiential field. The Earth is a vessel; it generates organic biological realities. Humanity is a vessel; it generates societal and cultural realities. Our cells, tissues, and organs are vessels; they generate human biological body realities. Artificial intelligence is a vessel; it generates virtual realities, and so on. The "experience landscapes" that each vessel creates are the realities that vessel lives inside.

Vessels emit particles of experience and weave "experiential patterns" inside and around them. That weaving terrain is what we call reality. If there is a reality, there is a vessel; if there is no vessel, there is no reality. You are the embodiment and the expression of all realities operating inside and around you.

There is a unique relationship between souls, vessels, their experiences, and the realities they create. As humanity evolves and further decodes our species' reality formation process, we will be able to create thriving conditions for all life forms — if we choose to.

Such reality creation requires soul-centric wisdom coupled with reality creation mastery.

I distinguish between ensouled realities, informed by the long-term wisdom of the soul, and constructed realities, informed by the short-term thinking of the mind (personal and collective mind). Our global mind and brain emerged as a result of an evolutionary necessity to better manage information to serve different vessels as part of the Soul of the World. It developed as a tool to organize, analyze, and process vast amounts of information to serve particular vessels surviving and thriving.

Humanity's global mind was formed to improve the survive-ability and thrive-ability of our species, and it excelled at it — until now. *Homo sapiens*' mind and its advanced communication and collaboration skills set us apart from our Neanderthal, Denisovan, and other "cousins." But now, humanity's mind has expanded its reality's domination and colonized the entire soul of humanity! Not only that, our global mind refers to the earth as a resource to be used, to children as labor to be exploited, and to humans as vessels to expand its hegemony.

Mind took a driver's seat, confusing itself with the person's soul and with humanity's soul. Mind and the realities that mind creates, such as language, conceptual thinking, and the internet and technological landscapes, are growing out of proportion. Mind realities are out of synch with the individual's soul, with humanity's soul, and with the soul of our planet. Enabling this confusion are primarily unconscious humans (who are allowing such a mind-colonization process to take place) and rapidly developing technologies devoid of souls.

We have been migrating to and living inside mentally constructed psychological identities, collective stories, and technological realities for a few centuries now. As Plato wrote in his 380 BC "Allegory of the Cave," we are captives, chained since infancy, gazing at the shadows flitting across the cave wall, considering this as our full reality. Comfortable in the chains of what we know to be true, we are unable and unwilling to live inside the full scope of our humanity, the full scope of our soul.

In addition, we have been using constructed systems and mental realities as pathways to understanding our existence, not realizing that these are halls of mirrors, reflecting to us who we are in the moment but not the essence and the soul of who we are — the bedrock that gives rise to all realities. We need to challenge ourselves by continuing to ask deeper questions. What actually separates humanity from its soul, from the earth, and from each other? How can we awaken and see the truth of life?

THE SOUL OF THE WORLD AND TECHNOLOGY

The Soul of the Word is a sentient organism field. It includes the totality of all ever-differentiated and actualized vessels since the inception of the universe. It includes all forms in all time, spaces, and realms. It can also be described as an ever-changing universal source code —an intelligent and actualized wave-function fabric — representing what it feels like to exist, to experience the world, in all times and spaces since its inception.

With the exponential growth of biotechnology, genetic engineering, nanotechnology, and artificial intelligence, we are in the midst of a human mutation. We are gradually migrating our life-force from the human soul to the "digital machine soul." Our collective human soul is becoming a hybrid of the two.

This convergence is occurring before humanity's soul has even begun to express its inherent, multidimensional, energetic, conscious, vibrational, soulful capacities. These capabilities are powerful beyond measure. These capacities are deeply embedded in our soul-seed DNA, which takes many forms, such as self-healing, the transformation of matter, remote viewing, remote hearing, remote communication, teleportation, and mastering the science of reality creation, to name a few.

From artificial intelligence to machine learning realities, from social media to mail-order CRISPR kits that allow anyone to hack an organism's

DNA with a genetic editing tool, technologically constructed realities are taking over our planet. Who are the young software engineers designing humanity's next mutation? How much soul maturity and long-term ecological wisdom are infused in their design? Soul wisdom is an intelligence that emerged out of millions of years of evolution. Who is overseeing our species' transfiguration?

The more humanity invests in scientific, industrial, and technological realities, which are external constructs, the less humanity devotes itself to inner, embodied, biological, psychological, soulful capacities and extrasensory perception. Slowly but surely, our life-force is migrating away from our body, our feelings, our sensations, our relations, our soul, our planet, and our collective, ancient, ensouled wisdom. Who are we becoming? Can we create an ecologically flourishing future that serves nature, culture, technology, and all life? Yes, we can.

Humanity's future depends on the rate at which humanity will embody its own soul. It also depends on our civilization's relationship to the earth and technology. What will be the growth rate of natural realities, ensouled realities, compared to technological realities?

▌THE SOUL OF THE WORLD TECHNOLOGICAL ALGORITHM

Humanity is now capable of designing algorithms to optimize thrive-ability for all life on our planet. By applying multidisciplinary, rigorous scientific research based on ecological and holistic soulful principles, we could harness the power of soul-consciousness combined with technological-consciousness to direct our culture toward a long-lasting renaissance.

We are now capable of designing an algorithm that nourishes all life and supports our evolutionary thriving. The purpose of the algorithm is to cultivate the right conditions for optimal thriving for all life. The algorithm is programmed by the wisest and most ensouled humans, as well as the most powerful, skilled programmers and engineers.

By embedding in the algorithm universal principles, such us reciprocity, collaboration, interconnectedness, complex systems dynamics, infinite games theory, long-term planning, ecological thrive-ability, and so on, the algorithm will then suggest the best course of action, taking into consideration all ways of knowing. Artificial intelligence will offer the best ways of applying and integrating such upgrades to humanity's systems and culture. A global wisdom council guides the application of all algorithms at all times.

Reality is fundamental to existence — as fundamental as (if not more) consciousness, energy, vibration, or matter. Therefore, elucidating reality will allow us to create conditions, systems, and technologies that will support our thriving evolutionary future.

As we converge all ways of knowing into a theory of reality and begin to discover the principles of reality, we create conditions that give rise to life-centric realities, aligned with universal principles.

▌OUR INTERCONNECTEDNESS

Our collective history, afflicted with wars, famines, and disease, has scarred us with deep physiological and psychological wounding. These are passed on to us from previous generations and are still imprinting our collective field.

Our wounds bind us to the pain of others and relentlessly push our society toward external progress, toward the external alleviation of pain. In the name of safety, security, and progress, we never again want to feel the pain of hunger, the humiliation of slavery, or the disgrace of abuse.

The abandonment of our personal and collective inner lives results in our blind use and abuse of Earth's biodiversity. Our attempt to gain security, stability, and comfort is leading us astray. When we focus on external progress alone, we pay a huge price, reflected in epidemics of heart disease, cancer, and mental illness.

When we starve our souls and sedate our consciousness, we cause tremendous damage to ourselves, our families, our countries, and the world. This damage is imprinted in our collective pain body realities. Therefore, a crucial step toward ensouling humanity is prioritizing healing and reconciliation of individual and collective trauma as soon as possible.

Healing humanity is an easy task. Take, for example, the COVID-19 period. It showed us our global capacity to create a new world order within weeks. Such a rapid global reorganization of the masses is a fascinating case study for years to come. When humanity is called to redirect its Earthship, it does. When countries need to collaborate, they do. When we are asked to change our ways, we do. In the same way, it is possible to heal and revive the soul of humanity on all scales within a short time.

We hacked the human genome. We put a man on the moon. We elected a Black President of the United States and just recently overcame the COVID-19 global crisis. Mastering the soul, art, and technology of reality creation could be next in line.

There is an intelligent co-creative dynamic between (1) our soul, (2) the reality we create, and (3) the world we experience. It's the first time in history that humanity's collective consciousness, coupled with cutting-edge technologies, could allow us to observe our moment-by-moment evolutionary happenings in real time. As humanity grows to master its agricultural, industrial, technological, and conscious skills, I believe we are now entering a new era of reality mastery, a period where we are creating, experiencing, transforming, and witnessing our realities in real time.

▌THE SPIRIT, ART AND TECHNOLOGY OF REALITY CREATION

From Sxp to vessels, from the Soul of the World to realities and back, how do we apply ensoulment reality creation principles and processes to serve our personal and global flourishing?

We begin with ourselves by:

1. Learning to discover, connect, and express our soul in our daily lives
2. Witnessing correlations between our soul (essence), our personality (mental construct), and the Soul of the World
3. Inquiring what plays a role in the construction of our reality, what gives rise to the quality of our experience and how?
4. Continuously healing and integrating pain, wounding, and trauma in our personal and relational field
5. Observing what experiences allow us all to personally thrive while continuously orientating toward global well-being
6. Continuously studying our personal relationships with our experiences, vessels, the Soul of the World, and the realities we create
7. Examining our reality creation process — how do we give rise to our everyday experience in our personal lives, intimate relationships, professional lives, creative lives, and family or social lives?

Then we move out into the world and apply the same discovery process to our social collectives and humanity's soul. We learn together. Who is the soul of our family? Who is the soul of our country? Who is the soul of humanity? How does the soul of humanity communicate? How does the soul of the planet communicate? What will support their thriving?

As we observe the human realities we construct, from social norms to media, from national to international relations, we vote with our attention and participation in realities. We vote by creating desired realities and inviting players to take part in these. Every thought we think, every news channel we listen to, and every word we utter shapes and empowers multiple realities. We become masters by choosing the realities we participate in.

We literally learn to decode conscious and unconscious patterns in our collective realities. We keep orienting ourselves toward personal and global behaviors that support flourishing at all levels: how we grow food (the soul of food), how we treat animals, and how we protect natural landscapes (the soul of nature). We delve into the soul of education, healthcare, politics, economics — you name it. When we source our perspective in our soul, we learn how to create realities that serve all of humanity and the planet with ease and grace.

Finally, we create processes and systems that cultivate life-centric reality inquiry.

To decipher humanity's reality creation process, we organize in groups, structures, and processes that act like greenhouses for cultivating reality inquiry on all levels and scales.

We gradually increase the importance and influence of multidisciplinary reality research. Since everything is co-arising simultaneously (cells, tissues, organs, people, nature, culture), the more synergetic, collaborative, and inclusive we are in our inquiry, the closer we connect to the truth of being.

How do we orient our collective life-force toward embodying "the soul of things"?

- Soulful food, soulful relationships, and soulful communication
- Soulful governments, soulful education, and soulful health care
- Soulful embodiment, soulful energy sources, and soulful trauma healing

One way to collectively embody the soul of things is to establish a multidisciplinary "Reality Exploration Program," and here is my proposal.

▌REALITY EXPLORATION PROGRAM/WISDOM COUNCIL – YOU ARE INVITED!

In 2022, I began conversations with a few globally conscious organizations to champion the creation of a "Reality Exploration Program," which acts as an incubator dedicated to cultivating inquiry about reality through (1) community, (2) research, (3) publication, (4) application, and (5) change-making.

The program includes artists, scientists, psychologists, sociologists, mystics, technologists, futurists, thought leaders, and spiritual leaders, to name a few. We come together and ask two primary questions:

1. What does human knowledge tell us about reality?
2. How do we integrate reality sciences into the fabric of humanity to allow life-centric thrive-ability?

The Reality Exploration Program/Wisdom Council's mission is to:

1. Position the field of reality research in public discourse
2. Scope the reality research domain and fields of inquiry
3. Engage in rigorous, collaborative, multidisciplinary, scientific research and artistic, social inquiry, constructing a Reality Theory of Everything (R-TOE)

4. Develop innovative reality models, tools, standards, perspectives, and worldviews

5. Develop technologies that optimize "reality patterns" and broadcast a "reality radar" (similar to the weather updates)

6. Publish, market, apply, and engage the public

7. Cultivate an open-source, nonhierarchical, transparent global community

▌SUMMARY

Wiser living in a planetary civilization requires deep and holistic knowledge of self, culture, nature, and reality. The fate of humanity depends upon the emergence of a life-affirming cosmological narrative that fosters an ecological understanding of our interconnectedness. The future is calling; will we answer the call?

Humanity is at a tipping point where our collective intelligence, power, and interconnectivity have matured enough to discover reality itself — not only consciousness, energy, matter, technology, or our psyche but also a comprehensive, integrated narrative that considers all perspectives and all ways of knowing.

A flourishing, regenerative, and abundant world is on the verge of birthing itself. It is sending its epigenetic codes through all of us — lovers, thinkers, scientists, and artists. Through every heartbeat, every inhale and exhale, the world is revealing what it could become through us. We belong to this planet; we belong to each other; we belong to this moment, journeying toward our essential truth before thought was created.

NOTES & REFERENCES

▌CHAPTER 29

ph

1. Bacchia, A. (2018). *Vedere Oltre lo Spazio-Tempo: dall'Era della Logica all'Era della Sapienza*. Milano: Anima Edizioni.; Bacchia, A. (2016). *ÌNIN Holographic Evolving: Toward a Civilization of Symphony. World Futures*, 72(1–2):83–92. https://doi.org/10.1080/02604027.2016.1143311 (Philadelphia: Taylor and Francis - 2nd revised Edition. Lugano: ÌNIN Editions, 2017); Bacchia, A. (2016). *Respiro Olografico - Il nostro Respiro, un flusso d'aria ubiquo e senza tempo*. Milano: Anima Edizioni.; Bacchia, A. (2015). *ÌNIN, an unexplored Experience of Akasha*. Lugano: ÌNIN Editions.; Bacchia, A. (2011). *ÌNIN One Earth Choir - Intercultural Project between Science and Art – Manifesto*. Lugano: ÌNIN Editions.; Bacchia, A. (2008). *How does 'what is not there' become 'what is there': A New Cognitive Approach, A New Experience of Information, New Awareness Spaces*. Helsinki, Finland: The 11th ISSEI Conference. (Reprinted in Lugano: ÌNIN Editions, 2008); and Bacchia, A. (2008). *The Emptiness Creating: How does 'what is not there' become 'what is there'? Intuitions where Cognitive Approach is Creation Process, is Life itself*. Lugano: ÌNIN Editions.
2. T. Torrance in: Bersanelli, M., & Gargantini, M. (2009). *From Galileo to Gell-Man: The Wonder that Inspired the Greatest Scientists of All Time: In Their Own Words*. West Conshohocken, PA: Templeton Press.
3. Renati, P. (2016). *Physical Analogical Foundations of Conscious Reality*. Lugano: ÌNIN Editions.
4. Merry, P. (2020). Impersonal Productivity. https://petermerry.org/impersonal-productivity/
5. op. cit. in note [2]

▌CHAPTER 31

6. Bohm and Hiley's concept of "active information" (1993: 35–38). See note [32].

7. Schore (1994). See note [32].

8. Schore (1997): 30. See note [32].

9. However, exposure to prolonged negative interactions impairs the infant's developing frontal cortex, producing enduring psychosocial dysfunction and later emergence of psychiatric disorders and instability in relationships (Schore, 1994). See note [32].

10. Sternberg (1986). See note [32].

11. Sternberg (1986): 119–122. See note [32].

12. The others are "Nonlove," "Liking," "Infatuated Love," "Empty Love," "Romantic Love," "Companionate Love," and "Fatuous Love."

13. This reports the results of a nation-wide, longitudinal study of 57 urban communes conducted in the mid-1970's (see Bradley, 1987). See note [32].

14. Field observations indicate that power relations function as an actualization hierarchy — *not* a hierarchy of domination.

15. A stepwise model, in which *only* these two structural measures meet the minimum statistical criteria for entry into a discriminant function analysis, correctly classified the survival status of 45/46 (97.8%) communes (Bradley & Pribram, 1998). See note [32].

16. Jahn & Dunne (1987): 293; bold and italics, added. See note [32].

17. Jahn & Dunne (1987): 339–340; bold and italics added. See note [32].

18. Such as, room temperature, the pH behavior of water, and fruit fly larvae maturation.

19. Tiller et al. (2005): 92; italics added. See note [32].

20. Tiller's concept of the "U(1) EM gauge symmetry state" is "Our present-day unconditioned, conventional physical [and cognitive] reality"; viz, the macroscopic domain of our spacetime reality (Tiller et al. (2005): 106–110 and 255, respectively; italics and bold added). See note [32].

21. Tiller et al. (2005): 37; italics added. See note [32].

22. See McCraty et al. (2006): 8–22; especially Figures 3 and 4. See note [32].

23. Tiller et al. (2005): 139; italics added. The term "heart coherence" is from McCraty et al. (2006). See note [32].

24. From Tiller et al. (2005), Equation #6.4: 230. See note [32].

25. Tiller et al. (2005): 230; bold and italics added. See note [32].

26. E.g., Nelson (2008), Radin (2006), Sheldrake (1999), Bradley (2020), and Radin et al. (2013). See note [32].

27. Nelson (2008). See note [32].

28. Bradley (2007). See note [32].

29. Marcer (1995). See note [32].

30. Prigogine & Stengers (1984), Chapter V. See note [32].

31. Adapted from R.T. Bradley (2022). See note [32].

32. Bohm, D., & Hiley, B. J. (1993). *The Undivided Universe: An Ontological Interpretation of Quantum Theory*. London and New York, NY: Routledge.; Bradley, R. T. (1987). *Charisma and Social Structure: A Study of Love and Power, Wholeness and Transformation*. New York: Paragon House.; Bradley, R. T. (2003). Love, Power, Mind, Brain, and Agency. In, David Loye (Ed.), *The Great Adventure: Toward a Fully Human Theory of Evolution*, 99–150. New York, NY: SUNY Press.; Bradley, R. T. (2007). Psychophysiology of Intuition: A Quantum-Holographic Theory of Nonlocal Communication. *World Futures*, 63(2):61–97. https://doi.org/10.1080/02604020601123148; Bradley, R. T. (2020). Group Intuition and Intentionality: Collective Action at-a-Distance? In Sinclair, Marta. (Ed.), *Handbook of Intuition Research as Practice*, 15:197–213. Cheltenham, UK and Northampton, MA, USA: Edward Elgar.; Bradley, R. T. (2023). The Great Adventurer: David Loye's "Hololeap" to Future Vision. *World Futures*, 79(1):1–28. https://doi.org/10.1080/026040 27.2022.2161788; Bradley, R. T., & Pribram, K. H. (1998). Communication and Stability in Social Collectives. *Journal of Social and Evolutionary Systems*, 21(1)29–81. https://doi.org/10.1016/S1061-7361(99)80005-8; Jahn, R. G., & Dunne, B. J. (1987). *Margins of Reality: The Role of Consciousness in the Physical World*. New York-San Diego, CA: Harcourt Brace Jovanovich.; Marcer, P. (1995). A Proposal for a Mathematical Specification for Evolution

and the Psi Field. *World Futures*, 44(283):149–159. https://doi.org/10.1080/0 2604027.1995.9972539; McCraty, R., Atkinson, M., Tomasino, D., & Bradley, R. T. (2006). *The Coherent Heart: Heart-Brain Interactions, Psychophysiological Coherence, and the Emergence of System-Wide Order.* E-Book (pub. #06-022), HeartMath Research Center. Boulder Creek, CA: Institute of HeartMath.; Nelson, R. D. (2008). The Emotional Nature of Global Consciousness. Paper for the Bial Foundation 7th Symposium; Pribram, K. H., & Bradley R. T. (1998). The Brain, the Me and the I. In, M. Ferrari & R. Sternberg (Eds.), *Self-Awareness: Its Nature and Development*, 10:273–307. New York: The Guilford Press.; Prigogine, I., & Stengers, I. (1984). *Order Out of Chaos: Man's New Dialogue with Nature.* New York, NY: Bantam Books, Inc.; Radin, D. (2006). *Entangled Minds: Extrasensory Experiences in a Quantum Reality.* New York, NY: Paraview Pocket Books.; Radin, D., Michel, L., Johnston, J., & Delorme, A. (2013). Psychophysical Interactions with a Double-Slit Interference Pattern. *Physics Essays*, 26(4):553–556. https://doi.org/10.4006/0836-1398-34.1.79; Schore, A. N. (1994). *Affect Regulation and the Origin of the Self: The Neurobiology of Emotional Development.* Hillsdale, NJ: Lawrence Erlbaum Associates.; Schore, A. N., (1997). Early Organization of the Nonlinear Right Brain and Development of a Predisposition to Psychiatric Disorders. *Development and Psychopathology*, 9:595–631. https://doi.org/10.1017/s0954579497001363; Sheldrake, R. (1999). *Dogs That Know When Their Owners Are Coming Home: And Other Unexplained Powers of Animals.* New York, NY: Three Rivers Press.; Sternberg, R. J. (1986). A triangular theory of love. *Psychological Review*, 93(2): 119–135. https://doi.org/10.1037/0033-295X.93.2.119; Teilhard de Chardin, P. (1967). *On Love.* New York: Harper & Row.; and Tiller, W. A., Dibble, W. E., & Fandel, J. G. (2005). *Some Science Adventures with Real Magic.* Walnut Creek, CA: Pavior Publishing.

CHAPTER 32

33.   During 'Abdu'l-Bahá's 1912 visit to the United States, a staff reporter of *The Palo Altan* writes about his visit: "The teaching of the Bahai is at once mystical

and practical. In effect, it challenges frequent comparison with the charity, illumination, and social service of that sweet mediaeval, Francis of Assai. We have something of the same close sympathy with the divine, combined with a splendid personal humility and eagerness to serve. Abbas Effendi leads his followers over what is elsewhere called the Mystic way; but wherever they march, they tread with practical feet..."

34. Lloyd-Roberts, S. (2016). *The War on Women: And the Brave Ones Who Fight Back*. UK: Simon & Schuster.

35. Discussed in depth in Mustakova, E. (2021). *Global Unitive Healing: Integral Skills for Personal and Collective Transformation*. Fort Lauderdale, FL: Light on Light Press.

36. See Nader Saiedi's discussion of the coherence of mind, feelings, and will in his critique of spiritual reason in Saiedi, N. (2000). *Logos and Civilization: Spirit, History, and Order in the Writings of Baha'u'Llah*. University Press of Maryland.

37. See *Unitive Narrative* at https://sdgthoughtleaderscircle.org/unitive-new-narrative/.

38. See *Frontiers of Learning* at https://www.bahai.org/frontiers/.

39. See *Declaration for Unitive Justice*, Elena Mustakova, Scott Alan Carlin, Robert Atkinson, Jonathan Granoff, Joni Carley, Jude Currivan, Audrey Kitagawa, David Lorimer, Chief Phil Lane Jr., and Earl Possardt in Robinson, J., & Kuntzelman, E. (Eds.). (2023). *The Holomovement: Embracing Our Collective Purpose to Unite Humanity*, Fort Lauderdale, FL: Light on Light Press.

40. Alliance for Unitive Justice: https://www.a4uj.org/

41. Clute, S. *Unitive Justice: Bending the Arc of Justice Toward Love*. (Scheduled for publication in 2023)

42. Part II in Elena Mustakova's book, *Global Unitive Healing*, is dedicated to an in-depth examination of the re-structuring power of an evolutionary spiritual language.

43. Lopez-Claros, A., Dahl, A., & Groff, M. (2020) *Global Governance and the Emergence of Global Institutions for the 21st Century*. Cambridge. MA: Cambridge University Press.

44. Atkinson, R., Johnson, K., & Moldow, D. (Eds.). (2020). *Our Moment of Choice: Evolutionary Visions and Hope for the Future*. New York, NY: Atria Books; Portland, OR: Beyond Words.

▌CHAPTER 33

45. Dante, A. (1921). *The Divine Comedy of Dante Alighieri*. trans. M. B. Anderson. New York, World Book Company.

46. Dawkins, R. (1976, 2006). *The Selfish Gene*. Oxford: Oxford University Press.

47. Novalis (1989). *Pollen and Fragments: Selected Poetry and Prose of Novalis*. trans. Arthur Versluis. New York: Phanes Press.

48. Plato, *The Symposium*. https://en.wikipedia.org/wiki/Symposium_(Plato)

49. Keats, J. (1819). "Ode on a Grecian Urn." *Annals of the fine arts* [originally published anonymously], 4(15):638–639. https://babel.hathitrust.org/cgi/pt?id=mdp.39015012982370&view=1up&seq=148

50. By dimension, I mean a plane of reality – this is not accepted in mainstream science, although mathematically, higher dimensions exist.

51. McLuhan, M. (1964). *Understanding Media: The Extensions of Man*. London & New York: McGraw-Hill.

52. Merleau-Ponty, M. (1962, 2002). *Phenomenology of Perception*. First published in Paris in 1945. London & New York: Routledge.

53. Haldane, J. B. S. (1927, 2017). *Possible Worlds*. London: Taylor & Francis.

54. Keith Devlin, referenced in Nahin, P. J. (2006). *Dr. Euler's Fabulous Formula: Cures Many Mathematical Ills*. Princeton: Princeton University Press.

55. Tarnas, R. (2006). *Cosmos and Psyche: Intimations of a New World View*. New York: Penguin.

56. Planck, M. (1944). Das Wesen der Materie [The Essence of Matter]. Lecture in Florence, Italy.

57. Pythagoras

58. See 'Map of Consciousness' in Hawkins, D. (2002) *Power vs Force: The Hidden Determinants of Human Behavior*. Carlsbad, CA: Hay House Inc., which maps out the resonance of various emotional states.

CONSCIOUS EVOLUTION: OUR SALVATION

ERVIN LASZLO

QUO VADIS HUMANITAS? Where are we headed, humankind? Are we staying on the traveled path, or do we have the vision and the courage to find a better way to live and act? The time has come to reflect on this existential question, the contemporary variant of Hamlet's famous "to be or not to be." Can we shift to a path leading to a peaceful and sustainable world? That is now the question.

With the roadmaps suggested by our world-renowned contributors, we have a set of alternatives in our hand. The suggested roadmaps are bold and daring, yet they are intrinsically feasible. They show the way to a better world, but they do not guarantee that we will take it. Entering on the paths envisaged here calls for a major change in our world — above all, in our thinking. It calls for a veritable revolution in our concept of the real world, and of our ideas of our place and role in that world.

The world that makes up the woof and warp of our everyday experience, and is implicit in the reports of the international media, is a world of real and foreseeable crises. It is unstable and unsustainable. It appears to head toward ever greater breakdowns and raises the specter of an ultimate collapse. It is very different from the upshifted world of the roadmaps. It appears that an upshift from today's chaotic and crisis-prone world to a world of peace and harmony is plain delusion — mere wishful thinking.

This is not a correct assessment of the situation. We are in the midst of a fundamental and radical systems-change, known in the systems sciences as a "bifurcation." A bifurcation is not only danger — it is also opportunity. It is the opportunity for a new system to be born. Today, the new system is foreshadowed, but not yet in place. How it will be born is yet to be decided.

One thing is certain — a new world will be born. It will bring fundamental change in the way we relate to each other and to the world around us. This could be a change for the better, or for the worse. If it is to be for the better, we need to interact with the process of its birthing. We must make our evolution on the planet conscious.

The presuppositions for conscious evolution are given. We have the human and the material resources as well as the technology to live and thrive on the planet. There is nothing holding us back but our obsolete vision — or lack of vision.

There have been crises in the world before the current one, with revolutionary tipping points and unforeseen consequences. The current crisis is not the first in history, but it is more embracing than any of its predecessors. Our problems and the challenge of coping with them are now greater than ever. Will we rise to meet them? We live in a global crisis in a globalized world. We could rise to the more limited crises of the past — we are still here. But will we rise to the current crises? This is not clear. The current path of our evolution would be a dead-end.

The outlook for the future is not entirely dark, however. There are signs that we are waking up. A spirit of cooperation and solidarity often arises in the midst of chaos.

We must not discount the evolutionary factor. The evolutionary impetus in the universe, the "holotropic attractor" is an ever-present motivation orienting the evolutionary process toward integral systems change. It made the universe into what it is, a coherent and complex whole, rather than a cloud of randomly interacting plasma, as it was at its birth in the aftermath of the Big Bang.

The great upshift can be and must be attempted. There is no time to waste and prevaricate. The chances of success are good. We have practicable roadmaps in our possession — those described in this book and a plethora of others. We are in the midst of a systems bifurcation, and there is growing openness to alternatives. We need not descend into terminal chaos. We can rise toward the wholeness that characterizes fundamental processes in nature.

Recognizing the existence of an evolutionary impetus is not a warrant for complacency and inaction. The response to the survival challenge may manifest independently of our conscious efforts, but how soon will it manifest — and at what cost? Clearly, the longer we wait, the greater the challenge and the higher the cost of meeting it. The naïve attitude of "just wait and see" would take us down the wrong path. The comforting belief that "in the end things will take care of themselves" could be suicidal.

The crisis we experience is deepening and spreading. We need to address its causal core and not its symptoms and corollaries.

We need to change the way we evolve on this planet. But how can we do it? There is no moral authority on Earth that could command or even recommend taking another path, nor is there any legal authority that could enforce it. The power to change does not lie above or beyond us. It lies *in* us. We must rethink and revise the narrow, materialistic, and exploitative way of thinking that still dominates the modern world. The root problem of our time is the obsolescence of the way we think.

Fortunately, the prevalent mindset is not engraved in stone, nor is it encoded in our DNA. It is subject to change. It has been changing throughout recorded history — every crisis brought a revised mindset. Today's crisis is no exception. Under the impact of mounting crises, more and more people are questioning the wisdom of continuing to live and think the way we do. But the new mindset that will take place of the old is not yet decided.

Changing the way we think and act is a realistic enterprise. It does not call for changing the mindset of every person on the planet, or even of a significant majority. It is sufficient to shift the mindset of a critical mass. The upshifted mindset of a small group of awakened people can spread and generate a growing wave of change that would constitute a new path for the evolution of humankind on this planet. Conscious evolution is possible.

The steps we need to take are clear. We need to upshift our physical and mental health and heal ourselves and our fellow beings. We must upshift our thinking to embrace the factors that are crucial for our well-being and even for our survival. We must deepen our intuition so that we are able to apprehend the evolutionary impetus and allow it to guide our steps. The alternatives before us are crystal clear. We either upshift to peace and harmony on the planet, or we downslide to conflict and chaos. Which will it be? On the surface, it appears that we are headed toward a world of conflict and chaos. But underneath, there is a deeper evolution unfolding: a great upshift toward peace and harmony on the planet. This book showed the way — it provided the roadmaps we need to upshift to conscious evolution.

The great upshift is before us. It is up to us to enter on the path that leads to it. The vision and the courage to do so could be, and will be, our salvation.

BIOGRAPHICAL NOTES

Robert Atkinson PhD is a developmental psychologist, educator, award-winning author of *A New Story of Wholeness: An Experiential Guide for Connecting the Human Family*, *The Story of Our Time: From Duality to Interconnectedness to Oneness*, co-editor of *Our Moment of Choice: Evolutionary Visions and Hope for the Future*, and founder of One Planet Peace Forum. www.robertatkinson.net

Anna Bacchia is a Researcher in Human Sciences and Cognitive Sciences and has focused on the *nature of the Cognitive, Creative and Intuitive processes*. For the outcomes of her Research, she is a Laureate of the *Luxembourg World Peace Prize* and Life Member of the *World Peace Forum*. Founder and Director of the *Consciousness Institute* in Lugano, Switzerland, her Educational Programs are even active within some Programs of the *United Nations*. www.AnnaBacchia.net

Gregg Braden is a five-time New York Times best-selling author, scientist and renowned pioneer in the emerging paradigm based in science, spirituality, social policy, and human potential. To date, his research has led to 15 film credits and 12 award-winning books now published in over 40 languages. www.greggbraden.com

Raymond Bradley PhD studies the role of love in human development, collective organization, and psychic phenomena. He is the author of *Charisma and Social Structure*, and co-author of *The Coherent Heart*, among 90

publications — including an award-winning quantum holographic theory of intuition. Soon to be completed: *The Lens of Love: Quantum Holographic Eye of Universal Consciousness.*

Gauthier Chapelle is an in-Terr-dependent researcher, stay-at-home dad with four kids, naturalist, biologist, and agricultural engineer. Since 2009, he co-facilitates workshops of "The Work that reconnects," and supports a school in the woods project. He has co-authored a number of books in the fields of biomimicry, agroecology, mutual aid, and collapsology.

Professor Allan Combs PhD is a consciousness researcher, neuropsychologist, and systems theorist at California Institute of Integral Studies where he is the Director of the Center for Consciousness Studies. He is the author of over 200 articles, chapters, and books on consciousness and the brain and of *Consciousness Explained Better: Toward an Integral Understanding of the Multifaceted Nature of Consciousness*; *Synchronicity*; and *Thomas Berry: Dreamer of the Earth* (with Ervin Laszlo). https://en.wikipedia.org/wiki/Allan_Combs

Jude Currivan PhD is a cosmologist, futurist, planetary healer, award-winning author — most recently for *The Story of Gaia* (2022), previously one of the most senior international businesswomen in the UK, and co-founder of WholeWorld-View aiming to serve the understanding, experiencing, and embodying of unitive awareness and conscious evolution. www.wholeworld-view.org / www.evolutionaryleaders.net

Kingsley L. Dennis PhD is a full-time writer and researcher. He is the author of over twenty books. His forthcoming book *The Inversion: How We Have Been Tricked into a False Reality* will be published in September 2023. www.kingsleydennis.com

Charles Eisenstein is an essayist and the author of several books. His recent work can be found on Substack. https://charleseisenstein.substack.com/

Michael Ellis, MD is an accomplished writer, futurist, and peacemaker, with advanced qualifications in medicine, healing, and the arts. He has dedicated his life to the study of mind, consciousness, global sustainability, and peace, and his latest projects are two courses, "Psycho Potential and the Cosmic Mind" and "Resilience in Times of Change." Contact: admin@psychopotential.com. https://t.ly/C_1u

From 6th Mass Extinction event to 6th Mass Evolution, edutainment producer **Alison Goldwyn** has spent decades party planning an epic music event to shift the Emotional Climate, root of nearly all our global ills. Co-hosted by the power of our imagiNations, Synchronistory® is a Party for the Planet celebrating every living being — broadcast live worldwide. www.synchronistory.com / www.jaimestones.com

Stanislav Grof MD, PhD is one of the founders and chief theoreticians of transpersonal psychology and the founding president of the International Transpersonal Association (ITA). His most recent book is *The Way of the Psychonaut* with a corresponding documentary film about his life and work. www.thewayofthepsychonaut.com / www.stangrof.com

Satish Kumar is the founder of Schumacher College and Editor Emeritus of *Resurgence & Ecologist* magazine. He is the author of *Radical Love*, *Elegant Simplicity* and his autobiography, *No Destination*. A former Jain monk, Satish completed an 8,000-mile walk from India to America promoting peace. He is a recipient of the Goi Peace Award.

Alexander Laszlo PhD is President of the Bertalanffy Center for the Study of Systems Science; Research Director of the Laszlo Institute of New Paradigm Research; Founding Director of the Social Systems Foundation; Co-Founder of Global Education Futures; Professor of Systems Science & Curated Emergence; and author of over 100 journal, book, and encyclopedia publications. https://alexanderlaszlo.net/about-me/

Ervin Laszlo PhD is a philosopher of science, leading systems theorist, author, co-author, and editor of over one hundred books, and was twice nominated for the Nobel Peace Prize. He was a celebrated child prodigy pianist and theorist of the Akashic Field. Ervin is the founder and president of the Intl. Think Tank — The Club of Budapest and The Laszlo Institute of New Paradigm Research.

Holding a PhD in Economics, **Thomas Legrand** is the author of *Politics of Being: Wisdom and Science for a New Development Paradigm* (2022). He leads the UNDP-convened Conscious Food Systems Alliance. He lives next to Plum Village, the monastery of Zen master Thich Nhat Hanh, in the Southwest of France. https://politicsofbeing.com / http://www.conscious-foodsystems.org/

Bruce H. Lipton PhD is a stem cell biologist and author of the bestselling books *The Biology of Belief, Spontaneous Evolution,* and *The Honeymoon Effect.* Bruce, recipient of the prestigious Japanese Goi Peace Award, has been listed in *Watkins'* global top "100 most spiritually influential living people" for the last 13 years.

David Lorimer is a visionary polymath who is Programme Director of the Scientific and Medical Network, Editor of *Paradigm Explorer,* and Chair of the Galileo Commission. His most recent books are *A Quest for Wisdom* (collection of essays) and *Better Light a Candle* (volume of poetry). https:// scientificandmedical.net / https://galileocommission.org

Pavel Luksha is a system scientist, change catalyst, and facilitator. He is Founder of Global Education Futures and the School of Evolutionary Leadership, and co-founder of The Weaving Lab, The Learning Planet, and Living Cities Earth movements. He is the author of several seminal reports on the future of education and work and a scholar of ancient and modern wisdom that can contribute to the evolutionary upshift of humankind. www.globaledufutures.org

Ted Mahr is a gifted psychic with "Out of this World Radio." An accomplished author, he has been in contact with the other side for 30 years and teaches people how to talk to Angels. The purpose of his work is to make this world a much better place! www.outofthisworld1150.com

Entrepreneur and Design Thinking thought leader, **Sunil Malhotra**, has relentlessly championed the cause of spirituality in the workplace. He founded (and runs) Ideafarms, a Design-in-Tech Advisory that pioneered Industrial Design approaches in Infotech. His forthcoming book (2023) explores the idea of co-evolution where Yoga and AI work together as friends.

Lynne McTaggart is the award-winning author of seven books, including the worldwide bestsellers *The Field*, *The Intention Experiment* and *The Power of Eight®*. She is also the architect of the Intention Experiments, a web based "global laboratory" to test the power of intention to heal the world. www.lynnemctaggart.com / www.wddty.com

Nitamo Federico Montecucco MD is a physician, neuropsychosomatics researcher, and President of NGO Global Village, Humanistic

Psychotherapy Institute. He lived for three years in India meditating and for three years in the USA studying neuroscience. In addition to offering University lectures at WHO Milan, Sapienza Rome, University for Peace UN, Cattolica Milan, Chieti, Verona, Cagliari, Sassari, Arezzo, he is the author of many articles and books. http://www.villaggioglobale.eu / http://www.progettogaia.eu

Elena Mustakova PhD is an evolutionary psychologist, social scientist, spiritual philosopher, educator, and public speaker whose global contributions in research, community development, and writing have received multiple awards. Senior Editor of the comprehensive volume *Toward a Socially Responsible Psychology for a Global Era*, her recent book, *Global Unitive Healing: Integral Skills for Personal and Collective Transformation*, has been called "a hymn to collective sanity."

As Chief Economist at a major consulting firm, **John Perkins** advised governments and corporations around the world. His eleven books, including *Confessions of an Economic Hit* Man, spent 74 weeks on *The New York Times* bestseller list and sold millions of copies in 38 languages. www.economichitmanbook.com

Stephen Rodgers founded Alchemy Advisors Consulting Agency, helping purpose driven people and businesses. He is a former Warren Buffett CEO, serial entrepreneur, and leader who has continually evolved as a Spiritual Business Activist, which is his ultimate, most important life's work. Steve focuses in business ecosystems as a consultant, executive coach, board advisor, podcast host, speaker, and author. www.thealchemyadvisors.com

Dr. Maria Sagi holds a PhD in psychology at the Eotvos Lorand University of Budapest and a C.Sc. degree of the Hungarian Academy of Sciences. She is the creator of the Sagi method of information medicine and the author of twelve books and over 150 articles. She is the science director of the Club of Budapest, and lives in Budapest. https://www.mariasagidr.com/

Dr. Karan Singh is an Indian parliamentarian, eminent educationist, environmentalist, and an authority on Indian spiritual systems. He was Indian Ambassador to the USA in 1989 and was Chairman of the Auroville Foundation for 20 years. He also was Chancellor of Jawahar Lal Nehru University and Banaras Hindu University and was formerly India's Member on the UNESCO Governing Board. https://www.karansingh.com

Anneloes Smitsman PhD is a futurist, systems scientist, entrepreneur, and award-winning pioneer in human development and systems change. She is the founder of EARTHwise Centre and architect of the EARTHwise Constitution and Game. She is the co-author of the award-winning best-sellers of the *Future Humans Trilogy*. https://www.earthwisecentre.org/anneloes-smitsman

David Talmor has gained extensive experience as a management consultant at major business consulting firms as well as through management positions in production and technology companies in the U.S. and in Israel. More information on his approach to Resonating~Business and on his Resonating~AI initiative can be found at www.ItsAResonatingWorld.com / www.resonAIting.com.

Arabella Thaïs is a writer, speaker, philosopher, and artist with a PhD in cosmology and consciousness. Committed to the evolution of humanity, her work explores the intersection of poetry, mathematics, beauty, and time, which she teaches at her online school of consciousness, *The Temple*. She uses various aesthetic mediums — such as music, film, and experience design — in order to communicate ideas and propel human transformation. www.arabellathais.com

Michael Charles Tobias is an ecologist, author, filmmaker, historian, explorer, anthropologist, educator, and non-violence activist. His field-research has taken him to well over 80 countries and from regions like Antarctica to many of the world's deserts, temperate zones, tropics, and boreal forests. For many years, Tobias has been the President of the Dancing Star Foundation which works assiduously throughout the world in areas of biodiversity conservation, animal rights, and environmental education. www.dancingstarfoundation.org

Kees van der Pijl retired as a professor of International Relations from the University of Sussex, UK, in 2012. His books include *The Making of an Atlantic Ruling Class* (1984, new edition 2012), *Nomads, Empires, States* (Deutscher Prize, 2008), and most recently, *States of Emergency: Keeping the Global Population in Check* (2022).

Alfred de Zayas is a law professor at the Geneva School of Diplomacy. He is the author of twelve books including *Building a Just World Order*. He is former UN Independent Expert on International Order (2012-18), Chief of the Petitions Department at the Office of the UN High Commissioner for Human Rights, and Secretary of UN Human Rights Committee.

Natalie Zeituny is a reality cosmologist and consciousness architect. She is a clairvoyant, energy healer, creator of "ensoulment," and an international speaker. She has published four books, and as a social entrepreneur, is dedicated to innovative applications of reality models that facilitate personal, collective, and planetary transformation. www.nataliezeituny.com

MESSAGE FROM THE PUBLISHER

Light on Light Press produces enhanced content books spotlighting the sacred ground upon which all religious and wisdom traditions intersect; it aims to stimulate and perpetuate engaged interspiritual and perennial wisdom dialogue for the purpose of assisting the dawning of a unitive consciousness that will inspire compassionate action toward a just and peaceful world.

We are delighted to publish *The Great Upshift* because there is nothing more important right now than peace and harmony on the planet. This vital book addresses this greatest of needs in the broadest and most inclusive of ways, by bringing together 35 of the world's leading thinkers to address comprehensively how and in what specific ways our individual and collective consciousness can and must be upshifted to the level needed to ensure the desired outcome of the world's ongoing crises. Ervin Laszlo and David Lorimer, drawing from their holistic expertise and global network, have assembled a stellar cast of contributors to decode the big picture, map our path forward, and offer exactly what is required to upshift our healing, our thinking, and our intuition to ensure a bright and beautiful future. This compendium of insights into solutions for a troubled world calls for the conscious participation of all of us to implement the verities herein.

We consider this book an essential guide with all the needed signposts for navigating our way through the process of global transformation currently spreading across the planet. We are extremely pleased to bring forth this watershed book when the world so needs it.

Managing Editors—

Kurt Johnson, PhD
Robert Atkinson, PhD
Nomi Naeem, MA
Chamatkara (Sandra Simon)

Printed in the USA
CPSIA information can be obtained
at www.ICGtesting.com
LVHW041530040124
767941LV00061B/1546